Transcending Darkness

A Memoir of Abuse and Grace

DENISE BROWN

Publishing services provided by  **Archangel Ink**

ISBN: 978-1-950043-37-8

This book is dedicated to my sisters, who have grown into amazing, beautiful women. I am so proud of all of you. I love you—always.

Contents

SECTION III: RESURRECTION

Introduction

My childhood was difficult and as a teenager I found myself in a bleak, hopeless place. I tried to break free of my pain with the help of friends, the distraction of a busy schedule, even with self-harm. Nothing I tried had the power to guide me to a happy life. Then at sixteen, I made God a promise that if he would lead me through the darkness, I would do what He asked of me. God took me up on that promise and set me on a path to healing and wholeness.

In college, I first heard His call to write my story. I began but did not finish it. Years went by and I had all but forgotten what God had asked of me. I was too busy, too preoccupied, and too ashamed of my past to resurrect my book for public critique. But God had not forgotten me and waited patiently until I was ready.

In the fall of 2012, I attended a weekend-long Presbyterian church retreat for women. We watched a video of Brené Brown speaking about her research on trust and authenticity. She spoke about being bold, about not being afraid of who you are. She said that people most respect those who are open and tell the truth of their story.

Hmmm, I thought, *the truth of my story.*

At the workshop, I felt God's pull in my heart. He was asking me to start working on my memoir again. But when I got home, I found that I was afraid, afraid that if I released my story to the public that it might mar my reputation in the community and damage my practice beyond repair. So I let it be and went back to the fulfilling work of treating patients and raising my son with my husband.

Two years later, I picked up the book *Half Time* by Bob Buford after it was recommended as a must-read business book. I was surprised to discover that it was about figuring out what God's plan is for your life and career, a guide to reassessing one's trajectory at midlife. I realized, somewhat reluctantly, that God was asking me to change my life course slightly. I knew in my heart that he was asking me to make my memoir my half-time career, but I was still too busy and too worried about the potential ramifications to pick it up again.

I began turning the idea of working on my story over and over in my head, weighing the pros and cons. I had not forgotten the promise I'd made to God in my youth that I would do what He asked of me after He saved me, but the cons seemed to always win the argument in my mind. I questioned this commitment. Was God really asking me to risk everything and rewrite my book? I started praying. A couple of weeks later, after dropping my son off for school, I prayed out loud while driving to the office.

"God, am I actually hearing you? Am I supposed to work on my book again? I need a sign. A real sign that this is what you want me to do."

As soon as I finished my prayer, I heard the song that was playing in the background ring out. It was "Write Your Story" by Francesca Battistelli.

I could hardly believe it. I had my answer. I was absolutely positive that God had asked me to finish my memoir. However, I hadn't traveled more than a mile down the road when I asked, "Okay, God, you want me to work on my story, but how in the world am I going to do that? When am I going to find the time?" I knew that the book I had written from age nineteen through twenty-two needed an overhaul.

The following Sunday, I sat near the back of the church in my usual pew. We were entering the season of Lent and my pastor was talking about making sacrifices for God for Lent. He said, "It's not always about giving something up. Sometimes it is better to add something into your life instead, such as setting aside a small amount of time to read your Bible, even if it is only for one hour a week."

God was speaking to me again, I knew it. He was asking me to spend one hour a week working on my manuscript. I could do that; I could find one hour a week or even two or three. I knew that it would take years to complete, but as an orthodontist I knew how to be patient, that very small, imperceptible movements over a period of a couple of years could transform one's appearance and, even more importantly, one's self-esteem. Of all people, I knew what wonderful effects could happen with minimal consistent motion over time.

And so I began the rewrite. This book is the fulfillment of the promise that I made to God thirty years ago. I am grateful that He held up His end of the bargain much sooner than I did.

SECTION I

CHILDHOOD

Chapter 1

Scared Silent

1980

The first memories I have of my mother, Deborah, are of her sitting on the couch, staring ahead, as if caught up in a daydream. I had to walk up to her and say, "Mommy?" before she would turn to look at me.

At the time my story begins, my mother was twenty-six years old. She was thin and just over five feet tall with oily mousy-blond hair that she wore parted in the middle. Her thick dark-rimmed glasses exaggerated her round face and blue eyes. When I looked into those eyes, it was like leaning over a dock, peering into the murky waters below. I knew there was life beneath the surface, yet I couldn't discern anything through the darkness. What's more, I had the uneasy feeling that the life lurking within those unknown depths was dangerous.

In the spring of 1980, we looked like the typical American family. I was five years old. My mother stayed at home with me and my sisters, Lillian and Mariah, who were three and a half and two and a half, respectively. My father left at seven in the morning each day for his job manufacturing radar systems. I helped my mother wash the dishes, change diapers, and clean the house—chores that wouldn't seem unusual to an outsider. After all, most parents teach their children to be responsible.

But the normalcy stopped there. I may have been able to greet people at the door with a smile, but inside, I was constantly in hiding, forever watching my step around my parents. I never knew when my mother would erupt in anger, damaging whatever or whoever happened to be in her path.

One Saturday, we were all sitting around the kitchen table waiting for our scalding canned beef stew to cool enough so we could eat it.

My father began fretting, "I don't know how we're going to pay to fix the car. We just don't have the money." As his words escalated in pitch and volume, my sister Lillian and I knew trouble was brewing.

"Then just don't drive," my mother yelled back.

Even as small children, we could tell her response did not make sense, but we didn't dare point that out to her.

As my father persisted in complaining about the repairs, my mother came toward me. I knew I was in a precarious position, so I tensed up and kept quiet.

"How am I supposed to get to work, then?" my father continued. He was responding as if she could think her way to a solution, but even as a child, I could tell she didn't have the capacity. Why couldn't he recognize that?

"If I don't have a car to get to work, how will I earn money? How will we pay for the groceries?"

"The car is all you care about," my mother shrieked. To my dismay, she was standing directly behind me. "That car always needs something."

I sank down into my chair. She was too close to me, and my father was at the other end of the table, too far away to help. I felt vulnerable and exposed. I instinctively scooted farther down in my chair, trying to make myself small and invisible. Unfortunately, she noticed this and advanced on me.

"Just what are you doing?" she screeched.

There was no point in answering. It would only make things worse. I remained quiet, trying to be inconspicuous. Suddenly, she grabbed a fistful of my hair and jerked backward. Then, as if I had challenged her, she slammed my face down into the bowl of steaming stew. I struggled to get out of her grasp and away from the burning liquid. My face was on fire. Just as suddenly, she let go. Perhaps my father had dashed toward her to stop her, or perhaps she simply felt she had made her point.

I sat there, stunned. I kept my eyes closed, trying not to breathe or make any noise that would bring her attention back to me. I tried not to feel the burn, but my face was seared. I mustn't cry. If my mother heard me sobbing, she might repeat the assault. My mouth hung open and my hands shook as I held them up alongside my face, trying not to make more of a mess. I might get punished for that.

I sat with my head just inches from the bowl. I didn't want to do anything to invite another attack. If I wiped the stew away, would something bad happen to the burned skin on my face? Suddenly, my father scraped a paper towel across my eyes, smearing the stew off of my skin. He was rough, not realizing the seriousness of the burns I had suffered. His cleanup effort was completely perfunctory and missed my hair and neck entirely.

When I opened my eyes, I saw that my mother had left the room. What she would later call an "argument" with my father—rather than a crazy moment that had swept me into her destructive path—was over. Her flair for ending "arguments" with unexpected and often violent drama relieved her tension but projected it onto those of us around her: usually her children. My father always seemed oblivious that part of his role as a father was to protect his children from their mother.

Before I could recover or even finish cleaning myself up, my father drove us to the babysitter. When I got to her house, she saw my scalded face and messy hair, flecked with pieces of stew, and she pulled me into her bathroom to clean me up. I stole a glance at myself in the mirror. My face was bright red, as if I had severe sunburn.

"Denise, what happened?" she asked several times, but I didn't answer. I just kept staring at the shiny bathroom tiles, too afraid to say anything. I would have to go back home, after all, and I was afraid of what might happen if it got back to my parents that I had tattled on them. I already knew not to discuss what happened at home with others. I knew I didn't deserve this treatment, but I still refused to tell her what had happened. Eventually, she stopped asking.

Life at home was quiet for a few weeks after that. The interval of peace in the house was directly proportional to the size of the previous outburst. If there was a particularly dramatic event, we might have relative calm for an entire month, but a small meltdown would only buy us a couple of days until the next explosion.

One afternoon later that summer, my mother went out for a walk, which she did regularly, and left me in charge of my sisters while our father was at work. Their long, silky-blond hair was tangled, and bits of their lunches were still stuck to their faces. It didn't occur to me to take on the motherly task of cleaning them up.

At the back of the basement we had an area we called our play-room. Under the stairs, a metal barrel that was painted white held our toys and stuffed animals. I was the tallest, yet even I had trouble reaching our playthings at the bottom of the barrel, since it was as tall as I was. I knew not to ask my mother more than a couple of times a day to fetch a toy for us from that barrel. When I asked, she had one of two reactions. She might bark, "I'm busy," implying I was an awful five-year-old for making such unreasonable demands on her. On the other hand, she might ignore me entirely. I knew she could hear me, but she wouldn't respond or even bother to turn her head to glare at me. When that happened, it was as if I were invisible to her. I felt like I wasn't even important enough for her to acknowledge. This response unsettled me; it was like the calm before a storm. Whenever she ignored me, I sensed I should back away slowly.

Even when she was gone, I dared not do something that would have angered her had she been there. So because we couldn't reach the toys in the barrel that afternoon, my younger siblings and I settled down to watch television.

The television was in our playroom. A large woven multicolored area rug covered the cement floor there, softening the fact that we were in a cellar. We each had a small plastic chair facing the TV, but we preferred to sit directly on the floor in front of the small black-and-white set with its rabbit-ear antenna and cheap metal stand. Next to the television was a door that led to a second basement room, known as "the plant room." We were not allowed in there, and we didn't dare enter even when my mother was gone.

Sesame Street was playing on the TV. I had prematurely outgrown the show and thought it was stupid. But I was too afraid of being punished to change the channel to find a cartoon. I never touched anything without permission.

Suddenly, the phone rang. That also posed a quandary: should I answer it without my mother being home? What if it was my mother calling to tell me something important?

I decided to answer, hoping it was the right decision. "Hel-lo?" I said hesitantly.

"Hi, is your mother home?" a woman asked.

"No."

"Is there a babysitter there?"

"No." I should have had the foresight to lie, but frankly, I didn't see the harm in being in charge of my sisters. I certainly felt mature enough, and we were all just sitting around watching *Sesame Street* anyway.

"Can I speak to an adult?" The woman's voice lilted in that sweet fake way adults sometimes spoke to me.

"No."

"Are you by yourself?"

"No, I'm watching my sisters."

"Oh, stay where you are, okay?" she spoke again with the lilt.

"Okay."

I didn't know where she expected me to go, so after hanging up, I sat back down with my sisters. Within minutes, there was a loud knock on the door. I went upstairs, opened the front door, and found myself staring at the crotch of a big man in a blue uniform.

"Excuse me, miss," he said gently as he scanned the room behind me. He must have noticed the stack of dirty dishes on the counter and the pile of empty, smelly cans of cat food in the corner. Something like pity flickered across his stern face. It was the kind of pity a person has when they come across a lost, dirty puppy. "Is your mother home?"

"No."

I peered around his leg and saw two police cars parked on the lawn filled with big men in blue uniforms, each one talking through a box with an antenna. The boxes crackled and spoke back like chattering insects. I realized in that moment that whomever I had spoken to on the phone had reported us to the police. Sending out more than one cruiser would have been excessive in most cities, but we were a small rural town where nothing particularly interesting ever happened. I decided to keep my mouth shut regarding any further information.

"What's your name, sweetie?" asked the officer.

"Denise."

"Would you mind if I came inside, Denise?"

Little girl, little girl, let me in. Not by the hair of my chinny chin chin...

"I'm not supposed to let strangers inside. Mommy said so," I said firmly. Surprise spread across his face. I stood in the doorway, feeling like Superwoman. I was keeping out the bad guys, even though they could easily have knocked me across the room if they wanted to. At that age, I considered anyone who could cause me grief with my parents to be a bad guy.

"Denise, do you know where your mother is?"

"No."

"Is there a babysitter home?"

"Yeah," I lied in a desperate attempt to cover up my previous mistake. I knew better than to make mistakes, and this had been a big one.

"Can I talk to her?"

"She's sleeping. If I wake her up, she'll get mad at me."

"If you let me inside, miss, I'll wake her up," the officer said. "Then she'll get mad at me, instead of you."

Faint laughter from *Sesame Street* echoed from downstairs. My sisters were quiet, oblivious to the officer standing before me. I was thankful they weren't underfoot, causing me to lose focus. "You can't come in," I said. "You're a stranger. Strangers aren't allowed inside." I was a worldly five years old, and I was Superwoman. I felt sure that the policeman believed me.

"There is no babysitter here, is there?" the officer said, trying to overcome my resistance.

My confidence turned to terror. I had been caught in my lie by a man of authority. There would be consequences. I had made the wrong decision… again! I shouldn't have answered the phone.

"How many sisters are with you?" he asked.

"T-two," I stammered.

"Can we see them, Denise? It's okay. We're not here to hurt you. We just want to make sure everyone is all right."

"You can't come inside," I repeated. "You're a stranger."

Behind him, I spotted my mother running up the hill, yelling. My heart sank. Before she could reach us, she was stopped by another police officer who questioned her for a few minutes. Whatever she said must have satisfied the officers, because they began to leave.

I tensed up, already worrying about how my mother might act once the officers left and I was alone with her. I silently sent the officer at the door a mental message, asking him to take me with him and away from my mother. Even as a child, I could sense that he cared about me more than my own mother did. As she approached the front door, my heart filled with fear. I would soon be alone with her again. I had been a bad girl.

Much to my relief and surprise, my mother did not punish me for answering the phone that day. She ignored me instead, refusing to acknowledge my very existence. While it didn't feel good, I preferred being ignored to being punished.

Later, when my father came home, there was no mention of what had happened. Instead, my parents took Lillian, Mariah, and me to the Awana Bible study program for kids at the neighborhood Baptist church. A few months earlier, they had brought me there after I'd asked to see the inside of this building, which I thought was so pretty. That visit, made out of curiosity, led to my joining the church's Awana program. I loved Awana and was happy that my regular evening there happened to fall on the same day as the scary incident with the police.

At Awana, we colored, sang songs, and listened to stories about God and Jesus. The teachers served us cookies, and we drank juice from tiny disposable blue cups, like the ones you swish with at the dentist's office. It was a calm, supportive environment where the adults seemed genuinely interested in us. Because of Awana, this fearful girl who was always terrified of what would happen next at home learned that God was always there if she became scared or needed a helping hand.

That evening at Awana, during silent prayer, I prayed that my parents would not punish me when I got back home. With fear dominating my thoughts, I didn't participate much that evening. When my parents came to pick us girls up, they were unusually happy, and we drove home as if we were a normal family.

My mother had difficulty completing the basic tasks other adults took for granted. Although she had obtained her driver's license years earlier with assistance from her stepfather, she wasn't able to translate that into competent driving. She did not wear makeup, she rarely bathed, and she hadn't had her hair trimmed since childhood, which was something both of my parents were proud of. Her hair was perpetually greasy, since she only washed it every week or two under the tub's faucet as she leaned over its edge. On the few occasions I saw her brush her hair, she fumbled with the brush, as if she had never mastered the simple technique of brushing hair in one long, fluid, continuous motion. At that age I didn't realize that was unusual, especially since I only bathed once a week myself and always had tangled hair.

However, I did realize that there were aspects of my mother's behavior that weren't typical. She never hugged us, never kissed us, never smiled when we showed her our artwork. If we tripped, fell, and started crying, she didn't rush to make sure we were all right. Instead, she stood awkwardly at a distance, as if she didn't know how to respond, as if she didn't know how to be a mother. I had seen mothers on sitcoms that hugged their kids and were excited to see them. If it was on TV, I reasoned it must be what all the other families were like.

Worse than her unusual awkward responses to us children were the fights that my parents had week after week, as if they derived satisfaction from the ritual. Once my father started yelling, he couldn't stop, prompting my mother to scream and strike at him.

"Go ahead and hit me," my father shouted one September evening that fall when Amanda, the newest addition to our family, was one month old. He rarely fought back. Instead, he would stand there, blocking her blows and protecting his head. In such moments, my mother went wild, swinging at him with open hands. Knowing how these crazy moments often turned against us, Lillian and I ran up to our room to hide and scrambled under the bed that we shared. Mariah had already scurried off somewhere.

Sure enough, we soon heard our mother screeching, "Deeeniiissse! Deeeeniiiisssse! Denise, come down here now. Liiilllly! Lillian, get over here, or I'll hurt you."

We desperately wanted to remain under our bed. Going downstairs would likely end badly for us. We hoped our father would come up to protect us, as he had a couple of years earlier when my mother had threatened to hurt us. At that time, my father had hidden us in the attic, stuffing Lillian, Mariah, and me into a large box and warning us to stay quiet. We had remained absolutely silent, and an hour later he had returned for us, once our mother had calmed down.

Now, as I hid beneath our bed, I longed for the safety of that box. But we couldn't hear our father coming to our defense, and our mother continued calling for us. We came out of hiding—we knew that she would come looking for us if we stayed hidden too long—and followed our mother's hoarse cries into the kitchen. Her glasses lay on the floor where she had thrown them, not far from our father's feet. They were bent, and one lens had popped out. Her pale round face, large nose, and squinting eyes made her look like an albino mole. Even with her half-blind eyes, she saw us slowly creeping toward the kitchen and commanded, "Call the police! Call the police! Call the police now!"

Our father screamed back, "Don't you dare call them. Go back to your room."

We stood there, frozen, not knowing whom to obey.

"Go back to your room," Dad insisted again. He grabbed the receiver off the wall and held it high in the air so we couldn't reach it. This prompted Mom to start throwing anything within reach, which at that moment, was a kitchen plate from the sink.

She screamed at us, "Go to the neighbor's house and call the police from there."

That was our out. As Lillian and I scurried for the door, our father shouted after us, "Don't you dare call the police!" He still held the receiver and had advanced on us as far as the cord would allow. We knew he wanted us back in our room, but we also knew that, at the moment, he didn't dare let go of the phone. If our mother won in this fight, she would find us in our room and mete out some punishment as our father retreated to the darkness of their bedroom. If our mother gave up first, she would run out the back door into the yard.

Mom lunged for the receiver, and Dad turned his focus back to her. Relieved that their attention was directed away from us, Lillian and I ran through the darkness toward the street. The September air was chilly, but we didn't care. We had no intention of calling the police; we were just relieved to be out of the house.

I could hear Amanda crying loudly in her crib upstairs, but no one went to pick her up. Mariah was still hiding somewhere.

As we approached the road, the harsh streetlight tore away the darkness that had protected us. We returned to the shadows and hid in the hedges along the driveway, hoping that our parents—and especially our mother—wouldn't find us. Although the light from the street filtered through the tiny branches and surely exposed us, neither parent came searching for us.

After that night, the hedge often served as our prickly sanctuary from our mother. Unfortunately, we had cause to run to it far too often.

Sometimes, while hiding in the hedge, I heard voices calling my name. I thought it was my mother calling for me. My body would twitch in fearful anticipation until I realized that the calls were coming not from the house, but from the woods on the other side of the dirt road that ran along the back of our property. It was not my mother's voice. It wasn't even a single voice, but rather the voices of several people, each calling to me separately. I didn't dare venture into the woods to find out what the callers wanted. Instead, I would turn to Lillian, who was always coiled into a tight ball, trying to hide by making herself smaller. I searched for signs that she, too, had heard these people calling out to me, but she only stared at the ground. It seemed she heard nothing at all. Since we both spooked easily, I decided not to tell her about the voices calling from the woods.

We dared not leave our hiding place too soon after these fights, as our mother often ran out into the yard, sometimes very near us. As if experiencing Pavlovian conditioning, I would start trembling as soon as I heard the front door slam—the signal that she was coming outside.

But she never came out to look for us. Instead, she would scream a single note, shrieking at the top of her lungs. That scream seemed to go on for an eternity before she had to stop and catch her breath. There was a moment of silence, and then she would start up again, howling at the top of her lungs. This eerie ritual would continue for at least ten minutes, sending waves of terror into my small body the entire time. My mother sounded like a banshee recently escaped from the depths of hell, bringing forth the fury of her imprisonment on Earth. Something about her shrieking made me feel as if I would go insane if I listened long enough.

Once the feelings weighing her down were exorcised, she would return to the house. If the night was warm, Lillian and I would stay outside until our father called for us, indicating that Mom had calmed down. If it was too cold for us to remain outside without jackets, we would tiptoe over to visit our neighbor across the street. She was a plump, kind lady with short curly hair. Much to my relief, she never asked questions. Instead, she would just call the police and serve us milk and cookies while we waited for the police or our father to take us back home. Calling the cops meant trouble for our parents, so most often we simply endured the cold as long as we could, and then Lillian and I would creep back inside and tiptoe up to our room. There, we would slip into bed, wondering when the next crisis would leave us exposed and vulnerable again.

Chapter 2

Flowers in the Basement

January–July 1981

One evening, Lillian and I were playing together in the down-stairs playroom with a couple of inexpensive baby dolls. Lillian, who was much more feminine than I, loved playing with them. She was a good "mommy." I preferred to play outside in the dirt and sunshine since I helped take care of Amanda, who always seemed to need her diaper changed. Suddenly, we heard our mother scream, "Deniiise! Liiillly! Come here!"

Instead of responding immediately, we froze in place, weighing our options to follow the call or run.

Her tone changed. It was calmer and quieter but more threat-ening, as though she were addressing someone close by—probably our father: "I'm going to hurt the kids. I swear to God, I'm going to hurt the kids." Then she switched back to her earlier long-distance screaming voice: "Deniiise! I said, Liiilly, *come here!*"

We couldn't escape outside from where we were, so we fled into the forbidden plant room next to the playroom in the basement. There, grow lights emitted a blue hue over two long green tables covered with large plants in matching terra-cotta pots. At another time, I would have reflected on how pretty it was in there with the lights and the leafy plants growing beneath them. But right then, Lillian and I could only think of the plant room as a good hiding place. Since our father didn't allow us in that room because he didn't want us near the plants, we hoped Mom wouldn't look for us there.

Decades later I would learn from my mother's sister, Aunt Clara, that they were growing marijuana and that my mother had been arrested for it.

Lillian and I scrambled under a table and huddled close together. We could hear Mom stomping around angrily upstairs. We knew she was hunting us down. Suddenly, the screaming stopped. Silence was not a good thing in this case. We knew that her tirade wasn't over until we heard the long terrifying siren shriek. The stomps started again, down the stairs. We heard our mother rummaging through the playroom, looking for wherever we might be hiding. Paralyzed with fear, we listened to her moving things around in the playroom. She was intent on finding us.

Again, she screamed, "Deniiise! Liillly! Come here! I told you to come here. Get out here *now*!"

We remained motionless and silent.

She continued screaming like this as she moved through the basement, eliminating all the places we weren't and coming closer to where we were. She approached the door of the plant room. It was the only way in or out of the room. We had no escape.

When she entered the room, she spotted us immediately. She grabbed Lillian by the hair before we had time to react. As she pulled her out from under the table, I ran to hide under the stairs behind our toy barrel.

Mom dragged Lillian across the floor and out into the playroom by her hair. "Denise, get out here now, or I'm going to hurt her. I mean it. Get over here now."

Lilly was howling in pain. Not knowing what to do, I curled up in a ball behind a mound of toys in the corner beside the barrel. The cold cement wall scraped against my skin as I cried and shook in fear. I peered out from under the steps and saw my mother holding Lillian up in the air by her blond mane. A patch of hair ripped from Lillian's scalp, and my mother was left holding the clump of hair as Lilly fell. She shrieked as she landed hard on the cement floor, and

I hoped she would escape, but my mother tossed aside the hair and regained her hold on my sister. Lillian, who was only five, was still screaming and flailing; her little feet kicked powerlessly in circles.

The whole time, my mother continued yelling, "Denise, I told you to come out. Get over here! I mean it, Denise. Come here, or I'm going to hurt her!" As if she hadn't already.

Silent tears burned my cheeks. I started to pray. I had been taught at Awana that God listens to prayers. "Please, God, make her stop. Please, God, make her stop," I repeated over and over again silently.

Nothing stopped. My mother suspended Lillian in the air again by her hair, probably because it prevented her from flailing. At Awana, they had told me that God would help us if we prayed to him and that He would be there for us, but that was not happening. God was not there. He was not saving us from our mother. Nothing was saving us. Not God and certainly not my father.

"Get over here, or I'm going to hurt your sister," my mother kept screeching, stuck in her crazy threat.

"Please, God, please come help us. Please!" I prayed.

When no one came to rescue us, I realized I was the only person who could help Lilly, who was still shrieking in pain. Despite my shaking, I pulled myself to my feet and exited my hiding place. I was now in full view of my mother. Slowly and unsteadily, I walked toward her, shuffling through the stuffed animals, barely able to move for fear of what would happen to me once this madwoman got hold of me. I didn't make eye contact with her, which I knew would incite her. Instead, I looked at the floor. But this also meant I couldn't follow her movements, which could turn against me at any moment. I came to a halt directly before my mother. I was quaking inside, and my little heart was beating so fast.

Luckily, at that moment, the basement door was flung open. My father filled the doorway at the top of the stairs. He was lit from behind by the bright florescent lights of the kitchen. "What is going on down there?" he demanded.

Looking back on it now, I wonder why he even bothered to ask such a question, as he had been there when my mother began her rampage and threatened to hurt us. It would have made more sense—and it certainly would have been more reassuring—to hear him say, "Leave the kids alone." He had seen her attack her children like this before, yet he almost never intervened. Somehow, he must have thought it was appropriate for her to unleash her rage on us, displacing it from him.

My mother released Lillian, who again fell to the cement floor. This time, she was able to scurry up the stairs past my father. I, too, used the break in attention to bolt away from my mother, completely forgetting about my desperate prayers to God to send help.

* * *

My family spent these early tumultuous years in a two-level four-square house built around the turn of the nineteenth century at the end of a cul-de-sac. Although my parents lived in a small apartment when I was born in January of 1975, we moved out when I was still too young to remember it, and my first memories are of the house that my physician grandfather bought for my parents. Our home was at the edge of town and backed up to the farms that straddled Bancroft Brook, a tributary of the Connecticut River. The house, which was nothing more than a plain box with dormer windows, was painted white on the first story and green on the second. The darker color higher up was an attempt at creating visual interest, but it just made the house look top-heavy.

We were fortunate to have many kids on our isolated road, which was hemmed in by farmland on one side and woodland on the other. Johnny, who was a year older than me and my best friend, lived halfway down the street. He discovered an old barn filled with hay, previously used as a tobacco shed, on one of his solo excursions and brought me to see it. He led the way as we jumped and ran through the undergrowth of the woods. We climbed up into the low rafters and jumped down into the scattered piles of hay. When he got bored with that, Johnny started walking along the crossbeams and dared me to do the same.

As I was climbing off of a hay bale, he suddenly stopped and called down from the rafters, "Hey, Denise, didja hear that?"

"No."

"I thought I heard your mom call you. You didn't tell her where we are, did you?"

"No, she doesn't know where this place is," I replied.

"I could've sworn I heard her call for you from the woods. Maybe it was an owl."

For a moment, I assumed Johnny had just heard my mother calling from the house, but then I realized we were too far away for that to be possible. Had he heard the same voices calling for me that I heard when I hid with Lillian in the hedges? I was relieved that someone else could hear the voices calling my name and that it wasn't just in my head. However, I wasn't ready to find out why I was being called.

* * *

One late summer evening, the neighborhood children gathered at dusk to play hide-and-seek with Keith, another friend who lived at the far end of the street. His parents had adopted three or four children and had a couple of their own. It was a wild scene. Nearly a dozen children were dashing about. Some had flashlights. Some wore dark clothing, which gave them the appearance of shadows as they ran howling through the backyards. One of the girls was crying over being caught.

Unexpectedly, my nearly four-year-old sister, Mariah, appeared. She had wandered down Ident Road, unsupervised and barefoot, looking for Lillian and me. She was still wearing diapers, and her diaper sagged, as if filled with rocks. Our grandmother had once told us that she was "special." We didn't know what she meant by that, but we did know that she wasn't normal like we were. Mariah wanted to play, but every time she approached someone, they ran away, screaming. The other kids pointed and laughed at her. A couple of kids sprinted up to her, called out, "Come and get me. You stink, Doo-doo Monster," and then darted back into the security of the shadows. Soon Mariah was just walking in circles, crying.

I thought this was hilarious—but only for a moment. Guilt pricked my throat and squelched my laughter. Lillian must have felt the same way because she and I remained silent in the darkness. We didn't want to be associated with Mariah by coming to her rescue. The streetlights glared down on my sister as she tried to find someone, anyone to play with her.

Fortunately, Keith's parents soon called in their children, and the rest of us headed home. Lillian and I kept well ahead of Mariah, pretending she wasn't behind us.

Mariah was like a gigantic, sweet baby. She loved to give hugs and kisses; more than that, she loved to eat. At this stage of her life, she was unusually compliant and rarely fussed, prompting our parents to say to Lillian and me, "I wish you two were more like Mariah. She goes to bed when we tell her to and without whining." Mariah's big round eyes sparkled with joy whenever anyone engaged with her, but we were embarrassed by her. We tried to leave her behind when we went out to play with the neighborhood kids, but she followed us whenever she had the chance. Mariah was a constant reminder that even when we tried to interact with other kids, we couldn't seem to escape our family and just be normal.

Chapter 3

Mother's Mayhem

July–December 1981

My mother controlled her temper better when she was out of the house, but even then, she reacted like a wild animal backed into a corner anytime she was confronted. She was anxious in the most ordinary situations, and that anxiety increased as social interactions grew more complex.

One afternoon late in the summer, I went on a walk through the backyard with my mother. I loved being outside and was happy to spend time with my mom when she wasn't having a meltdown. As we approached the edge of our property, she saw Tommy Erickson's mom walking along the dirt road that ran between our property and the small stream we children enjoyed playing in. Tommy was my age and lived in the nicest home on the street. His family owned a large piece of land behind several of the homes on our street, and they were thinking of subdividing it into lots for houses. As part of these plans, Tommy's father had recently widened the dirt road running along our property. My parents disputed the Erickson property line and insisted that the road had been partially built on our land.

Upon spotting Mrs. Erickson, my mother rushed over to her. "Why are you here? This isn't your land!" my mother shouted, going way beyond the claim that the road was slightly on our property.

"What are you talking about? I'm not on your land. This is my road."

My mother screamed something unintelligible, and I backed

away from the two women.

Tommy's mother answered reasonably but with authority, "The road is well behind your yard. We have the right to develop our own property. If you want to come with me, I'll show you the property lines."

I knew this meant trouble. No one ever spoke to my mother like that.

They walked along the road bordering the small stream toward an abandoned bus, arguing the whole way. I followed not far behind, but when they reached the bus, I hid near a clay mound so my mother wouldn't know I was listening. Tommy's mother most likely didn't expect what happened next, but I did.

A scuffle ensued when my mother grabbed Mrs. Erickson's pocketbook, and she resisted. My mother managed to pry it from her and then threw it, though I didn't see where since the bus was blocking my view. I was later told that it landed in the stream. Mrs. Erickson, perhaps finally realizing that she was dealing with an unstable person, hustled off back to her house, where she filed a complaint with the police.

A short time later, officers came to our house to arrest my mother for throwing Mrs. Erickson's pocketbook into the stream. They stayed at our house for what felt like hours, waiting for my father to get home and assume responsibility for us children. Then they took her to the police station in their cruiser while the rest of us followed them in our car.

I wonder now as an adult if this was when the police discovered the marijuana growing in the basement. As a child, I wouldn't have picked up on the muffled code words the officers used, and my parents never admitted to the incident. In their minds, bad things *happened* to them. They were never the instigators.

At the police station, I was tall enough to just barely peer over the counter. I stood close to my mother, wondering why they were pushing her thumb and then her index finger into black ink. She was released that evening and remained silent the entire way home.

A few weeks later, my family accompanied my mother to court. I sat on a wooden bench next to my father and siblings, waiting for my mother to be called to testify. I was the only witness to the pocketbook confrontation, so I too would have to testify.

The judge, a well-built man with gray hair and caring eyes, sat slightly above everyone else like a king on his throne. My mother was brought to the witness box, but she didn't say much—mostly just "yes" and "no."

Eventually, it was my turn. An officer of the court led me to the witness stand and swore me in after I figured out which hand was my right hand. It took a couple of tries. I had to stand in the witness box because only part of my head was visible when I sat on the wooden chair inside it.

One of the lawyers approached me. She wore a black well-fitting suit and was young and thin with straight shiny brown hair cut into a long bob. I thought she was pretty. She spoke to me in a flat voice: "Did you see your mother throw Mrs. Erickson's pocketbook into the stream? Remember, you have to tell the truth."

"No. I don't know. I don't think so," I said as I shifted nervously from one foot to the other.

As I looked out from the solid oak box that surrounded me, I felt a multitude of faces staring back, judging me. I scanned the blank faces in the courtroom, feeling completely exposed, as if they could all see directly into my soul. Of course, in reality, most of the people present in the courtroom were likely just waiting for their turn to talk to the judge.

Another lawyer, an older man, said to me, "You must have seen her throw the pocketbook into the river. You were standing right next to them."

"But I went home when they started yelling at each other," I lied. After all, I was the one who would have to go home with my mother later.

I was shaking from the interrogation, but I truly didn't know what had actually happened. I had been hiding, hardly paying attention to what either woman was doing. I'd been listening to the pitch and volume of my mother's voice to determine my next move and hadn't heard the actual words they were speaking. The male lawyer started to ask me about the pocketbook again, but the judge must have noticed my discomfort because he cut him off and let me leave the stand. I quickly walked back to my father, trembling from my first solo performance before an audience. I searched his face to see if he was angry with me, but he was just staring at my mother with concern.

After I returned to my seat, the judge straightened a pile of papers on his desk and slid them into a manila folder. It seemed he had already made his decision about my mother's case before either of us took the stand. He decreed that we were to attend a year of family counseling in exchange for dismissal of the charges.

A couple of weeks later, when it was time for our counseling to begin, my mother shouted at my dad, "You can't make me go!"

"But, Debbie, we have to go. You know that."

"No, I don't have to go. They all think I'm crazy, and I'm not. They're the crazy ones."

She started throwing random items, mostly plates from the counter, at our father to make him change his mind, but he stood his ground. "You have to go, and that's that. Now get into the car," he said firmly.

"You can't make me!" she screeched back.

"Debbie, you know what will happen if we don't go, so get in the car."

They repeated this exchange almost every time we had to go to family counseling. She would either relent at this point and agree to go with us or escalate the argument into a full-fledged fit. If she had baby Amanda in her arms, she would throw her glasses, and if she didn't, she'd start beating her fists against her head.

When my mother hit herself like this, it stopped me in my tracks.

I wasn't sure if she actually wanted to harm herself or if it was the ultimate form of manipulation. When she did this, I was afraid to walk past her toward the front door and would start praying, "Dear, God, please, please make her stop. I'll be a good girl. Please!"

My father would grab Mom's arm and half drag, half lead her out of the house and into the station wagon. We'd follow closely behind and quickly pile into the car, climbing over each other and jostling silently for the window seats.

Once we actually arrived, I enjoyed the therapy sessions. The therapist was a slender man with a full head of thick dark-gray hair. His office was a quiet, peaceful, orderly environment where I felt safe. He had a new joke to tell us each time we arrived. Then he would usher us into a large room with two short tables, each surrounded by red, yellow, and blue child-sized chairs. We children colored at one of the tables while the therapist spoke with my parents in a private office with a glass door that allowed him to keep an eye on us. Sometimes, he asked Mariah to join them. He was most interested in her. He knew there was something different about her even if my parents wouldn't admit to it. After about thirty minutes, he would walk out with my parents and ask us kids a couple of questions while ruffling our hair, making it staticky.

However pleasant the counselor was, the counseling itself had little positive impact on my parents. One evening after our session, while driving home along the four-lane Route 5, my parents started arguing. I sank into the shadows of the back seat, staying very still in order to avoid drawing attention to myself. I wasn't really listening to their argument; I was too busy making myself small. I knew it would take very little for my mother to reach back and rake our faces with her long, sharp fingernails.

Suddenly, my mother flung the car door open. Wind whipped our hair, yet we remained silent; we knew better than to say anything. "I'm jumping out," she screamed. "I swear to God, unless you stop this car right now, I'm jumping out."

"Don't be ridiculous, Debbie. Shut the door," my father bellowed at her. Despite his words, part of him must have believed her threat because he slowed down. My father had this odd ability to deny what was right in front of him despite being a realist who understood what was going on.

"Stop the car," Mom repeated. "I'm getting out now." She leaned into the breeze.

We remained quiet in the back seat as my father continued to slow the station wagon. Before he could stop, though, she threw herself out of the car. Through the window, I caught a glimpse of her rolling onto the grassy shoulder. I was relieved that there were no other vehicles on the road behind us, both for her safety and for my sense of embarrassment. I couldn't believe she had done that. No one in their right mind would do that, especially a mom.

My father slowed to a crawl, checking his rearview mirror the whole time.

"Aren't you going back to get her?" Lillian wailed.

"She'll catch up." My father sighed, finally stopping the car. He leaned across the front seat and out of the open passenger door, one hand still on the steering wheel, and hollered, "Debbie, get in the car now!"

Lillian, Mariah, and I turned around in our seats to peer out the back window—since it was the eighties, none of us wore seatbelts. Our mother stood up and started walking toward us. She hadn't bothered to dust the dirt off of her jeans, and her elbow was scraped and bloody.

"No, I'm not getting back in the car," Mom shouted. "I'm walking home."

"Debbie, get back in the car. We're on a highway."

We were surprised and embarrassed when she walked right past the car and kept going. A couple of cars passed us and slowed down to gawk at the scene she was making. My father started driving again and crept up to her, the door still ajar. "Debbie, come on. Just get in the car," he begged.

"No!"

"Okay, fine, walk home then," he snapped. He yanked the door shut but continued to follow her for a few minutes, rolling along the shoulder. She stared straight ahead, pretending not to see us. Finally, Dad gave up and drove home in silence, leaving our mother alone, dirty, and disheveled to walk the last two miles home.

Chapter 4

My Father's Breaking Point

1982

My father held our family together during those early years when my mother's emotional turmoil made normal family life impossible. She was incapable of managing, much less nurturing, four young children. And in January of 1982, she was pregnant with her fifth. Looking back on it now, I realize that any reasonable person would ask why such a couple would bring yet another child into their chaotic, unhappy family.

The little nurturing and protection my father provided in my younger years evaporated that winter. One cold evening two weeks after my seventh birthday on January 24th, my father walked into the bedroom I shared with Lillian. He was in tears. It was the first time either of us had seen him cry. His entire body shook as he sobbed, his shoulders rising and falling with each devastated inhalation. He eventually calmed himself enough to tell us that our grandfather had passed away.

I asked him what he had died from, and my father simply said, "Old age." I couldn't understand how someone could die just from being old. I prodded a bit more, and my father explained that my grandfather had had a stroke.

Since I had only met him once when I was an infant, I had no memories of my grandfather, so I didn't feel sad about his passing. My father's sorrow, on the other hand, was palpable. It thickened the air in our room and prompted us to cry along with him.

As an adult, I wonder why he came into our room to release his pain. Most men would not seek out their children in such a moment; they would go to their wives. Was it because he knew my mother was incapable of feeling empathy? Did he know that she would not—could not—be there for him?

A few days after my grandfather's death, my father, Lillian, and I left for the funeral in Virginia. My mother stayed behind with four-year-old Mariah and one-year-old Amanda because she was seven months pregnant. It was easier for her to stay home with them than to manage all of us on a plane.

This was the first time I had ever flown, and I was excited. I gazed out the window, watching the clouds interspersed with swaths of land the entire trip. It was mesmerizing.

My grandfather's house was not what I had anticipated. He had been a doctor and the son of a bishop, and I expected him to have a "rich person's house." After all, my mother was always going on about how much money my grandfather had and how he never gave us any. Instead, he had lived in a small 1950s brick ranch-style house in an aging neighborhood. My father's aunt, who lived a few miles away in the same town, let us in. Instead of a hotel room, we were staying there for free. When she opened the door, we were greeted by the heavy, musty smell of mothballs. I crinkled up my face.

We followed our father through the living room. It was tidy, with expensive matching wood-and-leather furnishings. It was very different from our house's mismatched furniture and filthy piles of garbage. However, it was also utterly devoid of life, like a long-abandoned museum. With a flash of insight beyond my years, I realized that my grandfather had left everything exactly as it had been at the time of my grandmother's death many years prior.

Trailing behind Dad like ducklings, we made our way past the spare bedroom and into the bathroom. It was late in the evening, and my father had not yet taken his shower and bath, which he never skipped. He would take the shower first so that he wouldn't have to soak in potentially dirty water. My father pushed aside the yellowed plastic curtain surrounding the tub; beige paint was peeling from the porcelain.

"Who paints the inside of a tub?" he asked no one in particular. He ripped off a layer of paint, and it crumbled in his hand. He pulled another layer from the tub and rubbed it between his fingers. It, too, fell apart. What we thought was paint was actually a layer of soap! How could a prominent physician's home be in such neglect? I peered into the tub lined with the baths of a thousand days past, the tub of a man who no longer existed, unable to reconcile the grand stories my father had told us about our grandfather with his worn, neglected, and modest home. My father started to clean the tub. It was a long task.

The next day, Lillian, who was too afraid to see a dead person, stayed with a babysitter during the viewing. I was curious about the whole thing and asked to come, so I rode with my father and some distant relatives to my grandfather's wake. It was raining that day and not at all cheerful.

When we arrived, I walked to the front of the viewing parlor. The rich wood paneling made it a dark space; even the dozens of flower arrangements failed to brighten up the gloom. I could feel the sense of loss in that room. My father and his only sibling, Uncle Richard, seemed to exhale their grief.

Peering into the casket, I saw not the face of an old man, but that of a carved shriveled apple. Wrinkles and dark-brown age spots covered his face even though he was only seventy-three. He was a chain-smoker who had even smoked in his practice. I wondered if I should kiss him on the forehead. Wasn't that the proper thing to do? I had seen it on TV. His skin looked pasty from the makeup, and I couldn't bear to bring my lips to it. Instead, I just stared at him.

Suddenly, I burst into tears, sobbing quietly. What was I supposed to do? I didn't even recognize this man. He had never so much as spoken to me on the phone. I had been invisible to him, yet I felt as if I owed him something for helping us financially over the years.

I bent over his casket and promised him that I would become a doctor, as he had been. That promise felt like a proper substitute for not kissing his cold, dead skin. Somehow the idea of becoming a doctor like my grandfather felt right to me. A doctor? Sure, I could be a doctor. I could be someone my dad would be proud of.

The next morning, the morning of the funeral, it rained again. What looked like hundreds of people lined the church, the steps, and even the entrance yard, forming a canopy of black umbrellas. Although my grandfather had lived in a modest house, he had clearly touched the lives of an entire community. These people were crying and telling us what a wonderful man he had been as we stood in line after the service, shaking hands. I knew almost nothing about him other than these stories.

Learning to live with his father's death proved to be difficult for my father. Although we hadn't visited my grandfather since I was an infant—and I'm not aware of Dad visiting his father without us—my father changed after my grandfather's death. He hadn't had a close relationship with his father, who was largely absent, spending upwards of fourteen hours a day in his medical practice. Yet it destabilized him somehow. I came to understand later in life that this response was not a natural part of the grieving process. It was as if something had mentally snapped in him; perhaps it brought to the surface the pain of losing his mother to colon cancer when he was twenty-two. It devastated him.

My father's mother had doted on him, the baby of the family. She had been a teacher prior to having her two sons and spent a great deal of time helping my father as he struggled through school, which he wasn't very interested in. He mostly earned B's and C's, much to the displeasure of his father. He should have been a straight-A student like his older brother, Richard.

Recognizing her second son's lack of interest in academics, my grandmother had looked for activities he could excel at. She saw to it that he had dancing lessons, and he became a silver-star-level Fred Astaire ballroom dancer. He was her golden boy, and he returned the adoration.

However, his mother was also demanding and authoritarian—volatile and unpredictable, like my mother. She would bestow affection and then withdraw it, leaving him unsure of what to expect. Her husband and sons found it difficult to navigate her impulsive actions and irrational behaviors, and Richard wondered in adulthood whether she had borderline personality disorder. She was a germophobe and believed that anything and everything from her husband's previous military career was contaminated with syphilis or gonorrhea. Her fear prompted her to cut up and burn everything she associated with his military days.

By the time he met my mother at age twenty-six, my father had grown his hair long and wholeheartedly embraced the hippy counterculture. His mother's death had propelled him into an extended adolescence, and he'd spent his time wandering, backpacking through Holland, and moving to Connecticut. By the time he married, he hadn't attained more than an associate's degree. Now, he had lost his father.

My father now had no one to turn to. His sense of security in life had come from his father's emergency funds, and now that was gone forever. Without his father in the background, my father couldn't deal with the financial, emotional, and logistical demands of his growing family.

* * *

Helen, who was born in March, after my grandfather's death, was now the baby of the family. We were five girls—all under the age of eight. Five children under eight would be a challenge to even a normal and emotionally healthy couple. My parents were more than challenged; they were overwhelmed.

For Easter in 1982, my parents gave each of us an Easter basket.

They often tried to do the normal things that other families did during the holidays. Our baskets were brightly colored, made of braided plastic, and filled with green paper grass and an assortment of cheap candy that my mother had divided up among us. The crown jewel of each of these baskets was a single hollow chocolate rabbit.

After receiving our baskets, we retreated to the basement playroom to watch cartoons and eat our candy. I remember being content that morning—even happy.

Mariah was chewing on the ear of a large chocolate Easter rabbit. As usual, her eating habits left much to be desired for a girl going on five. Chocolate ran from the corner of her lip to her chin. Amanda's rabbit was missing, and since she was not yet two, she started wailing at the injustice of it. It only took a minute for Amanda's cry to reach Dad, and he ran downstairs to find out what was upsetting her.

Amanda had been Dad's favorite since she was born. She was unusually small and had had to be brought to the hospital for regular checkups for the first year of her life. The doctors worried initially that she might have spina bifida, a condition in which the base of the spine does not close properly prior to delivery. She was also the prettiest of us all. She had giant hazel-green eyes, long curling lashes, and delicate facial features. Her light-brown hair, streaked with blond strands, fell in long, loose curls around her cheeks.

My father used to recite the poem by Henry Wadsworth Longfellow:

> There was a little girl,
> Who had a little curl,
> Right in the middle of her forehead.
> When she was good,
> She was very good indeed,
> But when she was bad she was horrid.[1]

---

1   Henry Wadsworth Longfellow, "There was a little girl," Poetry Foundation, accessed February 24, 2021, https://www.poetryfoundation.org/poems/44650/there-was-a-little-girl.

The truth was that Amanda was always good. She was terribly shy and never argued when asked to do anything. She was the ideal child.

My father was very protective of her and did anything and everything to calm her when she cried. That day, as he walked down into the basement, he asked, "What's wrong down here?"

"Mi-ah dook bunny," Amanda wailed.

"Mariah, give the rabbit back to Amanda," he ordered sternly.

"No, it's my wabbit. She wost her wabbit," Mariah replied with conviction.

"Dook bunny. Dook bunny!" Amanda continued to cry.

"Mariah, give her back her rabbit right now." Dad was losing patience. I could tell he had been angry about something before the rabbit spat, and he had brought that anger with him.

"It's not her wabbit. It's mine. She can't have it."

By now, our father was standing right in front of Mariah. His nostrils flared and his face reddened at her defiance. His hand whipped through the air, and he slapped Mariah across the face.

Suddenly, everything was red. Blood poured from her nose like water spouting from a rain gutter. Mariah started screaming. I looked up at my father; he was blurry. I had apparently started crying without realizing it. I wiped my eyes and stared at the bloody, single-eared bunny that had fallen into Mariah's lap. I couldn't bring myself to look at her face. I watched as her yellow dress sprouted red streaks. She continued wailing.

As if awakening from another mental state, my father started repeating, "Oh my God, oh my God."

After this incident, my father's anger would often explode unexpectedly. His rage turned him into another person, one who was brutal, but then he would snap out of his rage, as if he had been hypnotized. There was always a trigger for this sudden anger. Learning that it was time to run when he increased his volume saved me a lot of grief.

To some extent, after his father's death, my father was no longer present for us. What we had instead was a man who couldn't handle being a father of five children. Now we had to contend with two unreasonable, unstable parents.

* * *

Now that the family consisted of seven people—five of whom were constantly getting bigger—our house on Ident Road was becoming increasingly crowded. Lillian and I were happy to share a room, but there simply wasn't enough space in the three-bedroom house for all of us.

Within a year of my father receiving his inheritance from his father, my parents found a larger home. Before I understood what was happening and what it would mean, I was whisked away from my friends. I left my childhood home to be reborn into a new, foreign life. In many ways, things got worse, and my parents grew increasingly unreasonable and unpredictable. It was a life I couldn't escape from.

Chapter 5

Settling In

1983

T he last rays of sunlight had already vanished when my father's 1957 red Ford pickup truck pulled into the driveway of our new home in Winsted, Connecticut. It had not been a long ride from South Windsor, but the landscape changed radically. We had left behind the broad, flat farmlands with their scattered barns that I loved so much and entered the gorgeous hills at the edge of the Berkshires, where Winsted was nestled in a valley.

I was curled up on the truck's floorboard between my mother's feet. Lillian and Mariah sat on the bench seat between my parents, and both Amanda and Helen were snuggled up in our mother's lap.

Upon arriving at our new home, we all piled out and stood in the driveway, looking around. Emerging from the dusk was the most majestic brick Victorian house I had ever seen. Awestruck, I temporarily forgot how urgently I needed to use the bathroom.

After everyone took a turn in the downstairs bathroom, we went on a tour of our new home. In the formal living room, a massive mahogany door opened to the front vestibule, which had a second smaller door with an etched glass mural. I gaped in astonishment at the morning garden scene with a large dew-draped spider web at its center. To my right was a huge fireplace surrounded by an intricate wooden mantel with shelves, miniature railings, a stained glass window directly in the center of the flue.

The dining room was to my left. In the far corner of the room was a built-in bench seat covered with plush red velvet cushions. Two huge windows framed with stained glass stretched to the ceiling above them.

I turned to my father and asked in awe, "Is this our new house?"

He explained that there had been a fire on the third floor thirty years earlier when the previous owners rented it out. Instead of restoring it to its original condition, they had just replaced it with an attic, which had lowered its value. That was how we had been able to afford it.

Our parents led us through a cheap modern glass-paneled door, conspicuously out of place among the majestic woodwork and detailing of the other rooms we had seen. The door and a wall had been added to close off the downstairs from the upstairs hallway so that rooms could be rented upstairs without allowing renters free range of the house.

I felt like we had moved into a castle. Everything about it was spectacular. For just a moment, I felt like a princess.

However, my elation dampened as we continued our tour. Despite the house's beauty, it was permeated by a sadness I could not place, and it felt like someone else was already living in it. It was like that sensation you feel when you come home expecting the house to be empty, but you realize as soon as you enter that someone else is there, even if you can't yet see or hear them. It was unsettling.

Our bedrooms were upstairs. Lillian, Mariah, and I would share one, while Amanda and Helen would share another. After our parents showed us to our bedrooms, they asked me to go down to the kitchen to get a cup of juice for Amanda. For once, my parents had had the foresight to purchase some essentials.

Of course, another parent might have said, "You don't know this house yet, so let's go get some juice for Amanda together." Instead, my parents simply gave me an order. The house also had a second staircase, used by servants a century earlier. My parents told me to take that staircase because it would lead directly to the kitchen.

Following their directions to the back staircase, I passed several empty rooms. I hadn't been afraid of the dark in our old house, but this was an unfamiliar space. I couldn't bring myself to enter any of these rooms. I had the feeling that someone was following me, so I turned around, expecting to see one of my sisters. But no one was there.

As I looked down the back staircase for the first time, I felt fear. The steep, narrow stairs were lit by a single flush-mount dome light at the top. The air was so dusty it appeared murky in the dim light. Walking down the stairs, I felt a malicious presence watching me. Still, knowing I had to bring the juice back or face a reprimand, I rushed down the steps to the kitchen. I sensed it was important to avoid whatever it was that resided in that house. I had never believed in the bogeyman before, but that evening, I began to question my disbelief.

Alone in that kitchen, I felt like Alice in Wonderland. The cabinets towered above me, stretching nearly all the way up to the twelve-foot ceilings. Everything around me was huge, as if I had suddenly shrunk.

After pouring the glass of juice, I dashed back upstairs as fast as I could without spilling the liquid. When I returned, my family was still in Amanda and Helen's room, which was directly above the dining room.

One corner of their room extended out away from the rest of the house, forming a square turret. In the turret corner, four long, thin windows were topped by convex triangular pieces of Gothic stained glass. One had been damaged by the fire, though, and had been replaced with plywood. This window was like something out of a cheap horror movie. It made me feel insecure, even in the company of my family.

We unpacked over the next few days. My mother had insisted on bringing boxes and brown paper bags full of items she wanted to save but had no practical use for, such as our old school papers, worn clothing, our scribbled artwork, photos and memorabilia from her youth, and photos of my father's family dating back several generations. These items had to be stored in the attic, and we piled them on top of each other under the eaves where my father directed us to place them.

Nothing was unusual about the attic in daylight, but when darkness came, it transformed from a quiet sanctuary into a dark and sinister place. Going to the attic was different from climbing the back stairs. When taking the back stairs, I felt a chill pass through me, giving me goose bumps. But when I began my ascent to the attic, a tremor swept over me. Sometimes, I would shake so violently that I would accidentally drop what I was carrying. I never saw anything frightening, but I knew something was up there. I could feel it.

My mother, who never lifted any of the boxes destined for the attic herself, always seemed to wait until dark before asking me to carry them up. I started to wonder if she was doing this on purpose, due to my trepidation. Of course, she may simply have been more active during the latter part of the day. Whatever the reason, I felt sure she could sense my reluctance and enjoyed watching me acquiesce to her demands, despite my fear.

If I could coerce one of my sisters into coming with me, the attic was nearly bearable. Unfortunately, I usually made the trip alone because the girls refused to accompany me; they were afraid of the third floor, too.

Whenever I made it to the top of the attic stairs, I would sing or talk to myself and whatever it was I sensed up there. The silence of the attic mingling with the whistling winds was terrifying, and I tried to replace it with my cheerful chatter. It was my only defense against the thousand eyes I felt watching me.

"Now stay back! I'm coming up," I would say to the things lurking whenever I began my ascent. "I know you're up here. I'll leave as soon as I put this down, okay?"

I reasoned that the things hiding in the shadows could not hurt me, but I couldn't help envisioning gremlins jumping onto my back, pulling my hair, and then disappearing behind a box, laughing at and tormenting me. After a few trips to the attic after sundown, I began putting the bags and boxes in my room. Then the next morning, I would bring them up in daylight.

I didn't tell anyone about the things I believed were residing in our house. After all, how could I describe this feeling concretely enough to be believable? Plus, my parents weren't even persuaded by believable arguments.

After moving, it took my parents a few days to submit the paperwork to register Lillian, Mariah, and me for school. Since my father was working, he had to take an extra day off. As a result, we had a full two weeks off before we started classes at our new elementary school, which was within walking distance of our new house.

A late spring snow fell the night before our first day of school. It was the kind that freezes all the buds off the trees, causing locals to bemoan the fate of their gardens. Walking to school that morning, we were underdressed, as usual. While other mothers paid attention to things like winter coats, scarves, and hats, my mother was oblivious to it. Freezing air blew up under our thrift-store dresses as we approached a hill that reached several hundred feet straight up. Cars drove by and splashed us with road muck. I wondered what kept the descending cars from flipping over on this steep hill. While pondering this, I slipped on the slush-covered sidewalk. My dress was wet and spotted with dirt.

Once we finally arrived inside the stark-white cinderblock hallways of our new elementary school, I spoke to no one, and no one spoke to me. I knew I was a stranger who was attracting attention.

I didn't realize at the time that my gaudy floral dress was a decade out of style. Once a year, my parents went to the local Salvation Army store to buy us "new" clothes. They never paid attention to what the other kids were wearing, and in my old school, I had worn such clothes without embarrassment. It didn't occur to me that I stuck out.

In our first few days at the new school, kids ran past Lillian and me yelling, "Raggy! Raggy! Look, it's a raggy!"

My first thought was, "What the heck is a 'raggy'?"

I asked a girl in my class and found out that *raggy* was a local term for the poor people who had worked in the town's factories back in the early 1900s. They brought home leftover scraps of cloth from the textile mills to make clothes, quilt blankets, or use as rags around the house. Even after the Mad River flooded in 1955, leveling most of the factories, *raggy* remained a name for poor, dirty, or otherwise outcast people. I fit all three categories.

Since I only bathed once a week, my fine, straight, uncut hair was perpetually oily and dirty. I was starting to realize that, even though we lived in a mansion of a house, we were still poor. And I certainly felt like an outcast.

Barely a handful of kids acknowledged my existence those first few weeks in my new town; most of those who did mocked me. It didn't help that I had a lisp and stutter, which got worse when I was nervous.

I missed my old friends and desperately wanted to return to them. I was homesick, had no friends in Winsted, and was scared that the bogeyman living in our new house would attack me. Everything about this foreign town felt cold and desolate. I couldn't even find my favorite stuffed animal, since so many of our boxes were still unpacked, crammed into corners and scattered about.

In those early weeks, instead of looking to my peers for acceptance, I found myself trying to please my third grade teachers. I worked hard, always raised my hand, and offered to help out. I received straight A's for my efforts.

My mother was also stressed from the move, and she had started her bouts of screaming outside again. It made me nervous because we had so many neighbors close by. Dozens of homes were within earshot, and there were no fields to serve as a buffer. I was embarrassed by her and knew that her unusual behavior would only cement my status as a "raggy."

* * *

A couple of weeks after moving in, we girls met our next-door neighbor while playing in the side yard. Her house was slightly higher up the hill than ours, and a three-foot-high wall of huge granite blocks created a terrace-like step up to her yard. One afternoon, when she saw us outside, she walked to the wall's edge to greet us.

"I'm so delighted you moved in," said the slender Italian woman, who was old enough to be our grandmother. "I always wanted a daughter, and now there's... wait... how many of you are there?"

"Five," I said. I had to tip my head back to meet her eyes and answer her.

"Five! Well, you're in the perfect house for so many sweet little girls. My name's Alice, and my husband's is John. I've been living here for over thirty years."

"Wow, that's a long time!" I answered. I liked her instantly. Alice reminded me of the perfect grandmother, the type that always asks you to come visit. The type who has home-cooked meals simmering on the stove and greets you with a gigantic hug.

A few weeks later, she came to visit at the wall dividing our properties again, this time with brownies—the good, homemade kind with chocolate chips and walnuts. She bent to hand the paper plate of treats down to us.

"Last night, right before I went to bed, I thought I heard someone screaming. It was really unusual. You wouldn't happen to know any-thing about that, would you?" Alice asked with concern.

Lillian looked at me with wide eyes.

"No," I said in my best lying voice. "I didn't hear anything." Lillian and I quickly shoved brownies in our mouths so we couldn't say anything more for a moment. In an effort to change the subject, I nervously said around a mouthful of brownies, "Thank you for the brownies. They're really good."

"You're welcome, sweeties. You can throw the plate out when you're done." She turned and walked back to her porch, which faced our property. A wave of relief washed over me. I had narrowly escaped having to explain to our neighbor that my mother went outside to scream her head off after an argument with our father every so often. Even in our new home, we were not "normal."

* * *

A month or two later, my father was awakened by the sound of his bedroom door opening. He looked up and asked, "Who's there?"

A small child stood in the darkened doorway. Assuming that one of us wanted something, he sat up and leaned over the edge of the bed to get a better look. The child was completely covered in an unidentifiable black substance. For a moment, my father thought his eyes hadn't adjusted to the light. As he strained to focus on the child's face to figure out which of us it was, he realized its eyes were red. The child continued staring at my father. Though it didn't speak, he somehow felt it communicate to him that it had come from the basement. Then it turned away from him and faded into the shadows.

My father didn't tell us about this incident right away because he didn't want to spook us, but a few weeks later, something startled Mariah awake in our bedroom. For our first few months in the new house, I slept in the huge eastern room with Lillian and Mariah. Lillian and I slept together in a full-size bed, but Mariah slept on an old couch. She still wet the bed even though she was nearly six. When Mariah awoke on that couch, she saw a girl about her age floating in the air above her. Mariah could only see the girl from the knees up; the bottom half of her legs disappeared into a white haze. Instead of screaming, Mariah covered her face with her blanket and fell back to sleep.

When Mariah told us this story the next morning, we were sure she was lying—she often lied to get attention. However, it was always easy to catch her in a lie because the details would change dramatically within a few days. With this in mind, I later asked her to recount the story. She reiterated it with nearly the exact same details. I realized she was telling the truth. The experience had truly scared her and left a lasting impression. My father attempted to come up with excuses for what my sister saw, trying to convince us that she had dreamed it, but I kept telling him "something" was in the house. When I asked him outright if he had seen anything, he finally recounted his story of the child covered in black.

* * *

There were six bedrooms upstairs, but shortly after we moved in, my parents rented out three of them to make some extra income. The rooms had been converted to studio apartments in the 1950s. One had an attached dressing room, which had been remodeled into a kitchenette. The other two each had a small makeshift kitchen area. One bedroom had an attached bathroom, but the other two had to share a bathroom in the adjoining back hallway.

In order to close off our section of the house from that of the renters, my parents locked the door between the kitchen and laundry room, which exited onto a small back porch. The renters could enter the house through the laundry room and ascend the back stairs to their rooms. It was a good plan, except instead of repurposing the room into a mudroom for the renters and keeping it clean and orderly, my parents continued to use it as a laundry room. Since my father didn't do the laundry, my mother was left in charge of that chore. She never did more than two loads a day, regardless of the need, and she did not attend to it daily, so a massive pile of dirty laundry quickly amassed in the middle of the room. The unfortunate tenants had to walk around this mess. To make matters worse, because Mariah still wet the bed and soaked her nightgown each night, the room reeked of urine. Since our father was convinced that we would break the washer if we tried to use it, no one helped our mother with this particular chore.

No one in our family viewed this as abnormal. Having piles of unattended dirty clothes lying around was simply how things were. Of course, most other people didn't share this view, and tenants didn't stay with us for long. On several occasions, my father wondered aloud why he couldn't seem to find any "good renters." Lillian and I would just shrug our shoulders, oblivious to the festering pile of laundry, which our tenants obviously found distasteful.

Since Mariah wet the bed at night, it wasn't long before the stench from the couch in our bedroom made it nearly unbearable for us to sleep in the same room. Having been soaked every night for months, the couch took on a caustic rotting odor. It was so bad that even with the door shut, the pungent smell filled the hallway and wafted into the renters' rooms.

Early that fall, my father finally realized the smell wasn't good for keeping tenants, and they moved Mariah into a small room in the attic. She had a bed, a dresser, and a bouncy horse on a large spring that my parents had bought for her sixth birthday. She broke it within a few weeks due to her weight and lack of coordination. The attic was cold and drafty (the radiators on the third floor had been removed after the fire), so my father placed a space heater up there to warm her room.

I worried about Mariah up there, but I was also relieved that my parents hadn't tried to move me into the attic. *She probably isn't scared up there*, I told myself. *Maybe she'll even scare off the bogeyman with the smell.*

Of course, it would have made more sense to move her into "the library," but my father used it as his "study." In reality, it was a temple to his previous life, complete with his mother's bed, cherry bookcases filled with his father's books, and various antiques our grandparents had collected. This room was strictly off-limits to everyone but him. It was a secret, sacred place that none of us children dared enter. We certainly didn't mention it as an alternative for Mariah.

The few months when my parents rented out the three upstairs bedrooms were quiet, calm, and almost normal for us children. Both of my parents behaved better, yelled at us less, reigned in their out-bursts, and simply hushed us children if we got too loud. But the sweet college students who initially rented these rooms left for more pleasant accommodations, and they were replaced by men who smoked several packs of cigarettes a day and wore leather jackets with biker patches. They left piles of cigarette butts on the ground beside the back porch, overflowed the toilet, and failed to pay their rent. My father, who found it hard to kick out the deadbeat renters due to the long legal process and expense, complained about them until he was finally able to force them out.

This experience led my parents to abandon the idea of renting out the spare rooms. Once the extra bedrooms became available again, Mariah was moved back to the second floor and given her own room, adjacent to the back staircase. That helped save some money, since they wouldn't have to use the space heater any longer.

But something had changed in Mariah during the months she had slept in the attic. Her sweetness was gone. She was no longer cooperative and willing to give out hugs. She had become aggressive. A year or two earlier, she had developed a vocal tic that sounded like she was clearing her throat. By the time she moved back down to the second floor, it had become foul and exaggerated. "Shit. Shit. Shit. Fuck. Shit," she would chant rhythmically, as if she were speaking in time with a slow metronome. Her body would twitch and her head jerk backward when she did this. She was almost seven years old by this time.

I assumed she was swearing to draw attention to herself. She had picked up the obscenities from the previous renters. "Mariah, shut up! Amanda and Helen will hear you," I told her.

"*You* shut up, Niecy. Shit. Shit. Shit," Mariah said.

"What is wrong with you?" I shouted at her in frustration.

"Fuck you. Shit. Fuck."

Lillian and I tried to shield Amanda and Helen from her by steering Mariah away from them whenever possible. Luckily, they were still very young and didn't seem to notice her new behavior. I hoped that my parents would step in and send her to someone who could fix her or at least stop her profanities, but my mother said it was a phase she would outgrow. My father just ignored it. I didn't think it was a phase at all. I knew something was wrong with her, and it frustrated me that my parents wouldn't admit it. I started to press my father for an answer.

"What's wrong with her, Dad?" I asked in a calm, sincere manner, which was the likeliest way to get a response. "She's not normal like the rest of us."

My father had a way of being deaf when he didn't want to discuss something, so I kept asking every few days until he gave me an answer. It took a couple of months, but he finally acquiesced. "When your mother was pregnant with her, we painted the old garage behind the house in South Windsor. We think the old paint she was scraping off was lead paint and that she had lead poisoning before birth."

Like my mother's instability, Mariah's condition became just another thing we intrinsically knew not to discuss. At least she had been placed in the special education classes at school and would receive some help there.

Not long after Mariah moved back downstairs, I began begging for a room of my own. I loved Lillian, and she was a great roommate. She was sweet and cooperative, the type of sister that was also a great friend. But I yearned for my own space, somewhere I could have my trinkets lined up just so, where I could read alone, and where I could steal a few moments of peace.

My parents gave me one of the former renters' rooms with a kitchen in the corner. I loved it. Lillian temporarily moved in with me and slept on the floor beside my bed so she wouldn't be alone in her room. I read whatever book I was interested in at the time aloud to both of us at night before falling asleep.

Despite this positive turn of events, my mother's outbursts worsened after the tenants moved out and reverted back to the intensity she had displayed prior to the move. She went back to hunting us down after an argument with my father, now with the addition of an old belt she kept on a hook in her closet. Our father no longer came to our rescue as he had in our old house in South Windsor. In fact, at times, he joined her in beating us, using his own belt.

Fortunately, in this vast house, we quickly found better hiding places than we'd had in our previous home. Lillian and I had also become agile runners who could escape from Mom when she did discover us. My favorite hiding spot was behind the main upstairs bathroom door. I was so skinny, I could squeeze behind it, and it would still appear to be fully open. I was always careful not to disturb my father's pornographic magazines, which were scattered across the floor, just in case a rumpled corner might somehow give away my position. Lillian often hid under a discarded towel or blanket beneath the bed in her room. There were so many articles of clothing and stuffed animals piled on the floor that it made for an excellent spot. It was also easy to escape from. If my mother did find Lillian, she could shimmy out the other side and make a break for the door. Our mother typically gave up searching for us after ten or fifteen minutes and went outside to scream her banshee scream.

* * *

School provided a welcome reprieve from the craziness at home. Even though I was an outsider in Winsted, I eventually began to adjust and make friends. When I was with them, I felt like I was normal.

That fall, Dawn, whom I played with from time to time, approached me on the playground at recess one day as I was cleaning up. "Would you like to be my best friend? My best friend decided to be Jennie's best friend instead," she said.

"Um, okay, sure. Yeah, I'd really like to have a best friend," I replied. I didn't know what was required of a best friend, but if someone wanted to be my friend, I was delighted.

That fall, I realized that my teachers had also accepted me when I was offered a spot in the gifted program, called Resource IV. Six of the brightest kids in my class of approximately eighty were in it.

It felt wonderful to be recognized and accepted.

I was proud of my enrollment in Resource IV, but it presented a new set of challenges. I had developed perfectionist tendencies from home, where any minor error could result in swift and severe punishment. That caused me a great deal of anxiety.

That anxiety was amplified by the way my classmates ignored me when I wanted to be their friend. They saw me as a girl who was not "well put together." My tangled hair was forever untrimmed, my second-hand clothing from the Salvation Army was often worn, and I exuded the faint smell of cat urine that permeated my home. I had become so accustomed to the stench that I could no longer detect it, but my classmates could. It would be years before I recognized that how I was raised created these issues.

* * *

After school each day, I was thrust back into a state of hypervigilance as soon as I walked in the house. Shortly after I moved into my new room, my fears about our house were further confirmed when Lillian and I went down the front stairs one night. We had decided to get a drink before heading to bed, and as we approached the top of the stairs, we heard a loud creak from the bottom step. We stopped abruptly but heard the next step groan as if someone heavy had stepped on it. The noises continued up the staircase until the creaking reached a couple of steps below us. We snapped out of our frozen state and began screaming hysterically. My father flew to the bottom of the stairs.

"Who's hurt? What happened?"

"There's a ghost on the stairs," I cried.

"What do you mean?" he yelled, irritated.

"The stairs were creaking one after another, all the way up to the top," I whimpered.

"There's no ghost on the stairs," he said wearily. "It's just the pipes. They make the stairs crack and pop."

"But it was exactly like someone walking up them," Lillian implored.

"There's no ghosts," Dad said. There was finality in his voice.

Lillian and I exchanged uneasy glances and then quickly and silently made our way down the stairs. We slipped past our father and into the kitchen.

A few months later, I saw a figure on the stairs one day. It was a handsome man in his late twenties wearing a brown suit, white shirt, and dark tie. He had an expensive-looking fitted top hat and a carved cane with an ornate curved metal tip, though it was clearly only an accessory. For a split second, he smiled at me, and his smile was pleasant and warm. After that, I was no longer afraid of the ghost on the stairs.

Chapter 6

Home Is Where the Hurt Is

1984–Summer 1985

The following spring, just as the weather started to warm, my father came home from work one day to find sticky hot chocolate spilled on the cheap Formica table in the upstairs kitchenette that connected Lillian's bedroom with Mariah's second-floor room. If I had spotted the mess first, I would have cleaned it up to prevent an angry outburst from our parents, but my sisters had not come to me to ask for help, as they typically would have. When my father discovered the congealed liquid, he exploded with rage. "Denise! Denise! Get up here now!"

I bounded up the stairs, knowing I had better arrive immediately or there would be trouble. "Yeah?" I asked tentatively, already afraid.

"Who did this?" he shouted at me, pointing to the spilled hot chocolate.

It was pooled in a large, thick puddle. Obviously, too much powder had been added to the milk, and the mug had been tipped over as whoever prepared it stirred the sugary muck. For a split second, I wondered how my father had managed to discover this spill when he had been home for only a few minutes. Had my mother previously seen it and told him about it without asking me to clean it first?

"I—I don't know," I managed to spit out. "I—I—I had no idea someone had made a mess."

"You better find out who did this!" he screamed.

Terrified by his intensity, I ran outside to where Lillian and

Mariah were playing in the driveway. They were kicking a small ball back and forth in silence. They weren't really playing; they were listening, their ears trained on Dad's screaming, ready to bolt at a moment's notice while pretending to play. They knew how to avoid drawing attention to themselves. I scurried from one to the other, desperate for one of them to admit to her wrongdoing, but even after intensive questioning, neither confessed to being the culprit. Both insisted they hadn't even been in there that day. It didn't even occur to me to question four-year-old Amanda. Helen was still too small to reach any of the utensils to make hot chocolate.

I returned to my father, who was now downstairs in the family kitchen. I hung my head and stared at my feet. Dad was an intimidating six feet tall, with copious facial hair and long, frizzy, dark-brown hair that he wore tied back in a low ponytail. He was still wearing his typical work outfit of threadbare cotton work pants, light-blue button-up shirt, and the dark-brown belt he used to beat us. I stared at his scuffed black shoes. "I couldn't find out who did it. They both said it wasn't them," I whimpered, gulping down my fear.

My father took a couple of steps toward me. I wanted to run, but I knew he was close enough to grab me. It was safer to stay and hold very still. "You better find out who trashed the table, or I'm holding you responsible. You have five minutes," he hissed down at me, his face so close to me that I could smell his slightly sour breath.

I would have blamed Mariah, since she was the one who usually broke things and left behind messes, but for some reason, this one time, I didn't pin the blame on her. She had seemed so sincere when I questioned her. Instead, I told him the truth: "I don't know who did it."

I should have gone back outside. I should have given myself the five minutes of pretend questioning to let him cool down, but I was so scared, I wasn't thinking straight. I was responding in fear.

My father's face turned so red it looked as if blood might start oozing from his pores. I could swear he was able to smell my fear.

He lunged for the large wooden broom in the corner of the kitchen, and I took off in the opposite direction like a sprinter reacting to the starting gunshot at a track meet. I raced up the grand front staircase and spun in a circle at the top, desperately searching for the perfect hiding place. In my panic, I ran into the very room where one of my sisters had committed the damning infraction. My father had already made it up the stairs and would discover me if I made any noise. I squeezed myself into the two-foot gap between the exterior wall and the side of the refrigerator, trying to make myself small—to disappear. There, I crouched in a fetal position, holding my breath. I pulled my legs in tight to keep my shoes from sticking out.

I heard my father enter the room and squeezed my eyes shut, wanting to believe that if I couldn't see him, he wouldn't find me. I could hear him, huffing like a bull about to charge.

I remembered my lessons from Awana and started praying, "Please, please don't let him find me. Please, please don't let—"

My thoughts ground to a halt when the light filtering through my closed eyelids disappeared. A huge shadow loomed in front of me. I opened my eyes. Gray pant legs trapped me like prison bars. I leaned forward, hoping to somehow shimmy through them.

Suddenly, the wooden handle of the broom made contact with my scalp. The strike made a sound like a watermelon dropped on the driveway. It felt like my skull had been split in half, causing me to curl tightly into a fetal position again. I wrapped my arms around my forehead to protect my face and wailed in pain as he delivered blow after terrible blow to my head.

"Please stop," I wailed, my voice a small squeak. "I'll never do it again." What had I done wrong? I was innocent. I had told the truth. Why was he beating me?

Somewhere amidst the pain, I pissed my pants. Urine streamed onto the floor. My father backed up a couple of steps, perhaps in surprise at the puddling fluid, giving me just enough room to escape. I scampered off, leaving my father still standing in place, as if dazed.

The hot streams of urine trickled down into my socks in narrow, meandering lines. I hated feeling wet and smelly, but the instant warmth felt nice against my shaking limbs. When I made it to the bathroom, I was surprised to find that I wasn't bleeding.

Later, as I lay on my bed after changing into dry clothing, I cried and winced at the small volcano of pain erupting from the grapefruit-sized lump on my scalp. My father walked in and asked, "Are you okay?"

I sniffled but didn't answer. The truth was, I wasn't okay. But I knew that in this instance, the truth was the wrong answer. I knew what happened when I told the truth.

"I didn't mean to hurt you. Will you forgive me?" His face and voice reflected sincerity.

I slowly moved my head up and down in a blatant lie. It was the only time my father ever asked me for forgiveness, but I wasn't able to forgive him. Not then, and not for decades. He had beaten me mercilessly over literal spilled milk.

He left the room, seemingly at a loss for words, since I still wouldn't look at or speak to him. I curled up into a fetal position on my comforter and cried quietly enough that no one else could hear. I cried for the pain still erupting through my head and for myself, realizing that I was utterly alone in a brutal world.

* * *

As 1984 rolled into 1985, I began to seek out escape, at least within my own mind, since I was very aware that I was unable to take care of myself. I started playing the flute and writing poetry. I was much better at poetry than music, which I enjoyed but had to work hard at. I sent my poetic works to a children's magazine, but they didn't accept them for publication. My poems were gritty and stood in stark contrast to the cute works that filled the magazine's pages. Despite these rejections, writing became an outlet for me. It didn't require the acceptance of others. Writing poetry was my attempt to organize the senseless things in my life, acknowledge my fears, explain them, and explore them.

Even at that young age, I had already realized that there was *something* deeper, something hidden behind the physical reality we knew. I felt this *something*, but I wasn't sure what it was. From church and Awana, I knew that an eternal God existed and that I could communicate with Him through prayer. But I didn't understand where I, an unkempt girl, fit into His big picture. Was He really concerned about me?

Despite my uncertainty, I turned to prayer more and more. I prayed when my parents were upset, asking God to help them find a solution to whatever they were facing. If my father misplaced his keys, I prayed that he would find them within five minutes; and every time, just as the five-minute mark approached, my father found them. This seemed to work for most small issues, so I knew that God must be watching out for me, for us, and I took comfort in that. But there were too many times when I felt like God wasn't looking out for me at all. Where was He when I was fleeing my parents' blows or enduring their emotional battery? Where was He when I was numb with fear and didn't have the composure to pray for help? Was He still watching out for me then?

I had plenty of time to ponder my plight as I scrubbed the carpet in the hall once again. My sisters often spilled their Kool-Aid while rushing to catch their favorite show on the downstairs television. Crouched on my hands and knees, I endured my father's threat, "You better get it all out or else!" As he tossed a sponge and dish soap at me, I wondered, *Why me?* I felt like Cinderella, pushing aside and organizing the random scattered books, school papers, and garbage as I scrubbed away at the stain. Over time I rubbed sections of the rug threadbare, exposing the dark wood floor beneath.

At least twice a week, my father spent an hour or more yelling at me and lecturing me when my sisters did something "wrong." At such times, I stood by the kitchen table as far from this towering man as possible, staring at the table's shiny faux wood beneath the scattered piles of mail, dirty paper plates, and half-eaten donuts. I remembered little of what he said during these tirades, choosing instead to block out his words as I stood motionless. I would zone out in an almost meditative state, standing silent, like a nun shutting out the world.

Although the topics of these rants differed from day to day, depending on what we had done, there was a predictability that ran through them all: "You kids are killing me. You never do anything around here. I'm the only one who ever does anything. What exactly do you do all day?" he would screech, as if we didn't go to school and have homework to do.

Though I spoke when he demanded an answer, I knew better than to volunteer information or a defense. "It's only a matter of time before I have a heart attack. And then where will you be? I'll tell you where you'll be: you'll be living on the streets because not one of you can do anything. Who's going to support you when I'm dead? Huh? Who? No one! They'll take away the house, and you'll be living on the streets, all because of the stress you cause me. You stupid good-for-nothing sluts. That's what you are. No one respects me, not even one of you. But I'll be dead soon. You'll all wish you had respected me then, after I'm dead from a heart attack and you're on the streets."

As my father ranted, questions churned in my head. *Am I stupid, like he says? Am I no good? I must be for my father to tell me that. He knows me better than anyone and why would he tell me those things if they weren't true?* But even as these thoughts rose, I would come to my own defense and tell myself, *He has to see how much I help out around the house. Why does he claim I don't do anything?* I became mired in the swirling negativity.

If the pain of his words ever caused me to grimace or if I tried to distance myself from him by backing away during his rants, my father would bellow, "There's the door. If you don't like it here, then leave." It was a threat, not an offer, since he was standing beside the door with the broom behind him and could easily catch me if I tried to bolt. I only tried it once. He grabbed and squeezed my arm so hard I squealed out in pain. I never tried to run out of the kitchen again.

I often wished that I was old enough to leave, to run away in the middle of the night, but I knew I couldn't feed and house myself as a ten-year-old. Plus, who would be here to protect my sisters if I left? Our father would just choose one of them to victimize next.

While my father took his rage out on my sisters too, berating me seemed to satisfy him the most. I had become a surrogate mother to my sisters and often attended to household duties in the kitchen. It was easy for him to trap me there and vent all of the anxieties he should have been working out with my mother.

However, if any of us girls did something more egregious, such as breaking something valuable or talking back, the broom came out instead of the belts. Brooms were more dangerous, as they had reach and could inflict damage without our parents having to hold onto us.

My father was even bold enough to occasionally chase one of us out of the house, down the steps, across the yard, and onto the sidewalk with the broom in hand. Fortunately, he always stopped in front of our minister's house, two houses down, as if there was some invisible barrier there. We knew that if we could make it past the parsonage, we were safe.

Unfortunately, we didn't always escape.

When Lillian was young, she had an innate curiosity about the inner workings of mechanical things. That spring, when she was only eight, in a moment of curiosity, she disassembled the coffeemaker but couldn't figure out how to put it back together. She left the pieces in a neat pile beside the coffeemaker, hoping that our father could assist her later. When he found the coffeemaker in pieces that evening, he demanded to know who had taken it apart. Lillian admitted to her wrongdoing and tentatively asked him to show her how to put it back together. Instead, he flew into a rage, dragging her outside to the driveway and throwing her down on the rough pavement. I ran to the kitchen window, desperate to help her but knowing I couldn't.

Usually, when he did this—it wasn't the first time—he left his victim where he had thrown her. This time, though, something snapped inside him, and he began kicking and stomping her. She flailed around on the pavement, screeching and trying to escape, but he kept kicking her back down until she curled into a ball, crying and whimpering.

Finally, as he turned to reenter the house, I realized I needed to run upstairs to escape any of his unspent fury. I fled before he could see that I had been watching. I joined the three other girls upstairs in Lillian's room, where they were watching the twenty-two-inch television set that someone at work had given Dad instead of throwing it out. I made sure the volume was turned down. Helen and Amanda were still too young to have much sense of what might happen, but Mariah and I were both ready to bolt if we heard either of our parents stomp up the stairs. Often, the punishment of one girl generated punishments for another.

After a while, Lillian crept back inside. She was bruised and scratched. Since she had soiled her underwear, she changed before joining us in her room. She was whimpering quietly, and we commiserated with her in silence as we all sat together. I never saw her disassemble anything or even ask how something worked ever again.

My sisters and I were like a small flock of penguins huddling together in the winter of our lives, seeking warmth and safety, desperate to survive the cold of our family. We all seemed to understand that if we stuck together, we would be okay. There was no competition between us. Without ever having to speak of it, we knew that cooperating and supporting one another was the best way to survive the madness we lived every day. We all tried—except for Mariah, of course—to keep our heads low. Even five-year-old Amanda and four-year-old Helen were beginning to know when to disappear. We were like animals hiding in the underbrush, knowing that if the hunter couldn't detect us, we wouldn't get hurt.

To this day, it saddens me that such gentle girls with beautiful souls were subjected to this fear and denigration. I loved my sisters fiercely and would have given my life for them. I wanted to protect them as much as I could, while also insulating myself from the irrational and cruel onslaught of my parents.

* * *

In a way, my survival strategies—being forever careful and cautious, always watching my parents' actions and moods, and responding immediately when summoned—worked against me. Because my parents picked up on my intimidated and submissive manner, they demanded that I assist in every mundane task they felt too tired or overwhelmed to tackle. They would summon me at any time for anything. Since the house was so large, I didn't always hear when one of them called for me.

To help their voices carry through the thick walls, they created a calling chant. My mother would lead with, "One, two, three." My father would join her, and they would call out my name in unison as loudly as they could.

Whenever I heard this, a bolt of electricity shot through me. I would immediately jerk to attention in a Pavlovian response. "Coming!" I would reply as loudly as I could muster.

If I hesitated for even a moment, or if they didn't hear me yell back, they repeated their call, "One, two, three! Denise!"

I knew better than to make them call a third time. They projected their impatience on to me in the form of physical or emotional abuse. "I called you three times!" my mother would scream when I appeared. "What are you doing up there? Helen needs help getting ready for bed. You're useless. You never help. You just go up to your room and do homework, while all this work needs to be done down here. I hate you!"

My parents pulled me away from my homework—and the downtime a young girl needs—for any reason: to change diapers, to help my sisters get ready for bed, to give the younger girls a bath, to break up a fight, to clean up something someone had dropped. Sometimes, they even summoned me to fetch them a glass of soda or a bowl of ice cream so they wouldn't have to get up from the couch themselves. As much as I hated being dragged away from what I was doing, I knew that we girls were all better off if our parents stayed immobile on the couch.

Once my mother figured out that I was somewhat capable of preparing dinner, that too was added to my daily tasks. My family didn't have the benefit of an adult experienced in preparing tasty and nutritious meals; they relied on a half-grown girl with limited cooking skills. I could do little more than drop spaghetti into a pot of boiling water and then mix it with tomato sauce and grated sharp cheddar cheese. I would also open a can of vegetables to serve on the side and a can of fruit to serve as dessert. When we didn't have spaghetti, we had baked Spam or fried bologna. My sisters enjoyed watching it puff up in the center.

Chapter 7

Cinderella—the Early Years

1985

When I entered the fifth grade in 1985, my morning duties expanded. There were now four of us girls attending school—Helen was still too young—and I had to help them get ready each day. Our father left for work at seven, and it was best to leave him alone in the mornings. Our mother only got out of bed early if forced, and she would screech at anyone who happened across her path. We were all happier with me waking the three other girls and assisting them as needed. I didn't mind this task much, but as with cooking, I was too young to bring the attention of an adult to making sure my sisters and I were cleaned, dressed, and combed. As a result, we sometimes looked like homeless waifs—which, in many ways, we were.

My father had purchased a Smurf alarm clock for me for my birthday, and I set it for 6:20 a.m. each day. When my alarm went off, it sang, "Hey, sleepy head! It's time to wake up and get going. Come on now. Open your eyes. Big stretch and out of bed. Hurry, because it's going to be a beautiful Smurfy Day." I loved starting my morning with a positive affirmation like that, rather than a jarring, beeping noise, which always triggered a wave of anxiety in me. I loved that clock.

I always woke Mariah up first after starting the bathtub for her. She took the longest, since she had to bathe every morning. She continued wetting the bed until she was fifteen years old. Every morning, her entire body, including her hair, was covered in urine. Luckily, she was easy to wake up. All I had to do was say her name in a sharp whisper, and she would spring from the bed as if she had been waiting for me for the past hour.

Lillian was a bit tougher to awaken—when she was home, that is. Even as young as nine, she arranged to spend the night with one of her best friends most of the time. She often failed to bring a change of clothes and would wear her friends' clothes to school. I didn't blame her. In fact, I was a bit jealous. I longed for that kind of escape from the yelling, abuse, and endless chores. If I'd had friends whose parents were willing to take me in, I would have done the same thing. My parents never seemed to notice that Lillian was missing, and as far as I know, they never called to make sure she was okay. The parents of Lillian's friends didn't bother to call my parents to let them know she was safe and would be spending the night. These parents probably knew that a call was not wanted. As for my parents, they were most likely relieved to have one less child bothering them and one less mouth to feed.

While she benefited from the distance, I learned later that Lillian felt invisible and hated, feeling unimportant and overlooked by our parents. She wanted a mother and father that missed her and wanted her back, but of course, that wasn't going to happen.

When Lillian was home and sleeping in her own room, I would slip to the side of her bed and whisper, "Lilly, Lilly, it's time to wake up," until she woke.

I often gazed out her east-facing window at the sun rising over the steep hills as I waited for her to awaken. From this vantage point, I could see the warm orange hues of the stretching sunlight wrap around the tall, thin steeple of the Catholic church. It was a stunning view, and I delighted in breathing in the new day as I gently shook Lillian again.

Next came Amanda, who was very self-sufficient in the mornings, and even though she didn't always pick out an outfit that matched, she could at least put something together for herself. When I woke

Amanda, Helen typically rose as well, since they shared a room. Helen was the most stubborn of the group. I would hold up different outfits, trying to convince her how awesome each one was. She hemmed and hawed with her thumb in her mouth and her index finger alongside her nose until I begged her to just put on one of the outfits.

After she was dressed and ready for the day, she would tell us her favorite and only joke: "Why did the *tuttle cwoss* the *woad?*"

"I don't know. Why did the turtle cross the road?" I would respond with a sigh.

"No, you have to say *somethin' weal.*"

"Okay, to get to the other side," I would say, humoring her.

"No *silwy*, to get his *pil-whoa.*" She giggled every time.

Lillian and I would look at each other as if to say *that was the dumbest joke ever*, and then we would burst out laughing. We weren't making fun of her, just laughing at how adorable she was. Hearing her joke every morning, as if she were telling it for the first time, always made our day and made us realize how much we loved her.

Before heading out the door, I always made sure Lillian, Mariah, Amanda, and I had forty cents each for the reduced-cost lunch we qualified for. Even coming up with the forty cents per person was a challenge for our family; not because we couldn't afford it, but because it was difficult to scrounge up a quarter, nickel, and dime for each of us each day. A more aware parent would have set out a jar of spare change for us to pull from. But that didn't happen for us.

Simple organization was particularly challenging in our house. We ran out of milk every other day, as it was the preferred drink for all of us girls after Kool-Aid. But instead of buying three gallons at once, we could only purchase one at a time because the refrigerator was never cleaned out. Much of the food in it was over a year old. Whenever Lillian and I attempted to make room by cleaning out the fridge, our parents would scold us.

"How could you throw out that cottage cheese? It's perfectly good.

We can still eat that! That costs money—money we don't have," Dad shouted one day on such an occasion.

"But, Dad, it's got mold on it," I pointed out quietly.

"There's nothing wrong with a little mold. What do you think blue cheese is made of? There are kids starving in Africa, and you're going to throw out perfectly good food!"

Of course, Lillian and I noticed that he never ate anything rescued from the garbage, and neither did we.

While our father was apparently attached to the spoiled food in the fridge, our mother insisted on holding on to the baked goods that she left stacked high on the piles of papers, dinnerware, and random knickknacks on the kitchen table.

"Those were my cinnamon rolls! I hate you!" she screamed one day while gingerly picking pastries out of the trash, as if rescuing a kitten.

"But they expired three weeks ago," I said.

"And they're hard as a rock," Lillian added.

"Get out of here! Get out of here now!" Mom screamed.

Because the refrigerator only had enough space for a single gallon of milk, I had to walk down the hill to the local IGA supermarket three times a week to purchase more. While I was there, I would cash into change whatever assortment of dollar bills my father had given me for our lunch money.

The younger women working the registers would roll their eyes and say something along the lines of, "Now, how many nickels do you need again?" They would make a show of breaking open a roll of change that I could clearly see didn't need to be opened.

Whenever possible, I got into a line staffed by someone over the age of forty, even if the line was longer. The older women were more patient with my requests to get twelve quarters, fourteen dimes, and twelve nickels when breaking a five-dollar bill. They would even call me "sweetie" sometimes. Then I would trudge back up the hill, lugging the gallon of milk through sunshine, rain, and snow.

I actually enjoyed this particular chore, as it gave me a few minutes away from the chaos at home, where I felt weighed down by the oppressive refuse of our lives. On the kitchen counter, there was a three-by-two-foot pile of our old schoolwork not far from another tottering mound of paper grocery bags. On the floor beside the back door was a huge jumble of all the things we never put away from our hikes in the woods and our picnics. In the corner by the second refrigerator, which never worked, were bags of clothes that had been left on our front porch by well-meaning neighbors. We pawed through the bags after my father brought them in, took out any interesting pieces of clothing, and then pushed the nearly full bags aside. The stove was so cluttered that we had to move aside the pots and dishes and already-used paper towels that covered it in order to use the burners. At dinnertime, we pushed aside the random glasses, stale food, and junk mail on the table just so we could have a place to put our plates. On the floor near the sink were several bowls of water and cat food whose contents were perpetually spilled onto the floor.

Every room of the house was in a similar state. In the downstairs TV room, where we folded the laundry, empty potato chip bags, crumpled candy wrappers, and mounds of discarded clothes that no longer fit vied for space with clean laundry.

My parents blamed us for the mess and accused us five girls of never cleaning. However, on multiple occasions during the winter months when we were stuck inside all the time, Lillian and I spent hours organizing everything in that room into separate piles so we could put it all away. We gathered clothes into a laundry pile, pencils and pens into a schoolwork pile, garbage to be discarded, toys to return to our bedrooms, and dishes for the sink, only to have our mother walk into the room and, seeing the various piles, sweep everything back together into one large jumble with the dreaded kitchen broom, as if she were helping by uniting the scattered piles. She didn't appear to comprehend that the separate piles represented a way to organize and clean. I could only look on in exasperation as she thoughtlessly ruined our attempts to clean. Of course, I didn't dare speak up or reprimand her.

When I came home from school, I would often find my mother sitting in her rocking chair in the hall, even though we had many other rooms where lounging would have been more appropriate. Sometimes, she would be reading a book. At other times, she would just be staring blankly ahead as she rocked back and forth. In such moments, her eyes were empty and her face was like stone, as if she didn't even register that I was home. This creeped me out, and I would shudder as I slipped past her quickly and silently, hoping she wouldn't notice me. At these moments, although I was relieved she wasn't demanding that I complete some random chore, I also wished for a mother who might have hugged me and said something like, "How was your day, sweetie? It's so nice to have you back home. I baked some cookies for you girls. Would you like one?"

For my own sanity, I didn't dwell on such thoughts. Instead, I looked for a logical explanation. I wanted my family to make sense, so I began to rationalize what was happening. I was able to rationalize my father's behavior more easily than my mother's. I concluded that he had nowhere else to vent his frustrations and convinced myself that he meant well but couldn't control his rage. The stress he felt trying to support a family of seven overtook him and changed him into something he never meant to be. After all, there were still days when he did put some effort into being a good father; during those times, life was good.

I sensed that something was wrong with my mother. She seemed incapable of doing simple things: driving us to school, preparing dinner, cleaning, even giving us hugs, but maybe, I reasoned, she was just lazy and wanted me to be her personal servant. Despite my rationalizations, I knew that we girls didn't deserve the severe mistreatment our parents doled out to us.

Outside of the house, there were times when we were like a normal family. Every Saturday during the summer, my parents took us hiking. I loved being outside. We all did. My sisters and I would run up ahead of my parents as we searched for critters and flowers. We would pick colorful mushrooms and then run back to Dad to ask if they were poisonous—not that we were going to eat them. We found newts and toads and the occasional garter snake. We climbed boulders and scaled short cliff faces. We skipped from rock to rock over shallow streams like a band of sprites, our long, fine blond hair flying up with each hop. Then we would take off our shoes to wade in the cold shin-deep water.

Sometimes I would break free from the group and find myself alone on the trail. In such moments, I would stop and stand silently, tilt my head upward, and soak in the sun streaming through the dappled leaves. I would inhale deeply, breathing in the scent of the fresh, moist earth surrounding me. For a few precious moments, I could feel the promise of life coming to me. At Awana, we were told that God wanted us to live a good life, and during these moments of solitude in the woods, I could feel how that might be so.

When fall came, the sun set low on the horizon, casting a yellow glow on the hills and fields, making them look like they had turned to gold. At this time of year, we went to the fairs. We lived in a semi-rural area, and nearly every town nearby had its own fair to support the local 4-H. We packed sandwiches that I prepared and bottled soft drinks and ate our lunch outside by the station wagon prior to entering the fairgrounds. The parking area was in a large field that smelled of fresh-cut hay, like recently mowed grass but sweeter and stronger. If happiness were a smell, it would be that of newly baled hay. Our father bought us each a wristband for unlimited rides, and we petted every single animal in the stalls, never thinking twice about digging our hands into the lone basket of fries my father bought immediately afterward.

Even during these outings, there were difficult moments when either my mother or Mariah flipped out about something. Usually, it was because they were hungry or wanted to do something the rest of us had decided against. When one of them erupted, I slipped into the small crowd of onlookers that formed, hoping I wouldn't be identified as belonging with these irrational people. Mariah in particular embarrassed me because of her tendency to screech and stomp. It was obvious that she was a special needs child whom none of us knew how to manage.

And then there were Sundays. Every Sunday, no matter what the weather was like, we went to church. Our father joined us on occasion, but most of the time, he stayed home to enjoy some quiet time. Even though his grandfather had been an Episcopal bishop in Virginia, our father had little interest in religion or God.

Our mother was a member of the church choir, even though she was a terrible singer. Shortly after she joined, a couple of retired women from the church, whom we called the "church ladies," started coming to the house two hours a week to help our mother with the dishes and other random chores. One night, Helen had gone to bed chewing bubble gum, though we had warned her not to. By morning, her hair was a massive bubble-gum tangle and the church ladies tried to comb the gum out. When it was obvious the gum wouldn't cooperate, they cut her hair. We called Helen "the little Dutch boy" for months.

Amanda and Helen went to the nursery during the church service. They loved playing with the toys there, as they were different than the ones we had at home. Lillian, Mariah, and I were old enough for Sunday school, which we attended immediately after the children's sermon. It gave us the opportunity to make new and different friends from those we had at school. These friends never made disparaging remarks about how we dressed.

The Methodist church, conveniently located just seven houses down from us, was stunning. The massive granite-block structure had been built in the late 1800s and featured several two-story-tall stained glass windows surrounded by huge stone arches. Two square towers stretched skyward over the main entrances, one of which housed the bell that rang to announce the start of the church service every week. Grand granite steps ascended a steep incline from the road to the doors.

The massive stained glass windows intrigued me the most. Their scenes were mesmerizing Technicolor depictions of the angel at Jesus's tomb, Jesus teaching in the temple, and Jesus sitting with children. The mosaic of light from these windows poured into the sanctuary and the second-floor Sunday-school classrooms. Directly over the sanctuary, there was a thirty-foot-wide, dome-shaped stained glass skylight. The pastel colors arching out from the center glowed vibrantly in the morning light. During moments when the service seemed to drag on, I turned my head up and stared at the domed window, hypnotized by its brilliance.

We always sat in the same pew—third row from the front—and I occasionally sensed some people standing against the back wall behind the rest of the congregation. But when I turned to see who was there, I saw only the small tables that held the weekly programs. Still, I couldn't shake the feeling that someone was there. If I concentrated long and hard enough, I could almost make out forms resembling monks in gray robes. Sometimes, the figures held something at their sides that looked like worn leather-bound journals. These figures came not from my imagination but from my mind's eye, as if I were staring at a 3-D stereogram, the kinds of images popularized in the *Magic Eye* books. Just like in the images in these books, I could somehow see past the static of the empty space of the room and just barely make out their forms.

The figures always stood silently, never interacting with us. They exuded neither good nor evil intent; they were neutral, timeless, and ancient, as if they had existed before the fall of Lucifer when good and evil were first defined. They were neither unnerving nor unwelcoming. They simply were. I sensed that they were there solely as record-keepers, writing down our deeds, like in the Book of Revelation, where the dead are judged by the works written about them in the books.

I felt no concern over their presence, unlike the anxiety I'd felt when I heard my name being called from the woods as a small child. Whatever these monks' role, they had no malintent toward us. Mostly, I found it interesting that I was able to discern them at all. Why would they let me know they were there?

I named them "the watchers" but kept their presence to myself, fully understanding that no one else could sense them; otherwise, they would be turning around to stare at the back of the church as well. I knew how to keep secrets and suspected that trying to describe them to an adult would only make me seem foolish and crazy. I desperately wanted to appear normal and wasn't about to risk that by talking about invisible people in our church. Still, my conviction of their presence remained unwavering, and I knew I wasn't insane. "Insane" was a word that would better describe my parents or Mariah, not me. I simply accepted that I was somehow different and that, like the watchers themselves, my being different was neither good nor bad. It just was.

I loved everything about the church: its beauty, warmth, and most of all, the cookies and lemonade we enjoyed during the social hour following the service. In the reception hall where the social hour was held, there was a portrait of Jesus. He looked a lot like my father, with long, wavy chestnut-colored hair and a matching full beard and mustache. I wondered if Jesus had been a hippy like my father. I pictured Jesus spending years wandering from place to place, living off the land and, to a certain extent, the goodwill of others. As I studied his image, I speculated that Jesus was simply a well-intentioned, enlightened traveling hippy.

After church during the colder months, we came home to a huge breakfast of scrambled eggs, bacon, and toast or pancakes. While our father stayed home from church, he cooked up a small feast, and when we got home, we stuffed our always-hungry bellies. Sunday mornings were the best times in my family.

Chapter 8
Junior High School
1986–Fall 1988

In sixth grade, when I was eleven, I started junior high. I was getting taller and dramatically slender, with lanky arms and legs that I had not fully learned to coordinate, giving me the awkward stance of a fawn learning to walk. Along with my alabaster skin, it gave me an emaciated appearance. The kids at school came up with new, unique names and phrases for me, such as "ape-girl" and "close encounter of the third kind." Few of my peers wanted to be around me.

My clothes, which still came from the Salvation Army and donated clothing bags, were outdated and slightly worn, perpetuating the "raggy" label. I was so thin, I could never find pants that both fit my waist and were long enough. Since no one in my family knew how to alter clothing, I wore pants that were slightly short just so they would fit my waist. This high-water look made me appear even nerdier.

In addition, my father forbade me from cutting or styling my hair. Instead, it was long, straight, parted in the middle, and perpetually oily. This look, which my parents favored, had been popular twenty years earlier when they were young, but now it singled me out as being unfashionable. I dreamed of having layers of big curls with six-inch-long bangs like my friends; bigger was better in 1986. Even worse, my mother had forbidden me from taking a shower more than once a week. I didn't ask why. She would have taken it as a threat to her authority and would have lashed out. I might have washed my hair by kneeling over the bathtub and using the faucet, rather than the shower head, but I didn't dare do anything that might be seen as pushing her buttons.

Still a tomboy, I didn't mind getting my hands and face dirty. I didn't notice when I was filthy, but apparently my sixth-grade teacher did. My ivory face reddened with embarrassment one morning when she took me to the girl's restroom to clean my face with a damp paper towel.

I had not been taught that I should wash up or brush my teeth before leaving the house each day. Neither of my parents enforced or even required such hygiene practices. And since I helped the other girls get ready for school, my sisters hadn't learned to do this either.

One day, as I was eating lunch in the school cafeteria with my friends and shoveling down my food as usual, Dawn, my best friend, stated flatly, "You're a pig, Denise."

"Why am I a pig?" I asked, not knowing what she was alluding to.

"You're just a pig," she answered inarticulately.

"Leave her alone," Kelly interjected. Kelly and I had become friends after realizing we had moved to town at the same time. She never teased or looked down on anyone and seemed to genuinely enjoy my company. I was very fond of her and her upbeat personality.

I stared down at my food in silence, unsure of what had prompted her to call me a pig. I was too afraid to inquire further for fear it might be something I was unable to change.

After a few additional comments from Dawn, Kelly finally took pity on me and explained, "Denise, you're holding your fork the wrong way. You have your fist wrapped over it." She held up her fork in a more socially acceptable manner as an example. "See, you hold it like this."

At dinner that night, I asked my father how he held his fork. He showed me—it was the same position Kelly had taught me.

"Dad, why didn't you show me that when I was little?" I asked.

"I just assumed you'd figure it out," he replied.

I don't know how I didn't figure it out on my own, but social graces were not a strength of mine. My new insight caused me great embarrassment as I recalled how I had been eating for years, and I was mad at myself for not paying attention to how everyone else ate. But at the same time, I appreciated my friends who bothered to teach me these basic life lessons. Every lesson I learned I passed on to my sisters.

Still, I was surprised that my father hadn't noticed that I ate like a three-year-old. I expected this nonchalance from my mother, but my father had come from a "high-class" family. I was disappointed with him for paying so little attention to us. He was often lost in his own world. His body was present, but his mind was far off somewhere else. My mother was even worse. Not only did she neglect us, she expected us to care for her. I often felt like a feral child that my parents sometimes fed at the back door, and if I were really lucky, my father might pet my head from time to time.

* * *

My crowd of lunch friends all came from broken, dysfunctional families. We understood each other intuitively in a way that only kids on the fringe can. I loved spending time with them, especially when we had school field trips. My friends and I all sat together on the bus, giggling and joking. I loved these excursions, most of which brought us through a rural section of rocky hills that tumbled down into the Farmington River, called Satan's Kingdom. It was a place of incredible beauty. According to local lore, Satan had claimed the area as his own until the angel Gabriel decided it was too beautiful to be occupied by Satan and his minions. Gabriel then banished them from the area. I always felt a special connection to this area, and a profound sense of well-being settled on me as the school bus carrying me and my friends passed through it.

Kelly had the best family in the group, and her mother and stepfather truly loved each other. The way they interacted was amazing to me. But Kelly had not seen her biological father since she was a toddler, and that hurt her deeply. She was proud of her Native American heritage; later in life I suspected that was an attempt to connect with her long-lost father who never even called to say happy birthday. Still, Kelly stuck by me regardless of what I did. Her heart was big enough to overlook my many faults.

These friendships weren't enough for me to overlook the teasing from other kids, though. Not only was I dirty, but now they were also telling me that I was homely. I seemed doomed to play the part of the ugly duckling. Yet unlike the ugly duckling who becomes a beautiful swan, I was sure I would never transform. With my childlike lack of perspective, I was sure that I would always be what I was.

Despite all the name-calling, I found myself beginning to dream about having a boyfriend. I imagined he would love and accept me and thus change my life, but I didn't believe that anyone would actually be interested in me and return my adoration.

I developed a crush on Billy, one of my classmates, anyway. He had been held back a year and was older than the other boys in my class and thus more physically mature. He was gorgeous, a prepubescent girl's fantasy. Billy often boasted about how he was a "lady's man," although it was a bit of a stretch to deem any of us sixth graders "ladies" or a "man." He also had a girlfriend, so I kept my feelings to myself.

At lunch one day, I was sitting with a classmate, Jenny, at the school store cart, where we sold pink erasers and colorful pencils, when Billy walked up. Completely ignoring me, he struck up a conversation with Jenny. As they talked, I indulged my senses by staring at his arms, his chest, and his face. Watching him made me blush and giggle silently to myself.

I was still daydreaming when he turned to face me. I was in heaven; I held my breath, awaiting his words. My heart beat rapidly as his full lips moved to speak to me. Panic surged through me as I wondered what he would say and what I would say in response.

"Why are you so ugly?" he said simply. "And why is your voice so funny?"

My eleven-year-old self believed him: I was ugly. My world came crashing down around me, and my mind went blank. From a distance, I heard Jenny say, "Leave her alone. Stop being mean. Go sit back down."

"No, Jenny, I want to know why she's so ugly." He seemed sincere, like a child asking his mother why a paraplegic was in a wheelchair.

I stared at my lap, and my lips began to quiver as I responded, "I was born this way."

This exchange squashed my crush on Billy.

After that, I worked even more diligently at excelling in school, studying for every test for hours. Academics was the only area in my life where I felt like I could be a champion, where the harder I worked, the more I was rewarded. I loved the fact that I could *create* results—unlike in the rest of my life, where things just happened to me. Outside of class, I kept my head down as I walked through the school's hallways, trying not to draw too much attention to myself. But in the classroom, I could hold my head high.

That fall, I also joined the cross-country team. Running is a largely independent sport that doesn't require peer acceptance or cooperation. Distance running was also something I was already good at—as were my sisters. We had probably developed this ability from dashing away from our parents.

For the next year, I focused solely on academics and running, largely ignoring my peers, who looked down on me.

* * *

At home, Mariah's personality was changing again for the worse. By my seventh grade year, when she was ten, she started throwing regular temper tantrums. Sometimes, she would fling herself onto the floor or strike out at those around her by hitting or biting them. Although Lillian and I could fight back against these assaults, eight-year-old Amanda and seven-year-old Helen could only defend themselves by crying out, "Make her stop. Make her stop." Lillian and I would then come to their rescue.

Mariah's swearing tic had now been replaced by her snorting like a pig. It was the type of sound someone would make while sucking down a large ball of snot so they could spit it back out. It was so loud that we could hear her throughout the huge house. Whenever she snorted, she would tip her head back to open her throat and kick her right leg back and upward so violently, she often hit her own rear. She had been doing this motion occasionally since she was little, but now it was more pronounced, forceful, and violent. She snorted like this every two or three minutes when she wasn't speaking, eating, or sleeping. I could only imagine how difficult this was for her special education teachers at school.

If she found out that one of us had done something to upset my father, she started talking about it, staying on the subject for the rest of the day. If we left the room, she would start shouting so that we could still hear her, or she would follow us, trying to get a response. It was bad enough to have to deal with our father's wrath without Mariah echoing our missteps back to us. Sometimes I wondered if I had died and gone to hell.

One day that fall, Mariah called me downstairs, saying, "Niecy, Mom called for you."

It was never a good thing to let our mother call for more than a minute or two, so I appreciated that Mariah was looking out for me. But when I went to our mother and asked what she needed, she said she hadn't called for me.

I went back to Mariah, irritated that she would send me downstairs for no reason. "What the heck?" I grumbled. "Mom didn't call for me. Is this some kind of joke?"

"But I heard it. I heard her calling your name," Mariah said. Her sincerity stopped me from pressing her further.

Then, a few weeks later, I began to hear the call, too. Almost daily, a voice that sounded exactly like our mother came from downstairs, calling me. Each time I heard it, I ran downstairs to answer. Each time, she sent me away.

Was someone—or something—in the house playing games with me? I buried the thought, too afraid to explore the idea further. This continued for the rest of sixth grade and into seventh grade.

That next fall, Mariah started talking to herself before falling asleep. Sometimes, she woke up in the middle of the night, mumbling incoherently. Her muttering woke my sisters, since they slept in the next room, which was connected to hers by a doorway covered with a dirty mustard-yellow curtain.

After a few minutes of hushed murmuring, she'd begin repeating, "I am the devil. I am the devil. *I am the devil!*" Her voice slithered through the inky darkness around the curtain. It was high-pitched, twisting itself past her strained vocal cords. Sometimes, she dropped down an octave or two for an even more terrifying effect. Once she sensed that she had captured the little girls' attention, she started repeating, "I'm going to get you. I'm going to get you. *I'm going to get you!*" louder and louder, ratcheting up the volume dramatically.

Amanda and Helen pretended they were still asleep, but Mariah was relentless about getting their attention. She began personalizing her disturbing threats: "I am the devil. I'm going to get you, Amanda. I am the devil. I'm going to get you, Helen!"

If Mariah scared the girls enough, they eventually appeared at my door. "Please make her stop, Niecy. She keeps saying she's the devil and that she's going to get us," Amanda or Helen begged through their tears.

"Okay. You guys get back in bed. I'll make her shut up," I assured them. Then I'd make my way to Mariah's bedroom, yelling, "*Shut up, Mariah!*"

Her chanting continued, "I am the devil. *I am the devil!*"

"Shut up or I'm going to have to come in there," I threatened from just outside her room.

"I'm going to get you, Denise!" Mariah said in her creepy voice.

I walked over to her bedside and screamed in her face, "Shut up! Don't make me hurt you!"

Often, she simply rolled over and immediately fell asleep, as if she had been sleep talking and my threat had ended that particular dream. In such moments, I realized I was alone, in the dark, and standing over my sleeping sister, who appeared to have no idea of what she had just been doing. The hairs on my arms stood on end, and I wondered if it was Mariah speaking from a dream or if something else was speaking *through* her. I pushed the thought out of my mind. I stood tall, trying to suppress my rising fear even as my breathing quickened. I tiptoed out of her room and down the hallway to my room.

On other occasions, when Mariah wouldn't stop her chanting, I would slap her face. That would snap her out of her automatic chanting, and she would jerk as if awakening suddenly. I felt guilty for hitting her and would try to avoid doing so. At these times, when Mariah continued her verbal assaults and chanting, and my conscience prohibited me from striking her, I would gather my other sisters and have them come sleep with me in my room.

Mariah became my parents' scapegoat—when I wasn't the one blamed, of course. The rest of us girls teased her about being dumb and overweight. I realize now that this only made her behavior worse, but it was our only form of retaliation and defense against her. In truth, Mariah scared me, and I'm sure she scared the others, too.

In the fall of my eighth-grade year, as we were still struggling to deal with Mariah's behavior, my parents made an announcement. They were standing in the hall as we were heading up to bed when my father said to my mother, "Do you want to tell them?"

"I guess," Mom said, as if embarrassed. Based on her awkward behavior, I knew something big was going on. "We're going to have a baby," she stated flatly.

I certainly wasn't expecting that. Our family was already under so much strain, and our father didn't earn enough money to support the children he and our mother already had.

"Why would you get pregnant again?" I blurted out incredulously. "What were you thinking? You don't even take care of the children you already have. You just sit in that rocking chair in the hall all day."

"Shut up, Denise," Mom snapped. "Nobody asked you. It's my choice, not yours. I wish you were never born!" She was taken aback by my reaction. I got the impression that she thought I would be happy to hear the news.

"Well, I'm not taking care of another baby. You keep having children and then dumping all the responsibility for them on me. I don't want another baby," I shouted back.

"I hate you! Get out of here!" my mother shrieked.

I believed then, as I do now, that she was having children as an excuse not to get a job, and when I shared this theory with Lillian, she agreed.

At this point, I was getting all A's in school, working a few hours a week outside the house as a babysitter, and taking care of more chores than anyone else in the family. Another baby only meant more responsibility for me at a time when I was busier than ever. And my mother certainly wasn't grateful for the things I did to help her and the family.

She often complained, "You never do anything around here. I have to yell at you to get you to do anything. Why can't you just help without me telling you to?" She would say such things even as I was clearing the table or washing the dishes.

She often spat, "I hate you. I wish you were never born," at me. At one point, she figured out that this really got to me, and she made it her personal daily catchphrase. I was too afraid to ask what I had done to make her hate me so much. Questioning her often brought retaliation, so I just continued my work silently, trying not to listen to her rants. She failed to make any logical sense, but her words still stung. I often wondered if I really was a useless human being who didn't deserve to live, and I continued to shrivel up inside bit by bit.

Unpredictably, there were times when I was doing housework and she would say to me, "You're a big help. None of the other kids ever do anything around here but you. I don't know what I would do without you."

Because I never knew what she would say next, I couldn't take those words at face value. In the next breath, she could easily start to abuse me again. It would have been easier to guess a coin toss than to guess what she thought about me at any given moment.

I truly believed my mother loathed me, and she let me know it daily, even when I tried so hard to help out. This often brought me to tears as I fell asleep. I fostered deep feelings of worthlessness. During her pregnancy that year, barely a day went by when she didn't tell me that she hated me. I would often go outside for a walk just to shake off her toxicity. Although I knew she was worse when pregnant, probably due to hormonal fluctuations, her words still bit into my heart, confusing me and making me feel useless and unlovable.

Emotionally torn, I thought "Honor thy mother" meant that I should love her; therefore, I was a sinner because I didn't know *how* to love her. The guilt I felt knowing that God thought I was a bad person for not being able to love my mother sent me into a downward spiral. I was letting God down, and I felt as if my heart would implode.

For months, I remained silent, then one day, something inside me broke, and I snapped back, "Well, I hate you too, you bitch!" That shut her up for a while, but I could feel her loathing me through the space between us as we washed and dried the dishes in silence.

My father, noticing the tension in our house, tried to make us all happy with the little money he had by taking us out for pizza or to a fast-food restaurant on Friday nights. On Saturdays, we continued to go on our long walks through the woods or to the fairs, as we always had.

These few moments of fun did not make up for my mother and Mariah escalating their fits in public places. Mariah would whine until our mother yelled at her, and then one would start hitting the other right in front of everyone. Eventually, one of them would stomp off, screaming back at the other.

Parents would pull their children away from our vicinity as Mariah shouted obscenities. I hated feeling their eyes boring into my back as they looked on at our family's chaos. I would find a way to slip out of sight and pretend to be a bystander, but my long blond hair—just like Mariah's—gave me away.

Eventually, my mother and Mariah's scenes became too much for me to deal with, and I stopped going to the fairs with my family. I preferred staying home or babysitting, which gave me an excuse to get out of the house and a way to earn a little income of my own. I used it to buy issues of *Seventeen* magazine and makeup, which my mother never wore and would not purchase for us. I thought that by staying away from my family, I could be a normal, everyday girl, but even miles of space could not separate me from the person my mother and father had taught me to believe I was.

Despite the craziness and dysfunction, there were times of quiet and calm. These were times spent with my sisters. On Wednesday evenings, we went grocery shopping as a family. After putting everything away as best we could, since the pantry was already filled to the brim with the free government cereal boxes and powdered milk that had expired years earlier, my sisters and I sat down in the TV room for our favorite shows. We sat close together on a small clear spot on the red carpet directly in front of the television. We did this partially to get closer to the screen and partially because the couches were completely covered in piles of unfolded clothes and discarded potato chip bags and candy wrappers. On these evenings, the five of us girls would share a giant bag of Doritos, which we washed down with soda, iced tea, and a carton of strawberries—when they were in season. Otherwise, we scarfed down pastries or boxes of candy. Other than Sunday mornings, Wednesday nights were the only time I wasn't hungry.

We watched *Doogie Howser, M.D.* and *Danger Bay*. My sisters teased me that I was going to marry Doogie someday. I had a little crush on him, my sisters knew it, and they knew how to get a rise out of me.

"Shut up," I would whine back. "I'm not marrying Doogie Howser."

It wasn't that I wanted to marry him. I wanted to *be* him. Who wouldn't want to be a genius teenage doctor who wrote the most insightful journal entries every night? He was one of my idols, along with Oprah Winfrey, who had become a remote surrogate mother to me.

We watched *The Oprah Winfrey Show* in the late afternoon, just before our father arrived home from work. I would prepare dinner during the commercial breaks. As I watched Oprah speaking into the camera, I wanted to believe she was offering the sage advice directly to me:

"You are worthwhile."

"You have the potential to become successful. You can do it, despite the odds laid against you by your family or your community."

"You're a good, beautiful person, and wonderful things are waiting for you. You just hang in there. You'll see!"

She counseled me day after day while looking directly at me through the screen. While I believed her, I didn't see how I could possibly end up successful. On the other hand, if Oprah—a poor girl from Mississippi—could become such an accomplished yet grounded woman, I—a miserable girl from a small town in Connecticut—could become the person I was beginning to dream of becoming.

And if I could be anyone, it would be Oprah Howser, MD.

SECTION II

BURNING PHOENIX

Chapter 9

Resisting Evil
Fall 1988–Summer 1989

Around this time, after more than four years in town, my circle of friends was beginning to expand from the school lunchroom crowd to the church youth group. I started attending an evening youth group on Fridays, in addition to my confirmation classes on Wednesdays. Despite Wednesday being grocery night, my parents always let me go. I was grateful for that. While attending confirmation classes meant forfeiting the post-shopping camaraderie with my sisters that I enjoyed, the classes provided me with support from kids my age. They also provided me with a pastor who was interested in my religious views and helped me expand upon my beliefs, though I never opened up enough to tell him about the chaos at home.

I very quickly found myself with new friends who accepted me for who I was, used clothes and all. I felt safe and welcomed. Wednesday and Friday evenings became a sanctuary for me. As soon as I passed over the threshold of the church, I had no burdens, no responsibilities. I could be a thirteen-year-old who laughed and played without constantly looking over her shoulder to see if her parents were about to rage at her.

After ten weeks of attending classes, I was confirmed in the church and officially became a member. My youth-group leader gave me a gold-plated angel pin with its wings stretched wide. I pinned it to my backpack so I would have a little guardian angel watching over me every day at school.

At the same time, I was also spending more time with my friends from school, but the two groups remained separate. Once every couple of months, my parents allowed me to spend the night at Dawn's house as long as I was home by 8 a.m., before my sisters woke up, so I could get them dressed. As the fall slowly changed to winter, this meant I had to rush through the cold morning darkness to do a job that mothers all over town had accepted as their responsibility instead of handing it off to a daughter.

Dawn became fascinated with Ouija boards, and she swept me up in her enthusiasm. Ouija boards were reputed to be a means of communicating with the spirit world, yet they could be found in any toy store. We were sure that if we could get our hands on one, and if they actually worked, we could see into the future. We were ecstatic about the idea of becoming fortune-teller gypsies that could talk to dead people. However, we assumed they wouldn't actually work unless one of us pushed the pointer, called a planchette, around the board. Still, there was the tantalizing possibility that it *would* work, and that possibility—and the possibility of either accessing our immensely powerful subconscious or a spirit—fueled our zeal. We couldn't wait to try one.

Dawn asked her mother for a Ouija board for Christmas. After weeks of eager anticipation, Christmas came and brought with it the long-awaited Ouija board. A few nights later, Dawn invited me to sleep over. She hadn't tried to use the board yet, but upon my arrival she could barely keep her hands off of it.

To create the best ambiance for contacting ghosts, we decided to use the Ouija board after dark. Heavy wintry clouds covered the sky outside, so the night was as black as a catacomb. This only heightened our excitement. Dawn turned off the lights in her bedroom, leaving only a nightlight, which barely allowed us to see one another. Then she tore the plastic wrapping off the board.

The Ouija board had a pale taupe background with black letter-ing. It had an image of the sun in the upper left-hand corner with the word "Yes" beside it; the moon was in the upper right corner with "No" printed next to it. The word "Ouija" spanned the space between "Yes" and "No." Below this, the letters of the alphabet were arranged in two rows in an arc. The numbers 1 through 9, followed by a 0, were positioned near the bottom of the board with the word "Goodbye" beneath that. Simple enough.

As we placed our hands on opposite sides of the planchette, we started giggling hysterically and making silly ghost sounds. When we asked our questions, still mired in laughter, the board was mute. Apparently, Ouija boards don't work when laughed at.

For an hour, we repeated in various spooky voices, "Is anybody out there?" over and over again. We never tired of the repetition. The planchette sat completely still, except for the few occasions when we accidentally moved it due to our convulsive laughter.

Just when we were about to give up on the board actually doing something, the planchette twitched.

"Did you just move that?" I asked Dawn.

"No, did you?" she said.

"Nope."

It was time to get serious.

"Who are you?" Dawn asked.

The planchette began to move, slowly at first. It stopped at the sun. We assumed that was good, or at least better than the moon.

"Do you live here?" I asked

Our hands moved smoothly across the board together. It stopped at "Yes."

"How old are you?" Dawn asked, obviously excited.

"9-3"

"How long did you live here?"

"L-I-F-E."

Dawn began recording the letters with her right hand on the back of a discarded sheet of homework while keeping her left hand on the pointer. "Your entire life?" she asked. I could tell she wanted to know who had lived there before her.

"Yes."

"Did you die here?"

"No."

It was a fairly simplistic conversation, but it was a rush for us. It was like we had stumbled upon hidden treasure. From then on, we were Ouija board addicts. Eager to show our friends, Dawn and I introduced Kelly to our new game. Kelly then brought Sue and Chris over to Dawn's house, and she showed them all how to use the board.

With the five of us in regular attendance, we had unwittingly formed our own Ouija board club. If any of us were together at someone's house, there was a Ouija board in use. Dawn, Kelly, and I became adept at working the board. The spirits were stronger when one of us was using it.

Whenever we used the board, I experienced a strange sensation in my hands, particularly in my fingers. A tingling numbness, like a mild electrical current, ran through my hands as we slid our fingers over the board. During sessions when we had a particularly active spirit responding, I felt the energy run from my fingers up through my arms and into my body. Although I assumed my friends also experienced these strange sensations, none of us spoke about it.

Perhaps it was the feeling of power that lured us into the mysterious realm of the dead. We liked being able to do something others couldn't. I didn't realize we were lighting preternatural matches and tossing them around like a group of children playing with fire. Every so often, something would catch fire, and we would be delighted by the response at our fingertips. We had not yet gone beyond thinking of this as anything more than innocent fun.

By late winter, I was completely addicted to playing with the Ouija board. Dawn had the store-bought board her mother had gotten her for Christmas; Kelly made hers out of a piece of wood and used markers to write out the letters; I created mine from the back of a pizza box on which I wrote the alphabet, "Yes" and "No," the numbers 0 through 9, and the sun and moon with a pen. I took a used margarine lid and cut a triangular window out of the center to use as a planchette. I used my cardboard Ouija board daily to obtain knowledge about my test scores, when I would die, when I would lose my virginity, who my first boyfriend would be, and pretty much everything else a teenage girl would think to ask the dead. I consulted my board for hours at a time—on the weekends after completing my chores and during the week after everyone else had gone to bed. During these nightly "consultations," I'd fall into a trance that I had difficulty rousing myself from.

The more I learned, the more I wanted to know. I was desperate to find out if my life would improve or if I would continue on my path of wretched servitude. I wanted to know that I would be okay, happy even, but all I could envision on my own was more pain, more fear, and more abuse. I needed to know that my future would be better so I could have something, anything, to cling to.

That spring, on our eighth-grade field trip to Washington, D.C., Kelly brought her Ouija board with her. She, Jessica, Dawn, and I shared a room. We were at the top of our class and normally didn't cause trouble. Quiet time was at 10 p.m., but we were up until three in the morning, making a terrible racket. The Ouija board told us that we would all lose our virginity that night to someone named "Stupid" and that there would be a huge orgy in our room with thirteen guys. We couldn't stop giggling.

Close to 3 a.m., I asked it again when I would lose my virginity.

"W-H-E-N G-O-D O-R-D-A-I-N-S," was the answer. This would not have been peculiar if we had known what "ordains" meant. We looked the word up when we returned home. It meant "to decree by virtue of superior authority." That was the first time I considered that we may have been speaking with a truly intelligent being.

* * *

Gabrielle was born shortly after my Washington, D.C., trip in May. I had to help take care of her, as I had anticipated, but I didn't mind as much as I thought I would. I loved that sweet little baby, even though she added more work to my already packed schedule.

In eighth grade, despite everything happening at home, I managed to finish third in my class and successfully balance all of my activities. I had become a Red Cross volunteer and a candy striper at the hospital, and I continued to be active in my church, all of which helped get me out of the house more often.

My father started talking to me about attending Princeton University. He had heard that tuition would be free if I could get a scholarship since we were a low-income family. My high grades led us both to believe that I might be able to attend an Ivy League school someday.

At my June graduation from junior high, I received several awards and brought home more accolades than anyone else. I was on top of the world, or at least of the school. My father gave me a pat on the back and told me that he was proud of me. It felt wonderful to receive such positive feedback from one of my parents.

The night of graduation, we had a dance at the school. As usual, the boys huddled together in small groups, unwilling to dance. I walked around the floor, attempting to persuade the guys to dance with me. No one accepted my invitation except for Mike. He had been in all my classes that year. I didn't know that his mother, who was a chaperone, had a camera with her. Years later, I learned that I was the first girl he had ever danced with, and she had the photos to prove it. No wonder he stepped on my feet so much! I was just delighted that he agreed to dance with me. I was moving on in my life, and the new life I was aiming for included boys.

But before those plans could materialize, in the summer before high school, something sinister came into my life.

With my junior-high years over, I waited anxiously for high school to begin. That summer, as I read the books I had been assigned as preparation for my freshman year, I dreamed about how wonderful the next four years would be. How could they fail to be exciting, since Dawn and I were planning on wearing tight, sexy clothing so the guys would notice us? We'd be popular and get invited to all the cool parties. In my fantasy, the boys were already tripping over each other to ask me to dance.

In between housework, reading, getting up at night with Gabrielle, volunteering, babysitting, phone calls, trips to Kelly's pool, sleepovers, and fantasizing, I was still regularly using my Ouija board.

Our sessions with the board had gotten darker over the months. We had been told dozens of times by "S-A-T-A-N" that he would kill us. In fact, "Satan" had muscled his way onto our board so frequently that we nicknamed him Louie, short for Lucifer. He was the strongest spirit we ever encountered, but I never felt that his threats were anything more than someone's slightly twisted imagination. I was still grappling with whether we were moving the planchette subconsciously or if we were actually communicating with spirits.

The summer after eighth grade was turning out to be the best summer of my life until the day I walked into my room and noticed my Bible sitting neatly in the center of my bed, back cover up. As I picked it up to move it, I felt strangely compelled to open it. I had never felt a compulsion to read the Bible before. In fact, despite attending church services regularly, I had never actually read the Bible, preferring to leave it buried in the bottom drawer of my dresser. There were too many words I didn't know how to pronounce; it wasn't my idea of leisurely reading material.

That day, as I picked up the Bible and turned it over, I wondered, *How did it get out of the drawer and onto my bed?* I flipped it open and started casually reading the page it opened to. I began at the top of the page, halfway through 1 Samuel 17 of the New International Version:

> And David girded his sword over his armor, and he tried in
> vain to go, for he was not used to them. Then David said to Saul,

"I cannot go with these; for I am not used to them." And David put them off. Then he took his staff in his hand, and chose five smooth stones from the brook, and put them in his shepherd's bag or wallet; his sling was in his hand, and he drew near to the Philistine.

And the Philistine came on and drew near to David, with his shield-bearer in front of him. And when the Philistine looked and saw David, he disdained him; for he was but a youth, ruddy and comely in appearance. And the Philistine said to David, "Am I a dog, that you come to me with sticks?" And the Philistine cursed David by his gods. The Philistine said to David, "Come to me, and I will give your flesh to the birds of the air and to the beasts of the field." Then David said to the Philistine, "You come to me with a sword and with a spear and with a javelin; but I come to you in the name of the Lord of hosts, the God of the armies of Israel, whom you have defied. This day the Lord will deliver you into my hand, and I will strike you down and cut off your head; and I will give the dead bodies of the host of the Philistines this day to the birds of the air and to the wild beasts of the earth; that all the earth may know that there is a God in Israel, and that all this assembly may know that the Lord saves not with sword and spear; for the battle is the Lord's and he will give you into our hand."

When the Philistine arose and came and drew near to meet David, David ran quickly toward the battle line to meet the Philistine. And David put his hand in his bag and took out a stone, and slung it, and struck the Philistine on his forehead; the stone sank into his forehead, and he fell on his face to the ground.

So David ran and stood over the Philistine, and took his sword and drew it out of its sheath, and killed him, and cut off his head with it. When the Philistines saw that their champion was dead, they fled.

I dropped my Bible with a quiet gasp. An eerie feeling settled over me. I knew something was about to happen and that I was meant to read that passage, but why? I couldn't shake the feeling that there was a message in that story for me. I tried to shake it off and told myself that I was being silly, but I still prayed to God for an explanation.

Then I hunted down my sisters to find out who had been messing with my stuff and had taken my Bible out of its drawer. They all denied going into my room with a look of true innocence, and I believed them. Plus, if they had been in my room, they would have been rummaging through my clothes or makeup. It didn't make sense that only my Bible had been moved.

Two weeks later, alone in my room and bored of the usual questions, I asked my Ouija board, "How do spirits have any fun?"

I began to taunt the spirit, telling it that it couldn't go on picnics, party, eat, drink, or make love.

I knew many spirits had a dark sense of humor, so I thought it was amusing when he told me that he was going to rape me. "Oh yeah, how's some dead guy going to rape me?" I taunted the board.

It answered, "W-I-T-H M-Y H-E-A-D."

"You don't have a head," I told the board. "If you don't have one, you can't use it, so there!"

I don't know what I was thinking, teasing a spirit like that. I was still fairly certain that I was the one in control and that it was only me, but why did I take that chance?

I pushed the spirit, asking, "So when are you going to rape me?"

"M-I-D-N-I-G-H-T T-O-N-I-G-H-T," was its answer.

Suddenly, this game had become serious. After this, the board was relentless. When I changed the subject and asked it other questions, its insistent response was that it was going to rape me. Chills ran through me. This session was different. Something was wrong.

This spirit was stronger than Louie. I had never interacted with it before, and when I had asked it early on in the session whether it was good or evil, the planchette had immediately pulled itself to the sign of the moon. Every response was spelled out in fast, jerky movements. I could barely keep up with the planchette as it flew around the board.

As I continued using the board, a sick feeling welled up in the pit of my stomach, and I started to shake. I told myself that I was being stupid and that this was just a child's game I was playing on a harmless piece of cardboard. It was all in my mind. It couldn't harm me. Yet deep down, I knew I was dead wrong.

My intuition was screaming at me to stop. I had crossed a line and was afraid I had connected with a spirit beyond my ability to control. It was no longer just a game. For the first time, as I read that repeated threat of rape, I was truly apprehensive about what the board said. I returned my Ouija board to its hiding place in the small spare bedroom off the back hall that no one wanted to sleep in because it was "too scary" back there.

Since I had first started working the board with Dawn, I had sensed something ominous about the game. Now, to my horror, I was being proved right. I realized with a shock how easily it had drawn me in. I was like the high school kid who, wanting to fit in, starts experimenting with drugs, certain he can stop at will. Using the Ouija board had been an escape from my home life, but I had become obsessed with it—addicted, even.

For the rest of the day, I tried to forget the session, but I couldn't shake my irrational fear. Too soon, pink clouds lit the sky and a veil of pale stars appeared. Fear inched down my spine like a black widow creeping across her web to suck the life out of a trapped insect.

Just after eleven, everyone in the house had finally gone to sleep except for me. A strange terror gripped my body and kept me wide awake. *Come on, Denise. It's all in your mind. Go to sleep. All you have to do is fall asleep before midnight. It's just a stupid game messing with your mind,* I told myself. Yet as much as I tried to fall asleep, I couldn't.

Waves of nausea suddenly surged over my entire body from the fear, prompting me to curl into a fetal position. I stared at my alarm clock, attempting to focus my eyes. It was 11:30.

The night was otherwise a comfortable one. A gentle breeze floating through the window beside my bed smelled of the promise of rain. Because it was a warm night, I had only a sheet covering me. The sheet was old and worn, with little yellow flowers splattered across it. It clashed with the thick horizontal blue-and-white stripes on my nightgown.

I heard something buzzing, and my nervousness spiked. The sound started as a low whisper, with more tones joining in until I realized it was the chorus of hell. The chainsaw-like buzzing rumbled through my head like a freight train. I opened my eyes, squinting into the darkness. There was something moving on the ceiling. When my eyes finally adjusted to the dark, I saw that it was a cluster of huge black houseflies flying in a circle around my ceiling. They had not been there just a few minutes earlier. It was as if they had materialized out of thin air. I thought there were at least a hundred of them, but they probably actually numbered ten or twenty.

I closed my eyes again as terror tore through me. It was coming true: whatever was in the Ouija board was coming to rape me. I wrapped my arms around myself to calm the trembling in my limbs. That's when I noticed it wasn't just me shaking; the bed was shaking too.

I lay there immobilized, my mind racing in a bramble of thoughts: *Get up. No, I can't. Yes, you can. Move your feet, Denise. Come on. Where am I going to go? Why aren't I moving? I'm going to vomit. Oh my God, help me.*

I looked at the clock. It was 11:43.

What am I going to do? Pray. Okay, I can pray. "Our Father who art in heaven, hallowed be Thy name. Thy kingdom come, Thy will be done, on Earth as it is in heaven. Give us this day our daily bread and forgive us our trespasses as we forgive those that trespass against us. And lead us not into temptation, but deliver us from evil, for Thine is the kingdom, power, and glory, forever and ever. Amen."

The prayer and the thought that God might answer my call was the one thing that gave me solace and kept my last morsel of sanity from slipping away.

I slowly rolled over to the edge of the bed, but my terror only intensified. I lowered my shaking arm to the floor and picked up the Bible I had placed there earlier that evening just in case. It felt like it weighed a thousand pounds. When I finally dragged it onto the bed, I was too weak to open it.

"Please help me, God. Please, please," I whimpered.

I watched a minute tick by on the clock and then whispered the Lord's Prayer again. I clutched my Bible to my chest as I lay on my side in a fetal position, the bed still shaking beneath me.

Whatever it was, it was coming.

Burning tears rolled down my face as the clock clicked over to 12:00 a.m. At that moment, I felt a force enter me, the same force I felt in my hands when I used the Ouija board, but now it was in my entire body and it was stronger. It was like static electricity times ten. All the hair on my body stood on end. The only place this force did not permeate was my head. I was relieved that it did not control my thoughts, at least not yet.

"Please, God. Please..."

At that moment, I lost control of my body and was engulfed in darkness both inside and out. A heavy feeling of doom enveloped me, and an acrid taste bubbled up and burned the back of my throat. It was the taste of terror. I swallowed down vomit, heaving, still lying on my side.

I became aware of the buzz of the flies again, but now it was louder. Their hum accelerated until I was dizzy from the noise. Their wretched sound filled my head, and I thought it would explode. I hated the flies, but I knew there was more to this than them. Whatever controlled them was attempting to control me as well.

I felt powerless in this struggle. I curled up tighter into a ball and covered my exposed ear with my free hand. My other hand still clutched my Bible, my lifeline. My pulse sped up. My chest heaved. My breath left my mouth, tasting foul. Tears raced down my face. I kept praying, but my prayers didn't alleviate the buzz of the flies. I couldn't abate the onslaught of whatever demonic force had come for me.

The shaking bed was even more terrifying than the flies. It became so violent that the bed was nearly jumping off the floor. Incredibly, it made no noise, not even a single groan, yet the turbulence thundered through my rigid body and echoed through my bones. I was paralyzed and desperate to scream, but when I opened my mouth to cry out for help, I couldn't even squeak. I lay there helpless, silently praying.

Believing that Satan was about to drag me into the pits of hell, I feared my soul was in jeopardy. I was just a kid; I knew I didn't belong in hell. I began making God all kinds of promises: I would be good, I wouldn't use the Ouija board again, and I would do whatever He asked.

My right arm started to move, but I was not the one controlling it. It shook as it moved out from under the sheet, followed by my left arm.

Stop! I silently commanded my limbs. With all my strength, I willed my arms to stop, but they continued to move. I was a puppet that belonged to a hideous puppet-master playing for nightmares. I didn't want to think about what might happen next.

Gingerly and in spite of my commands, my hands began sliding the sheet down my body. I was no longer shaking; I was incapable of doing even that. I was barely even breathing. Air could neither escape nor enter my immobilized body. I certainly couldn't cry anymore. The seconds seemed to slow into years as my alien hands removed the sheet. An odd chill swept over me like the wind preceding a storm.

By then I was in shock. I had stopped praying and was barely able to think. I had accepted my fate.

Once the demonic force had pushed the sheet from my body, it gained strength. Now, it directed my hands to undo the three buttons at the top of my nightgown. One by one, I unbuttoned the gown. Then slowly, too slowly, as if the spirit were toying with me, I pulled the nightgown over my head and was left wearing only my pink underwear. No longer in control, my fingers slid the pink cotton down my white legs.

I lay on the bed helpless, nude, and full of terror. I was sprawled out on my back, my fingertips touching the sides of the mattress, legs splayed open. My fear was so much more than the simple fear of dying. I had been taught that when my body died, my soul would transition back to heaven. I sensed that this entity wanted to break my soul and shred it, to permanently erase my very essence. If it had its way, my soul would not survive this ordeal. The force now controlling me would slowly, bit by bit, disassemble first my sanity, then my very existence.

Every cell in my body screamed in silent terror. A revolt rose from deep within my soul, and I came to my senses. I realized I could still fight back. There was still time, but I had to make a move, now.

I addressed the entity for the first time, screaming in my mind, *No, I don't want you here. You are not allowed. I rebuke you in the name of Jesus Christ, Our Lord. I rebuke you in the name of the Father, the Son, and the Holy Ghost.*

I don't know where the words came from. I had never used the word "rebuke" in my life, but it was there in the forefront of my consciousness, and I grasped it as if it were a life preserver thrown down by God.

I slowly took control of my fear. I repeated my silent reprimand to the spirit. Suddenly, my will came rushing back to me like a tsunami about to overcome the evil force.

"You are not invited!" I croaked, speaking aloud now. My voice was a whisper, but it felt like an amazing achievement. "In the name of Jesus, I command you to leave! I rebuke you in the name of Jesus Christ, Our Lord."

I repeated the words again and then again slightly louder. Feeling came back into my arms and hands. They were no longer numb. I hadn't even realized they were. Suddenly, I broke free entirely, reclaiming control of my body. I seized the moment, jumped off my bed, and took a deep breath, as if I had just surfaced after nearly drowning. I could control my body again, but I didn't know for how long.

I knew exactly what I had to do. Dressing quickly, I picked up my Bible, fled the room, and searched the house for matches. After finding them, I headed to the spare bedroom where I had hidden my Ouija board that afternoon. I yanked it from its hiding place, snuck outside into the darkness of the cool night, and burned it, plastic margarine lid and all.

The terrifying experience was over for the night. I hoped that would be the end of it, but in my heart, I knew better. That may have been the end of my obsession with the Ouija board, but I feared the demonic spirit I had let loose would return.

The days, weeks, and months that followed were filled with new strange and unusual occurrences. The flies in my room did not die off for months. They were resistant to bug spray and fly paper. I wondered what they thrived on.

My bed shook for weeks. I tried other beds to see if they would shake too, but they didn't. For a few nights after that terrifying encounter, I slept in Lillian's room while she was staying with her friends. I was scared to fall asleep, but even more terrified of what might happen if I stayed awake. I dreaded each nightfall and eventually asked Lillian and Amanda to sleep in my room with me so I wouldn't be alone. They reluctantly agreed. Sensing that I was scared spooked them too.

My room had a closet that had no door, and my sisters complained that they sensed something scary in it. They preferred sleeping in their own rooms. I agreed with them about the closet, as I sometimes thought I saw a dark shadow, blacker than the surrounding darkness, flit past the closet entrance. I assumed it was my mind playing tricks on me.

One night a couple of weeks after my terrible experience, as I was on the verge of sleep, I felt my sheet move slightly. I thought it was just the breeze from the window, but as I lay there, I realized the wind was blowing in the opposite direction; the sheet had moved toward the breeze. Then it moved again; it was being pulled off the side of the bed. I got up, raced across the room, and fetched Amanda to sleep on the floor beside me. Whatever was in my room wanted me, not my sisters, and I felt far less vulnerable with them by my side. I knew they hated staying in my room with me and that they only did so to help ease my fears.

I prayed to God constantly. Only prayer stopped the flies from buzzing and allowed me to sleep. I knew I was responsible for these events and that I had released something dark and sinister into our home. I sensed that it couldn't physically touch me again, but it was still lurking in the darkness and tormenting me. Even though I had been indirectly taught in church not to dabble in the occult because it would lead me into the fires of hell, I had been naive and hadn't heeded that advice. I hadn't really believed in the occult at the time, and my church didn't have much to say about Satan. It was not relevant to my life. Now I knew better. The Bible was right on that topic.

From time to time, I wondered, *Why me?* Was I an easy target for evil? Did I somehow deserve this? Lots of other kids played with Ouija boards without anything bad happening to them. Why would God bother to warn me and then come to my aid? And why wasn't this over?

At least daylight was my reprieve, or so I thought.

One bright September day, a few days before high school started, I was reading a book in the rocking chair in the hall. It was unusual for me to sit in this chair, which my mother often used, but the sun was so warm in that particular spot that it drew me in. The noonday sun shone brilliantly through the windows and reflected off the glass door in the hallway that led upstairs. As I closed my eyes to enjoy the warmth on my face, I heard the glass door creaking softly. My eyes sprang open. The door opened by itself, stopping only inches from me. Then it closed on its own at a leisurely pace.

Is there a window open upstairs, creating a draft that moved the door? I wondered. As I pondered this, the door opened again, faster this time, and then closed at the same speed. I sat paralyzed in my chair. I watched the door quickly reopen a third time and shut itself again.

That was enough for me. I threw my book down and ran into the kitchen. It took me a while to compose myself. I reasoned that there had to be an open window upstairs, and I decided to go up there and prove it to myself. After calming down, I climbed the stairs and looked in every room. Then I searched the rest of the house for an open door or window.

To my horror, they were all closed.

The door was only one of many objects in the house that moved without cause. My radio turned itself off and changed stations for no discernable reason. Empty bags and loose papers on my bedroom floor drifted from one side of the room to the other and sometimes back again. This spooky activity terrified me. I chose to blame it on drafts—our house was old, after all—but there had never been drafts like this in our house before. I resolved to stop leaving things on the floor.

The problem was, it wasn't just light objects floating across the room. One night, I heard a light shuffling coming from my dresser. I turned around to see two of my cross-country trophies teetering on the edge of the dresser, three inches from where I had carefully placed them. I knew they had moved because I could see lines in the light layer of dust I had neglected to clean.

I also began having nightmares. I was always running in the dream, typically down a road, but sometimes across a field. I was terrified, dashing away from something evil I could not see. My heart raced, and sweat dripped down my face. Sometimes, my entire body was drenched as if I had been running for my life for miles. I didn't know what I was trying to escape from, but I could feel an evil presence behind me. In every dream, I turned my head to look over my shoulder and see how far behind me the danger was. I was relieved to see that nothing was there. But when I turned my head back forward again, a demon would be standing right in front of me, grinning. I always ran right through it. It usually took a black, wispy form, like a huge smoky, translucent human figure. As I entered that black mass, I experienced pure evil, like I was entering the mind of a psychopath. There was no empathy, only feelings of hatred, disgust, manipulation, ridicule, and the intense desire for the death and suffering of others. I screamed as I passed through the form, then awoke shaking and drenched in sweat.

I was terrified to stay awake at night and equally afraid to fall asleep. Even my dreams were haunted by whatever I had let loose from the Ouija board. I slept with my Bible under my pillow every night or held it in my hands in a death grip, clinging to it as I would a life preserver. The only way I could fall asleep was by repeating the Lord's Prayer as if I were counting sheep. Every night, I prayed that I wouldn't have nightmares and that, eventually, the terror I was experiencing would fade and I would return to normalcy—if there were such a thing in my family. I prayed for protection from the force I had released.

I didn't tell anyone about what had happened—not even Lillian or my friends, Dawn and Kelly. Lillian and my younger sisters were already scared of the house, and I didn't want to add to their fear. I was too afraid of my parents to talk to them about anything, and I assumed they wouldn't believe me anyway.

When the morning came, I hid my fear by metamorphosing into a different person. During the day, I prevented myself from thinking about the impending night by shutting the demonic specter inside a door in my mind, where I could no longer see it. Living the nightmare at night was hard enough; I couldn't bear to live it by day as well. It was a classic case of denial.

When I stepped out of the house each morning, I left it all behind, as if the terror of the night before had never occurred. I tried to shift my focus to school and the new person I hoped to become.

Chapter 10

Luxaya

Fall-Winter 1989

My first day of classes at Gilbert High School was the start of a new adventure, and I was excited to meet my new classmates. I looked forward to seeing old friends and making new ones. Since our high school's student body was composed of people from two towns, there were many new faces. Like my classmates, I was fired up with the expectation of wonderful things about to happen in high school. The world lay open before me. Down a hallway or around a corner, something special was waiting. My history in junior high was no longer important. My new story was just waiting to be written. I was sure it would be amazing.

As I entered the huge hallways for the first time, I felt slightly overwhelmed and hid within the throngs of my fellow students. Many, obviously from the other town, were strangers. We freshmen stayed close to our homerooms, as if attached by leashes. For all the feelings of opportunity and change, few dared to explore the vast unknown yet.

My first class of the day was English. Our teacher explained that we would no longer be spoon-fed information or told what to study. I heard her speaking but barely listened. I was distracted by the boy sitting beside me, Mark, a student from East Hartland. Mark was built like a quarterback. He had chiseled features, a strong body with wide shoulders, and an alluring, quiet air. Half an hour into my first class, I had a crush on him. *High school is going to be wonderful*, I thought as I smiled and looked over toward Mark.

By October, my infatuation with Mark had only grown. While reading *Romeo and Juliet* in English class, I imagined him reciting Romeo's lines to me as I quoted Juliet's. When the class was working on grammar exercises, I gazed at his handsome face. He was trying hard not to notice my overt staring. *If I were prettier, Mark might talk to me*, I thought to myself.

Against my father's wishes and in an effort to be fashionable, I permed my long, straight blond hair. After all, it was 1989. I ended up looking like a cross between a member of the band Whitesnake and a sheep, but I loved having "big hair." Despite my father's disdain for my new look, I rejoiced in finally getting to create my own identity.

After waiting several weeks for Mark to approach me, I concluded that he would not, and I decided to talk to him first. I said "Hi" to him every day... in my head. My mouth never seemed willing to open around him. It was time for a new strategy.

I decided to write him a love poem and slip it into his locker. Dawn told me not to do it, but I ignored her words of reason. I composed my best love poem—it took up three entire sheets of paper—and spent another week working up the courage to walk to his locker, the folded paper with my amorous verses clutched in my sweating palms. Shuffling through the hallway, I tried desperately to look inconspicuous. At Mark's locker, I ran my hand down its hard, smooth surface before brushing my fingers across my cheek. I imagined him kissing me but snapped out of my fantasy at hearing the clatter of students around me. I had to hurry off to my next class. It was now or never. I quickly slid the sheets through the vent into his locker and then shuffled quickly down the hall.

Just as I reached my next class, my courage failed me, and Dawn's words of wisdom hit me. *Oh no, what have I done?* I thought in a panic. I had just dropped a love poem into Mark's locker, the locker of someone I had only said "hi" to a couple of times.

It was too late now. What was done was done. I didn't see Mark for the rest of that day. I'd just have to wait for his response in English the next morning.

But the next day, he didn't seem to have any kind of reaction to my profession of love. Nor the next day. Nor the day after that. A week passed without a word from Mark, even though he must have read my poem.

The homecoming dance was fast approaching, and I grew bold again, despite Mark's silence. I decided to have someone ask him to go to the dance for me. A girl named Karen, who had been friends with Mark since third grade, sat next to me in history class. She seemed nice, so I felt comfortable soliciting her help and asked her to ask Mark to the homecoming dance for me. She came back later that day with the message that he would give me an answer when he found out whether or not he was busy.

I was young and naive, so I waited patiently for Mark's answer. When homecoming was just a week away and I still had no response, I decided to ask him myself. I was too inexperienced at that time to pick up on his intentions. I saw him standing alone at his locker between classes and approached him through the crowded hallway. I had been rehearsing what to say to him the previous night, but those words vanished as soon as I walked up to him. The air ceased to enter my lungs. I started shaking and sweating. As I stood beside him, watching him stare into his locker, obviously not wanting to acknowledge me, I felt my mouth open and heard myself ask him to the dance.

Mark did not look at me. Instead, he sighed as he fixated on his locker. I felt the anguish I was causing him. With eyes full of sadness, he turned to answer me. I already knew what his response would be.

Why didn't I get the hint when he didn't respond earlier? The thought flickered through my consciousness.

I could see that he didn't want to hurt me, but he had to say something. "I'm sorry, but..."

That was all I heard. I watched his lips move, but I couldn't hear his voice over the maelstrom that filled my mind: *How could you be so stupid? What were you thinking? You're not pretty enough for someone like him anyway.*

"Well, thanks anyway," I managed to choke out as I walked away. I'd finally heard it directly from him; he wasn't interested in me. My crush ended with an aching heart.

Since I didn't have a date for the homecoming dance, I made arrangements with Dawn and Kelly, who were also solo, to go to the homecoming dance as a group. We had a great time and hung out in the bathroom together during the slow songs, complaining about how none of us had a date. Mark didn't even show up.

Embarrassed by my own forwardness, I avoided Mark whenever possible after that. I'd started high school feeling so hopeful, but now I settled into the familiar pattern of making myself as invisible as possible.

* * *

I had joined the cross-country team that fall, and my running career could not have been going better. I placed well for the team at meets all season, and my coach praised my abilities. Despite this, I often reproached myself for running too slowly. My perfectionism never let me rest.

During our training sessions, our coach would lead us through the woods in the hills that rose above the high school. As I ran along these forest paths, the peace of my surroundings and the gentle rhythm of my footsteps allowed me to disappear into a utopia of my own creation. In these hills, I could forget about how awkward I had been with Mark and about the demonic forces that still haunted me in my dreams nearly every night, preventing me from getting a full night's rest. I could forget about my mother's unreasonable demands and about my father's erratic behavior that left me guessing what he would do next.

About once a week, I would return to these hill paths, where I was in another world. After satisfying my mother's whims, I would slip out of the house. As I began my trek up the hills that bordered the quiet houses of my town, the tensions of my life slowly gave way to the peace I felt being among the trees, boulders, and insects.

My favorite path was a deeply grooved dirt road. After a mile-long gradual incline up a granite hill, it leveled off as it led to the summit. All along the hill's staggered rock face, patches of dark green moss extended upward from clumps of leaves and grass. Small trees found places to root in the crannies of the broken granite. As the trail wound up and away from the clamor of civilization, even the screech of birds faded into the background. Silence saturated the air. The hill emanated a sense of calmness I never experienced at home. I was drawn to its summit, perhaps hoping the stillness would quell the fears I tried to push down deep inside. It was a place of solace and meditation.

Typically, I stopped along the way, about half a mile before the summit, to sit on a ledge that was part of a rocky outcropping that dropped off suddenly at the edge like an infinity pool. There was a wide expanse of moss growing on a large flat boulder that was also speckled with small, crooked trees. A rotting lichen-covered log lay near the edge of the boulder. Due to the sheer drop, there was a natural part between the tall oaks and maples, revealing a view of the rounded hills stretching to the horizon. I was instinctively drawn to this place and returned to it again and again.

Here on this rocky outcropping, carpeted by moss and surrounded by stunted trees, I created a fantasy world. One day the name "Luxaya" popped into my head as I sat there, daydreaming. The name Luxaya just seemed to fit, as if the place had named itself long ago and had just whispered its name to me in a dream.

Here in Luxaya, I would rest on the bed of moss, with my head propped up on the log, and escape my mean, unloving world. I could simply exist as myself. I was a girl full of dreams, though I could not yet imagine how any of them might come true. Here, I imagined I had parents who said, "I love you." I imagined I had a mother who would take me shopping for clothes at the mall and who could actually drive a car to get us there. I imagined I had father who called me his "little princess." I imagined I had transformed into a beautiful woman and had a boyfriend. I imagined I wasn't afraid anymore.

When the silence seemed too long, I prayed out loud: "Dear God, please send someone to love me. Please make whatever evil I released from the Ouija board go away. Please help me grow up to become someone special and help me do well in school. Make me beautiful someday. Please, God, rescue me from this life."

When I had trouble settling down into the stillness, I quoted lines from Shakespeare's plays that I had read in English class. I was Hamlet, reciting the first few lines of his soliloquy by heart:

> To be, or not to be, that is the question,
> Whether 'tis nobler in the mind to suffer
> The slings and arrows of outrageous fortune,
> Or to take arms against a sea of troubles
> And by opposing end them? To die: to sleep;
> No more; and by a sleep to say we end
> The heart-ache, and the thousand natural shocks
> That flesh is heir to, 'tis a consummation
> Devoutly to be wish'd. To die, to sleep;
> To sleep; perchance to dream: ay, there's the rub;
> For in that sleep of death what dreams may come
> When we have shuffled off this mortal coil.

Then, I would transform into Juliet and ask:

> O Romeo, Romeo! wherefore art thou Romeo?
> Deny thy father and refuse thy name;
> Or, if thou wilt not, be but sworn my love,
> And I'll no longer be a Capulet.

Then I would skip a few lines to:

> What's in a name? That which we call a rose
> By any other name would smell as sweet.

I desperately wanted someone to love me as Juliet was loved, and I didn't want to be judged simply because I was a "Brown." At some point over the years, being known by my last name became a worse fate then being called a "raggy." By that time, our family was infamous around town. More importantly, I was debating whether life was even worth living. Perhaps it was better to die. Perhaps, in death, I would be free of my suffering, and all those who hurt me would come to understand my contributions. Maybe they would even miss me. Heaven must surely be better than this Earth with all its miseries. It seemed like a romantic idea.

In the safety of Luxaya, it wasn't uncommon for me to act out parts of Shakespeare's plays with a crooked stick for a sword. I would jump down to where the outcropping dropped down a foot, ambushing and slaying the villain in my imagination. Only later did I realize that this role-playing was an effort to combat the angst growing within me. Sometimes I froze in place as the silence of the hill became too intense for me. As I listened to the silence, goose bumps rose on my skin. I shivered for a moment and then, wanting to be distracted, I returned to my plays or recited poems of my own creation. Speaking aloud pushed back the growing stillness that threatened me.

A dying tree beside the log became one of my characters, a headboard for when I wanted to lean back, and a friend. Two small branches, barely alive, stretched outward from its trunk like arms toward a patch of sunlight. It was a mute mourner when I bent over in front of it, crying. It was a confidante who would not judge me, who understood my desires and fears, and who accepted me as I was. It was an unremarkable, ugly tree, but to me, it was special. Luxaya was my sanctuary, my haven.

However, I never lingered to watch the sun set or experience the day turn to dusk in those woods. As soon as the sun crouched at the horizon, my heart raced at the mere thought that darkness would soon engulf me, and I ran toward town. The woods receded behind me. Dogs barked as I passed. My feet hit the street's hard pavement just as the sun dipped below the horizon and the streetlights popped on, bathing me again in light. I took a deep breath. I was safe.

While I was glad to escape the coming darkness of the woods, I was returning to the chaos of my home and to the emotional entropy sucking the life out of me and my sisters. But return home I did. I had to prepare dinner quickly before my father arrived home from work.

After a typical meal of spaghetti or Spam, there would be calm for twenty or thirty minutes. I would go to my room to do homework, but soon, too soon, I would hear from downstairs, "One, two, three! Denise! Denise, get down here now!"

It made no difference if I had told them I had a test coming up or a paper due. The easiest route was to do what they wanted immediately.

Much of Gabrielle's care fell on me in the evenings, just as I had anticipated. A common complaint from my parents was, "The baby's diaper needs changing," as if I already knew and was purposefully shirking my duties.

One night, when I walked into the kitchen to discard Gabrielle's soiled diaper, my father stood on the opposite side of the table, as if trying to block access to the phone and door. It made me nervous.

As I fumbled with the sticky, stained garbage can lid, he started lecturing me. His face was stern, hardened, and devoid of tenderness. He wore his long, frizzy hair pulled back in a low ponytail, as he had for years; his clothes were worn and faded. He was no longer the slender man he had been a few years earlier. In fact, he had gained a considerable amount of weight, which made him stockier and much more imposing. He looked like a middle-aged member of the Hells Angels.

Now that I was in high school, his diatribes often started with, "Are you pregnant?" This evening was no different.

"No!" I exclaimed, unintentionally backing into the foot-high pile of mail and vitamin bottles on the stove. His question surprised me each time I heard it, even though he had grilled me on the subject dozens of times.

"Tell me the truth. Are you pregnant?"

"No, Dad, I don't even have a boyfriend," I said, staring at the ground. I hoped I hadn't disturbed the pile of things on the stove too much and was afraid that the mail and the bottles might topple over.

"You know, there's this guy at work. His daughter was on the honor roll her entire life. Then she went to high school, and by the time she turned sixteen, she was pregnant. Do you know what she did?"

I continued staring at the ground. The pile had not shifted, since it was braced by the yellowed porcelain teapot. I leaned away from it to avoid disturbing it further.

"Answer me!" His spittle landed on the table, spraying the boxes of partially eaten Danishes and piles of junk mail. "Do you know what she did?"

Of course, by now, I knew what she had done. I had endured this lecture at least a dozen times, but I answered, "No." Answering, "Yes," only enraged him more.

"She dropped out of school. That's what she did. And do you know what happened next?" his voice boomed from his bright-red face.

"No," I sighed in a whisper.

"Her parents had to take care of the baby because she was good for nothing. She ruined her life, and her parents had to take care of the baby. You better not ever show up here pregnant! Do you hear me?"

Even as a young teen, the irony of this did not escape me. My parents had children they could not care for and dumped much of that care on me. Did my father really see himself and my mother taking care of my baby when they didn't even care for their own children?

"Yes," I said, knowing that was the only answer that would quickly get me back to my homework.

"You better not show up here pregnant! You sluts are only good for one thing. Do you hear me? You better not show up here pregnant!" He shook as he shouted at me.

"Yes, I hear you. I haven't even kissed anyone," I cried in exasperation as I bolted from the kitchen back to my room, the very room that terrified me with its still-swarming flies and moving objects. Even that was preferable to my father's outbursts.

I was hurt by my father's insistence that I must surely be pregnant. Why didn't he see what a good girl I was? Why couldn't he acknowledge how much I helped out? Instead, he suspected me of being pregnant, despite my being so thin that I wore a belt to keep my jeans from falling off. Once he latched onto a thought or belief, he was adamant that he was right, even if the evidence pointed to the contrary. At least with this, I knew he would be proven wrong within the next nine months, and then he would act as if he had never made such an outrageous accusation. He would either forget or deny it so completely that it would be pushed out of his memories entirely. In his world, I was the crazy person for remembering what he so vehemently denied.

While my father believed I was sleeping around, the kids at school certainly did not. They knew I went to church three days a week and was as spotless as the freshly fallen snow. In fact, a group of kids a year ahead of me often teased me about my virginity.

"Sex is wonderful!"

"Why don't you make love to someone? I bet you've never even kissed anyone," they taunted, their cigarette butts hanging out of their mouths.

"We'll find someone for you! Just so long as it's not me!"

"No, thank you. I'm good," I'd say as cheerfully as possible. I tried to pretend that they weren't getting under my skin.

If they weren't busy laughing hysterically at my awkward reaction, they would offer me a cigarette.

"No, thanks. I don't smoke, either," I would say.

"What, do you think it's going to bite you?" they would say and collapse in hilarity.

At least I brightened someone's day, I thought bitterly. Overall, they were a harmless annoyance on my way to class.

* * *

One afternoon in early winter, I found myself hurrying to band practice. Snow was falling outside the fifty-foot-long bank of windows lining the hallway to the band room. The way the large snowflakes danced on the light wind was mesmerizing. Distracted, I stumbled over something and fell face-first on the gray carpet leading into the room.

As I lay sprawled across the carpet, Brian Davis, a clarinet player, reached down to help me up.

"I'm sorry," he chuckled. "Let me help you up."

I had tripped over Brian, who was sitting with his legs outstretched.

As with Mark, I was immediately smitten, but I knew better than to make my feelings known. Because he was a sophomore, I only saw Brian during band, where he sat across the room facing me but was oblivious to my furtive glances. I had always thought he was cute but hadn't considered him as a possibility until that day.

One afternoon, as we were leaving the band room, I overheard Brian talking about volunteering for the Special Olympics swim team. The following day, I volunteered as well. There wasn't even a try-out. At practice, I wore a long T-shirt so Brian wouldn't see my scrawny body. I was five-foot-seven and still size three—not a model's size three but an angular, skeletal size three. Although he didn't pay any attention to me, I was perfectly happy with just getting quick glimpses of him.

At one point, Jen, a mutual friend, told Brian about my crush. After that, he started saying "Hi" to me in the halls. I would smile, turn red, open my mouth, and say nothing. I wanted desperately to speak to him, but I couldn't manage a single word.

In addition to volunteering for the Special Olympics, I was already a member of the Junior Classical League (the Latin club) and active in the Red Cross, where I was working with a few other teens to open a local teen center. I had between two and four hours of homework a night. And, of course, none of this excused me from my daily chores of waking and dressing my younger siblings, preparing dinner, cleaning, and catering to my parents' every whim in the evenings. My activities did, however, cut back on my mother's access to me after school. Still, I was starting to feel overwhelmed with commitments.

Because of the demands on my time, my average dropped to a ninety-four on my next report card. This was a four-point dip in my grades from the previous year.

My father took one look at my report card and began a tirade: "You'll never be accepted into Princeton with grades as poor as these. How are you going to be a doctor if you can't get into a good school? You need to keep your grades up so you can get scholarships because I can't afford to send you to college even if you do get in."

Princeton was the only college he ever mentioned. It was either a full ride to Princeton or nothing. My father's vision of the world was completely black and white. Either I was number one or I was nobody, a complete and utter failure.

"Then what are you going to do? Have you thought about that? You have to keep your grades up. All these extracurricular activities are fine and good, but they're worthless if they keep you from getting into Princeton. The only way to make it in is to be first in your class, and even then, that might not be good enough."

His lecture continued for an hour. The irony, of course, is that I could have been devoting that hour to studying.

When he finally calmed down, I walked back to my room, crying, humiliated, and wondering if becoming a doctor was my idea or his. Had I really wanted to be a doctor when I made that promise to my grandfather? It had seemed to fit me so well at the time, but maybe it was just a fleeting fantasy that my father had latched on to. I didn't know who I was anymore or what I wanted for my life. The only thing I truly desired was an escape.

* * *

For my fifteenth birthday in January, I asked my father to take my friends and me to the mall, and he reluctantly agreed. The celebration started at my house, and my grandmother, whom we called Grammy, came over to celebrate with us.

At one point, while Dawn, Kelly, and I sat talking in the kitchen, Lillian came in and swiped her finger through the frosting on my cake and licked it. Catching her in the act, Grammy slapped the offending hand, and Lillian ran upstairs, crying.

My mother immediately turned toward Grammy and started shouting, "Don't you hit my daughter! If you ever hit her again, I'll kill you!"

"Somebody needs to teach her that you can't go around sticking your fingers in other people's cake," Grammy retorted.

"You have no right to hit her," my mother shrieked as she lunged at my grandmother and started beating her on the head with her fists.

Grammy, who outweighed my mother by at least eighty pounds, stood up and started swinging back. Between punches, they pulled each other's hair. My friends and I stood there, our mouths hanging open in astonishment. Then I ran to my room, mortified, in tears. I just left my friends at the table, dumbfounded. A few minutes later, they snuck upstairs and coaxed me back down. I was embarrassed and ashamed but soon felt guilty for leaving my friends behind.

My mother, who was still fuming at my grandmother and wanting to get away from her, decided to go shopping with us. My father tried to convince her to stay home, since we already had to cram seven people into the station wagon, but she was adamant.

My friends and I remained mute in the car during our ride to the mall. My father was the first to break the silence: "My emissions sticker expired last month. Police patrol the parking lot, especially on the weekends, so I'm going to park across the street. Is that okay with everyone?"

"No!" yelled my mother. "I'm not going to walk all the way across the street and the parking lot. It's too cold. I'm not walking through all that slush and snow. There's no police at the mall. All you ever do is worry."

We all knew that the state was extremely strict with their emissions and pollutions standards, or at least that's what the lawmakers wanted the public to believe. People were ticketed all the time when they parked in public places for being out of compliance, and it was a big risk for us.

"Fine," he snapped. "We'll park in the parking lot. But if I get a ticket, it's not my fault."

Once we parked, my friends and I ran inside. We looked through dozens of stores and giggled over the mismatched outfits we put together. None of us had the money to buy clothing at the mall, but we did get ourselves some ice cream cones and had a wonderful time. Too soon, it was time to leave.

When we got outside, we were in high spirits—until my father noticed a piece of paper stuck to the windshield: a ticket.

We crowded into the car. As soon as the doors closed, my father started the tirade I feared was coming: "I told you I'd get a ticket! Denise, this is all your fault. You're the one that demanded we go to the mall. Now look. Look at what you did! Now I have to pay $125 or they're going to take my license away. I don't have $125. So now what? They're going to take my license, and I won't be able to drive to work! And then what?!" His bellowing ricocheted through the car. It was nearly deafening.

Dawn, Kelly, and I scrunched together in the seatless back of the station wagon. We were lying on our bellies with our heads propped up on our hands, trying to stay as low as possible, while Lillian,

Mariah, and Amanda slid down in the seat in front of us. We knew to remain silent.

"I'll tell you what! They're going to fire me, and you'll all be living on the street because no one can do anything in this family but me! You girls are all good for nothing. Every single one of you. And not one of you respects me. I never get any respect in this family..." His rant continued.

"Don't worry, Neeze. We'll be home soon," whispered Kelly, trying to comfort me.

I appreciated the effort, but I wasn't sure that "home" was really where I wanted to be.

Chapter 11

The Dreams That Come
Winter 1989–Spring 1990

As winter's rigors quietly abated and spring's grace spread through Winsted, Gilbert High School's band and choir were scheduled to attend a music competition in Myrtle Beach, South Carolina.

Kelly sang in the chorus, so I sat next to her on the bus ride down to Myrtle Beach. My friends Paul and Jake sat across the aisle from us, and behind them was Steven Davis, Brian's brother. Late that night, as the bus rolled southward, I awoke from a light slumber and overheard a troubling conversation.

"Have you ever thought about suicide?" I heard Steve ask Paul and Jake over the backs of their seats.

"Yeah, once," one of the boys answered in a whisper.

I have, too, I thought. I didn't want to give myself away by saying anything, so I pretended I was still asleep.

Steve got up from his seat and leaned in toward Kelly, who had been sleeping against my arm for over an hour. "Either of you guys thought about death?" he asked.

Neither of us answered. Presuming us both asleep, he moved on. As Steven asked around, I was surprised to hear over half the kids say they had thought about suicide.

After taking his informal poll, Steve returned to Paul and Jake and started talking about how difficult it had been for him to kill himself when he'd wanted to.

This conversation was too intense for me. For months in Luxaya,

I had been contemplating death as an easy escape from my misery, and I was afraid of exposing my dark desires.

Once Steve returned to his seat, I straightened up and slipped the book that had been lying in my lap into the bag at my feet. It was about a father's search to understand why his daughter had killed herself. In my paranoia, I was sure Steve had seen it. While I yearned to ask him why he wanted to die, I was afraid he might turn the question back on me.

In time, the gentle movement of the bus lulled me back into a fitful sleep. When I awoke the next morning, Steve was talking again, this time about Brian's new girlfriend.

Girlfriend? What girlfriend?! I tried to listen for her name, but if Steve said it, I didn't catch it. Disappointment and sadness tumbled through me like an avalanche. Perhaps because it was still so fresh in my mind, I began thinking about suicide again. The more I thought about it, the more romantic it seemed.

Once we got to the hotel, I broke away from the group after unpacking to take a brief walk on the beach. I needed to return to nature to process my feelings. The salty breezes blowing through my hair and caressing my face helped me relax and feel less anxious. It was a welcome reprieve.

On our first day at Myrtle Beach, we went sightseeing. That night, I ran three miles along the shore. Track was important to me, and I loved to run, so going out in the mild South Carolina evening was an indulgence. The warm evening air, coupled with my effort, made me sweat, but I hardly noticed. I leapt over the rivulets created by the low tide, relishing the feeling of freedom and pure enjoyment. When I returned to the hotel, tired but exhilarated, I walked past Brian on the stairs.

"Wow, Denise, what have you been doing?" he asked. "You're dripping sweat everywhere."

"I just finished jogging along the beach. I have to stay in shape for track," I said.

"Hey, we should have gone jogging together! I just finished a run on the beach, too."

I was elated that Brian had spoken to me, but was too timid to ask if he wanted to jog with me the next day. That night, I fell asleep smiling and happy. That contentment was short-lived, though, as nightmares soon charged across my dreamscape.

I had more than one nightmare that night, but it was the second that shook me the most. In it, the band and choir were on the way home when the bus hit something large. The bus tipped over and burst into flames. Nearly everyone, including me, escaped through the back door or the shattered windows. Once we were all out, a large group of my classmates circled the bus while singing "Amazing Grace." As I walked toward them in a daze, they took my hand and drew me into the circle. I became another link in the chain. From this position, I could see someone trapped in the flames inside the bus, trying to escape. Whoever he was, he kept urgently calling my name.

I tried to break free from the group to rescue the person left behind, but my hands were held too tightly. "Let me go. Let me go," I screamed at them, but they continued singing. I was desperate to help my classmate, but the others held me back. I couldn't tell if they were trying to protect me or if they just couldn't hear the cries from the bus.

When the fire was finally extinguished, EMTs pulled a charred body out of the wreckage, laid it on a stretcher, and wheeled him past me. Moments later, an EMT approached me. "He wants to speak to you," he said.

I looked in horror at the protruding bones and melted skin on the stretcher. I could not tell who it was. Slowly, the cadaver's mouth opened. "Denise," he said. Then his jaw fell off.

I awoke from that dream and sat bolt upright in bed, crying and shaking. I was glad that I hadn't woken Kelly, who was sleeping soundly beside me.

The next day, I couldn't recapture the exhilaration of the previous evening's jog. The nightmares had riveted my attention on death, as if Death itself had called out to me. I decided that the best way to kill myself would be to dive off the railing of my hotel balcony. My head would crack open, and I would die a painless—or so I thought—death. I would finally escape from the misery that dominated every day of my life.

I tried to judge how many feet I would fall before hitting the ground. All I could envision for my future was an endless trek through an emotional desert. I felt like everyone hated me. Looking back, I realize how false that perception was and that I was just externalizing my parents' words, but I absolutely believed I was a useless unwanted hindrance. If I died, everyone would be spared having to look at my homely face. But would I actually have the courage to kill myself?

As I stepped outside toward the railing, I whispered into the breeze, "Dear God, please help me do this. Help me end this life now." I was so accustomed to praying for everything that praying for the courage to commit suicide didn't seem inappropriate.

As I leaned over the railing and looked down, I noticed a girl who sat near me in band sitting on the balcony below mine and eyeing me. "Get away from there," she shouted. "You're going to fall. I don't want to have to go down there and scoop you off the pavement with a spatula. Come on, get down."

I leaned forward and laughed. "I'm not going to fall off. I'm still up here, aren't I?"

"You're not funny, Denise. I mean it! You'd better get off of there."

"All right, all right," I said, shifting my weight to the inside of the railing and heading back inside.

We had our performance the second morning in Myrtle Beach. There were thousands of band students in the arena from dozens of schools along the Eastern Seaboard. It made me realize just how small and isolated my town was.

Immediately after our performance, we headed home to Connecticut. As the bus lurched back toward our school, I felt I had experienced a lifetime's worth of emotions in a few short days.

Chapter 12

The Crushing

Spring–Summer 1990

That spring, as the 1990 track season was getting into full swing, I was running at my best. However, my habit of self-effacement and my feeling that I was never good enough prevented me from acknowledging my "wins," which were piling up.

I competed in four distance events at each meet and placed in the top three in at least one event at each meet. At one particular meet between three schools, I finished the 3200-meter race in first place, lapping the second-place girl and missing the qualifying time for state-level competition by just a few seconds. I also came in third in both the 1600- and 800-meter races that day.

After my third race that day, one of my coaches standing at the finish line said, "Congratulations! You've earned more points for the team than anyone else here. Good job!"

Unable to accept the compliment or acknowledge that third place was still pretty good, I blurted out, "I'm sorry about finishing the 1600 and the 800 with such bad times. I'll run faster next time."

Although I was the third-highest point-scorer for the team my freshman year, I did not feel proud of myself. Instead, I wallowed in what I had been taught to think: that I wasn't good enough. I had learned to live with criticism, even from myself, and didn't know how to praise myself or accept it from others.

When my parents told me that I was lazy and useless, I assumed they were right. After all, if they weren't right, then what were they—liars, crazy, or perhaps even evil? It was easier to believe they were telling me the truth and that I was the defective one, not them.

I was as tough on myself with my schoolwork as I was with track. After the winter's ninety-four percent average—a "low" grade that my father berated me for—I tried to raise my grades back to where they had been in junior high, but I found high school to be more academically challenging. Once again, I felt like a failure. I had proven I was worthless. I was already envisioning a rejection letter from Princeton showing up in our mailbox, and I hadn't even applied yet.

While I desperately wanted to live up to my father's expectations, I sensed deep down that I wasn't good enough for an Ivy League school. I wasn't a genius, and I hadn't accomplished anything particularly remarkable. What I had done up to that point wouldn't make me stand out among thousands of other applicants. But as my dad always insisted that it was either Princeton or nothing, I believed it. In the back of my mind, I knew I wouldn't get in. I started to question why I was trying so hard. The idea of death continued to take root and grow in my thoughts. It would be so much easier just to give up.

In addition, life at home had become considerably more difficult. That spring, Mariah began complaining about feeling ill. At first, we made nothing of her complaints. We only began to worry when, on the fourth day of her claiming to feel sick, she started to smell like a rotting pumpkin and was unceasingly thirsty. Our father called the doctor, and the office's medical assistant told him that the doctor could see her in a couple of days and that she probably had the flu.

Having lived with her difficult personality for years, my sisters and I were not kind to Mariah, saying things like: "You pig, you drank all the Kool-Aid again! How can you drink so much? Stay away from me. I don't want to catch whatever you have."

The sunken purple-brown circles under her eyes, combined with her sallow complexion, made her look as if she were dying. The odd rotting-pumpkin smell radiated from all her pores. I told her to take a bath. She snapped back that she had.

Mariah stayed home from school on the fifth day, too sick to walk far. The dark circles surrounding her eye sockets turned black and seemed to be spreading out across her pale skin. She went to the bathroom every fifteen minutes or so, and the smell of her urine was pungent, filling the entire house with a foul odor. At one point, she drank an entire gallon of milk in half an hour. We nervously teased her about looking like the Grim Reaper.

Mariah stayed home from school again the following day. She wasn't talking much, which was unusual for her. Our father often claimed she had "diarrhea of the mouth." Now, she was mostly silent.

That day, Lillian arrived home from school before me, since I had track practice. As she went up to her room, Mariah was slowly climbing the stairs ahead of her, trying to make her way to her bed. At the top of the staircase, she collapsed. Lillian ran back down-stairs, screaming and demanding that my mother have someone take Mariah to the hospital. My mother still would not drive—even in an emergency like this. Instead of calling an ambulance, she phoned my father at work. It took him nearly an hour to arrive. While they waited, Mariah lay prostrate and motionless on the floor while thirteen-year-old Lillian waited helplessly by her side.

When I got home from track practice, our father was pulling out of the driveway, finally taking Mariah to the hospital. Lillian filled me in on Mariah's condition. I was glad I hadn't seen her fall. It took the responsibility that I would have carried forward with me off of my conscience. An hour later, our father came home to pick up our mother. Mariah had apparently contracted a virus that had triggered a reaction, making her diabetic. According to the doctors, if she had been brought in just a few minutes later, she would have had serious brain damage; a few hours later, and she would have died.

The emergency room doctors had never seen blood-sugar levels as high as hers. They were worried that her brain was swelling and decided to put her on a helicopter and send her to a hospital spe-cializing in pediatric emergencies. She was there for the next week.

While the doctors weren't able to locate any definitive brain swelling on an MRI, they seemed to suspect that she had sustained some level of neurological damage due to the prolonged illness.

We visited her in the hospital, where I learned how to prick her finger so we could read her blood-sugar level on a glucose test strip and give her the insulin shot she would have to take twice a day for the rest of her life. Although the nurses who trained me assumed I was only a backup for when my father wasn't around to do it, as soon as we got home, I was made entirely responsible for giving Mariah her insulin shots. My father claimed he didn't have enough time before work, and my mother flat-out refused the job via her typical shriek. It took Mariah six months to learn to give herself the prick test and shots. The nurses must have scared her terribly about the potential for death with her condition because she cooperated with me without complaining, even though I caused so much bruising on her thighs that she appeared to be covered in purple polka dots.

Either due to the constant fluctuations in her blood sugar or the potential brain damage, Mariah changed again for the worse after this. When she became angry, which happened two or three times a day, she started banging her head against the wall, hitting her head with her fists, breaking things, and screaming. This could be set off by the simplest actions: my mother asking her to dry the dishes, one of my sisters teasing her, someone accidentally bumping into her or even asking her a question. If one of the other girls was in her path, she would push her aside and strike out at her. In the past, an outburst like this might have occurred only once every week or two and seemed more like a simple temper tantrum. This new anger was like an unquenchable violent rage. Mariah had experienced a terrible transformation that we would all suffer from.

Mariah could sense when people were in a bad mood the moment they stepped into her presence. When she noticed this, she would start harassing them. She thrived on the negative attention they gave her in return. If any of us expressed dislike for something she did, she would repeat phrases she knew would get under our skin until we snapped. If it had only gone on for a minute or two, we could have ignored her, but after thirty or forty minutes, all we could do was screech in angry frustration and then run away in tears. Mariah brought out anger in me that I didn't even know I was capable of. I felt rage toward her bubbling up from deep down. I wanted to punch her, but I did my best to control these wild emotions. I often thought of her as a new form of torture.

Even the teachers in her special ed classes at school didn't know how to control her. Although she made an attempt to be civilized there, she sometimes swore at them and the other students, banged her head against the lockers, and ran down the hallway screaming. These outbursts were infrequent, but they permanently damaged mine and Lillian's reputations at school. We were insane by association. We were "Browns." To make matters worse, when Mariah came home, all the stress of the day burst out like an explosion.

We all hoped Mariah would grow out of her violence and insolence, but I knew better. Even though the doctors hadn't been able to find concrete evidence of it, I was sure she had suffered brain damage, which only compounded her social and emotional issues.

* * *

I continued to escape from my family problems, crushing perfectionism, and overbearing self-criticism by withdrawing to Luxaya. As my freshman year came to a close, Luxaya was at its most breathtaking. The budding leaves burst with new life. The town of Winsted was spread out below me, but it wasn't intruding. Alone and at peace in Luxaya, I could imagine a better life. I even sometimes imagined Brian holding me in his arms. Although I still had a crush on him, I had not spoken a word to him since the band trip. Terrified of making the same mistake that I had with Mark, I remained withdrawn, silent, and invisible.

My time in Luxaya helped me overcome my fears somewhat,

and I decided to leave him a "screw tab," the tab from a soda can, which had been carefully removed so that the inside ring was still attached. It was mainly meant to be a joke—a sexual rain check that the receiver could cash in if they wanted the same as the giver. It was the latest fad at my school.

I carried a tab in my pocket for several days, terrified that someone might notice its faint outline through the fabric of my jeans and ask me what I was doing with it. One afternoon after school, when the hall was empty, I raced up to Brian's locker and shoved the tab through one of its vents. It was a silly and impulsive thing to do, given that he had no way of knowing who had dropped this random piece of trash in his locker, but it satisfied my longing to connect with him in some way. Predictably, nothing resulted from dropping the screw tab, and my freshman year ended without a word from Brian.

A few days after school got out, Dawn invited me to sleep over at her house. She and her mother had recently moved into a new apartment, which happened to be directly across the street from Brian's home. I wasn't sure if that was serendipitous or just torturously coincidental.

That evening, as we were sitting on her porch, Brian and his friend Andy drove by in their car. They shouted out the window at us, "Do you two want to go for a ride?"

Yeah, I thought, but didn't dare say.

As they passed us, Brian threw something small and shiny out of the car at us. It clinked to a stop in the gutter a few steps from our feet. Dawn and I walked over to the item and picked it up. It was a soda can tab.

Had he figured out I had dropped the tab into his locker? Or maybe he was just making a pass at Dawn—or me.

Although my summer started out with this moment of excitement, the brief connection was not enough to sustain me. In fact, the more I thought about my life, the more miserable I became. I was slowly spiraling downward when Luxaya was destroyed in a windy thunderstorm a couple weeks after school let out. The rain smashed the dying tree into pieces, snapped the branches from neighboring maples, and tore up the delicate moss. An oak was felled by lightning and became caught on a neighboring tree, blocking the view. Part of me had expected Luxaya to be an immortal refuge, and when I realized it was not, I walked away disheartened. I never returned. My only sanctuary had been destroyed.

After the destruction of Luxaya, my summer continued its turn for the worse. My parents veered further into irrationality. They questioned my every action and became even more demanding. My father insisted I prove whatever I said—even with small things, such as when permission slips were due for my sisters' summer camp field trips. They were incapable of taking care of a one-year-old and a sick, violent daughter, so they placed it all on me.

* * *

I desperately wanted to talk to someone about how much I hated my life and myself, but I didn't. I should have been able to open up to Dawn, who was my best friend, but I was too nervous and too used to rejection. Besides, Dawn had a critical side. It was something she had acquired from her mother who, in stark opposition to my parents, was a relentlessly spotless housekeeper and organizer.

Dawn's life wasn't much better than mine. She spent just as much time cleaning and doing chores as I did. Talking back and whining were not allowed, and she was grounded if she ever came home with less than high honors. Her mother frowned on her joining extracurricular activities and grounded her for neglecting even minor chores. Despite this, Dawn loved and respected her mother. When Dawn was little, her mother had divorced her alcoholic husband; afterward, she and her mother lived in a tiny shack of a house, sometimes eating pickles for meals because they were so poor. All they had was each other, which drew them together and toughened them emotionally.

Dawn often gave me the impression that she was not allowed to cry and that it would bring forth a reprimand. She had a "get over it" toughness to her and seemed to expect the same self-control from her friends. Because of this, I feared she wouldn't be supportive or offer the help I needed. I was afraid that if I revealed too much, she would turn against me and I would lose my best friend. I couldn't afford to be further isolated. I thought she would just say I was being too emotional and blowing things out of proportion.

Looking back, I had other friends who would have appreciated me opening up to them and who would have been supportive and helpful. But at the time, I ruled them out. I reasoned that if I couldn't lean on my best friend, there was no one to turn to for help. It was Princeton or nothing all over again.

Still, Dawn did serve as a lifeline from my turmoil. She called me often that summer, and for a time, our superficial conversations pulled me out of my darkness. She was more fun than anyone else I knew. She introduced Kelly and me to a teens-only dance club that had opened a few miles from our homes. Every so often, either Dawn or Kelly would convince their moms to drop us off there for a few hours. Since it was summer, I always made sure that my household duties were finished early so my parents would let me stay out for the evening. Dawn sometimes loaned me a dress since I had none that fit, and she even washed them for me afterward, as I was still not allowed to use the washer or dryer at home. My father never stopped believing that my sisters and I would break the machines and relegated that chore to my mother, whose mountain of smelly laundry had continued to expand over the years. He never helped her get caught up.

At the teen dance club, Dawn, Kelly, and I would dance until sweat poured down our bodies, our hair stuck to our faces in clumps, and we smelled like the boys' locker room. During the slow songs, we would pout in the bathroom about how none of the guys ever asked us to dance. In those priceless moments, I felt like I truly belonged.

Other times, I would go to Dawn's place after satisfying my

parents' requests for the day. We'd sing songs by the Doors in her basement or explore the nearby woods. If we couldn't find anything else to do, we'd pop a video into the VCR and let our tongues hang out of our mouths as we watched the latest hunk trot across the screen.

Despite my friendship with Dawn and Kelly, which anchored me in the first half of the summer, by the middle of July a devastating emptiness settled over me, and my thoughts once again wandered to the idea of ending my life. This overwhelming sadness was slowly smothering my desire to live.

At last, I understood—at a deeper level than ever before—what my parents had been telling me about myself for years: that I was *pathetic*. The future became too difficult to contemplate because all I could see before me was more work and more pain. The thought of death as a release became my truest friend and comfort. I could escape everything through death: my nightmares, my parents, my inability to do anything right, my ugliness, and even the flies and moving objects that continued to terrify me in my room. I felt trapped inside my life, unable to escape despite the occasional reprieve with my friends.

One evening, I was shaving my legs with an open single-edged razor blade. I had snuck this blade out of the garage a couple years earlier before I had a job and before my parents had bought me an electric razor. But the electric razor left stubble, and whether out of habit or cheapness—probably a combination of both—I continued to use the open blade. Once I finished the task, I left the blade on the white porcelain sink that occupied a corner of my room.

Later that night, after I helped everyone else get to bed and returned to my room, the razor blade caught my eye. I was inexplicably drawn to this shiny object in the dim light of my bedroom.

I picked up the blade and rotated it between my middle finger and thumb, not quite taking it in, as if I were in a trance. Then I slid it gently down my wrist in a slicing motion. The feeling exhilarated me. It felt somehow powerful. I drew it against my wrist again, harder this time, leaving a slight scratch. That felt even better. This sensation brought me out of my trance. I was feeling something. Perhaps it was the same feeling of choice I had come upon at Myrtle Beach. I realized that perhaps I really could do it: I could actually end my life.

But then I put the blade down. I had done enough for one evening, enough to momentarily pull me out of my dark mood. The mood returned the next morning when I heard my mother shouting, "Denise, get down here and help me with the dishes." Since there was no room on the counter for the dishes to dry, one of us would wash while the other dried and put away the dishes wherever we could cram them into the cluttered cabinets.

I bounded down the stairs, asking, "Why can't one of the other kids help for once?" It wasn't that I was opposed to helping, but I was always the one called upon for chores, while Lillian and Mariah continued to play, watch television, or hang out with friends.

"Because I told you to!" she snapped.

"What about Lillian or Mariah?"

We'd had this conversation many times before. Depending on her mood, she would either repeat, "Because I told you to!" or she would spring over to the large broom propped up behind the kitchen door to beat me back into submission. By the time she reached me, I'd be at the sink starting on a dish, and she would back off.

There was something about this particular chore that was a trigger for my parents. If I waited until later in the day and my father arrived home before I had attended to the dishes, he would start a tirade. "You kids have all day to get things done. What are you doing all day, sleeping? I wish I could stay home and sleep all day. I'm the only one who ever does anything around here. Not a single one of you cunts is useful for a damn thing." He would continue on like this for at least thirty minutes. I soon learned to wash the dishes before he came home.

Meanwhile, there was a multitude of other tasks for me to attend to: waking up and assisting Helen and Amanda; making lunches for my father to take to work and for my sisters who went to summer camp; tending to Gabrielle, dressing her, changing her diapers, and holding her; giving Mariah her insulin shots; feeding the cats, the dog, and the rabbit that lived in the basement; folding and sorting endless piles of laundry; and going through the school papers that sat stacked on the counter, none of which had been discarded during the school year.

Three days a week, I worked at the local Red Cross office for four hours, helping them with minor secretarial duties. Those four hours were a nice reprieve, and the minimum wage I earned provided enough money to buy some makeup and personal items. However, the rest of my day was entirely subject to my parents' whims. They disliked it when I left the house for more than an hour in the evenings, since that meant they couldn't count on me to do random tasks.

They called for me so much, I despised the sound of my own name and constantly tried to escape to my room so I could read a book or play video games on the Nintendo I had won the year before by selling the most popcorn and knickknacks for the band. Yet every time I did so, my mother would call me back downstairs within fifteen minutes. She was like a vulture, screeching before it swoops down to pick the bones of abandoned carrion.

Despite everything I did, in nearly every interaction I had with my mother, she would inevitably say, "You never help around here anymore. I always have to yell for you to get you to do anything. I wish you were never born. I hate you." Having heard this so many times, I truly believed it. I even agreed with her: I, too, wished I had never been born. I didn't quite understand why she hated me, though.

I prayed to God that He would take me home to Him. With God, I would feel loved and safe. If He wouldn't take me to heaven to be with Him, I prayed that He would at least help me endure my life.

One night after praying, I had a dream. I was in a long white hallway. The light was so bright, it was blinding, yet I could see everything with intense clarity. God and Jesus were there, and they were both in human form. They were accompanied by a boy of about six, with pale skin and light-brown hair. He wore a golden crown with seven spikes, and he was giggling and running in circles around God and Jesus. I couldn't figure out who he was, yet all three of us loved him intensely. The feeling was palpable.

Then the boy turned to me as if he were saying "Follow me." We walked down the corridor together, and it opened into a field of dried, twisted, waist-deep thorns that extended far up a steep hill. I knew I was meant to travel through them, but I couldn't see a path through the brambles. The boy silently took the lead. I followed him as a convoluted yet discernible path opened before him. Eventually, we made it to the top of the hill, and I could see that the opposite slope was covered by lush green grass.

I awoke suddenly, but the feeling of intense love was slow to fade. I intuited that God was trying to tell me that he was there, leading me through the brambles, and that I was going to be okay because a path would eventually open up. But I didn't have the patience for "eventually." I wanted the everyday reality of my life to change now. After all, this glimpse into "eventually" did not change my parents' screaming and their abuse.

It was easier for me to escape into thoughts of fantasy. Brian continued to permeate my every thought, and I dreamed about him frequently. In one dream, I was a princess wearing an ivory Victorian-style gown while picking daisies in a field of wildflowers. Brian came along dressed in a flowing white linen shirt and knickers and riding a white stallion with black speckles. He stopped beside me and hoisted me up. As we traveled back to our castle, we became lost in the dark woods. Then, after riding along a crumbling cliff to a field of boulders, we sat together and watched a pair of emerald-colored dragons swimming in an onyx lake. When the sun disappeared behind the hills, Brian leaned toward me and pressed his lips to mine in a sensual kiss.

As I awoke from my wonderful dream, happiness coursed through me. It was wonderful not to be awakened by a nightmare. I felt as if I had really lived this dream, and it only fed my infatuation. I kissed Brian's picture in the yearbook every night. A single glance at his face made my heart beat wildly inside my chest. I wondered if my lips would ever touch something other than the paper his image was printed on.

One day in July, as depression was descending on me, my fantasy about Brian crashed. While riding my bike through the town park, I saw Brian walking hand-in-hand with his girlfriend. I ducked behind a large tree so he wouldn't notice me. I held my breath for a moment, unsure of what my next move should be.

I peered around the tree just in time to see her let go of his hand. He reached for it again, as if he needed it. He sat to lean against a tree, and she lay down beside him, placing her head in his lap. He slowly stroked her dark, shiny hair while whispering to her. I desperately wished I was in her place, instead of hiding and watching them. I felt small, hideous, and stupid.

As I watched them, the deep passion I felt for Brian shot through my body and then instantly turned to a painful, heavy sorrow. A fist-sized lead weight seemed to form in my chest and then sink slowly downward. I scooted back behind the tree and out of sight again, pausing for a moment to catch my breath as the flood of emotions began to wane. The unbearable emptiness that followed was filled with words like "dumb" and "pitiful." I slunk back to my bike, leaving in the direction I had come, hoping he hadn't noticed me. I felt sure that no one would ever love me.

Chapter 13

Beauty or the Beast?

Late Summer 1990

T hat August, I was one of three high school students my church sponsored to attend a Methodist youth conference in New York City. I packed my suitcase with all the essentials, including my flute, which I had been told to bring for a talent show, a small desk light, and my razor blade. I was afraid it might disappear while I was gone; without it, I would lose my chance to *feel*.

On my first day at the conference, I was walking through the lobby of the New York University dorm where we were staying when I came upon a group of other teenagers attending the conference. One of them was Robert. He was sixteen, muscular and stocky, and had dirty-blond hair. I noticed how his small straight upturned nose complemented his wide smile.

Robert and I began talking, and we soon separated from the group to continue our conversation on our own. I was amazed at how much we had in common: Robert was on the A honor roll, he was an excellent runner, and he loved biking. We talked about where we had grown up. We discussed our future plans. He told me that he wanted to be an engineer, and I told him that I wanted to be a doctor.

As we talked, he took my hand in his, interlocking our fingers. His sparkling teal eyes, a color I had never seen before or since, glanced at me seductively. "So, how many guys have you gone out with before?" he asked.

"I haven't exactly gone out with anyone. None of the guys I like ever seem to like me back. I guess I'm just too ugly," I said, trying to make a joke of it.

"What are you talking about? You're not ugly. You have gorgeous hair, beautiful eyes, and a great—well—very attractive figure," he said flirtatiously.

"Thanks, but you don't have to lie," I said lightly. However, as soon as the words came out of my mouth, I thought, *Maybe he means it, even if he's wrong!*

"I'm not lying. The guys in your school just don't realize what they're missing out on." He stared deeply into my eyes as he said this. I felt like he was trying to peer deep inside me.

A hardness within me, a hardness I hadn't even realized was there, suddenly softened, and I smiled. It was the first time a boy had ever told me I was pretty. I wanted to believe him, but I found it difficult.

The conference had over 250 participants, and it was the practice to group participants together into "family" groups of twelve chosen by lottery. Grouping into "families" was their way of bringing more intimacy to the conference experience. "Families" went on excursions through the city together and checked in with each other every evening about what we had experienced during the day. That evening, after dinner, we all went to our assigned "family" group. By pure chance, Robert happened to be in my "family." I was surprised and secretly delighted to see him there.

That first evening, we also picked a prayer partner, a person we were supposed to pray for every night. We chose our partner by pulling a name out of a box. I closed my eyes and reached in. Incredibly, I picked Robert's name.

"Cool, you get to pray for me every night," Robert said when he glanced over my shoulder and saw the name I held.

I considered the coincidence. There were well over two hundred participants, and yet, out of everyone there, I had picked Robert's name.

"You weren't supposed to look at that. It's supposed to be a secret," I whispered back.

"I'll let you look at mine then."

When he pulled out his slip of paper, he opened it so we could both read it. My name was scrawled across it. I was shocked for a moment before I realized that this had to be God's work. I knew that being each other's prayer partner was not coincidental and that for some reason, God meant for us to be together—at least for the week.

I turned toward Robert, who was grinning in amusement. "Cool," he said. "I guess that I get to pray for you, too."

Robert made me intensely happy from the first moments we spent talking. When I was by his side, I felt secure and fulfilled. Unfortunately, he flirted with nearly every pretty girl at the conference. For the first couple of days, this didn't bother me; Robert was just a friend, and he could do as he pleased. But it did confuse me when one minute we were staring into each other's eyes, and the next minute, he was following another girl down the hall. I didn't really know what to think of him.

The second day of the conference, several girls from Robert's church youth group approached me while I sat in one of the NYU lounges. The one who had designated herself their spokesperson cautioned me, "Denise, stay away from Robert. All he's going to do is break your heart. He cares only about himself. I wouldn't get involved with him if I were you."

"Uh, okay," I responded, not knowing how to reply to their warnings.

At one point while we were hanging out, Robert asked me if I thought a particular girl was beautiful. I happened to think she was stunning, but his admiration of her made me feel uncomfortable. The warnings of the girls from his church sprang to mind.

But Robert's attentions were so soothing and so nurturing, I found it easy to be forgiving. No boy had ever reacted to me the way he did. It was all so wonderful that I couldn't pass it up, warning or no warning.

On one of our excursions in the city, we visited the World Trade Center, where we waited in line for an hour to get in the elevator that brought us to the observation floor. Robert stood behind me the whole time, the warmth from his body penetrating my clothing and dancing along my skin. Whenever I took a step forward, he would move with me like my shadow. I wished time would stop, leaving me in his arms like this eternally. I wanted to feel like this forever: attractive, wanted, perhaps even loved. Everything I had prayed for so fervently over the past year, yet had never experienced, was finally happening. I knew deep down that because we lived in different states, we only had this one week, but I didn't care.

After the tour that day, Robert and I had planned to have dinner with a mutual friend, Jill, before the closing night talent show. We went to her dorm room to fetch her and lingered inside her room as she finished changing in the bathroom. As we waited for Jill to emerge, I was leaning against the door when Robert suddenly placed his hands against the door frame, pinning me there with his body. He stared into my eyes with a gaze that made me gasp for breath. He looked as if he was about to kiss me when, to my great disappointment, Jill opened the bathroom door. I, who had never kissed a boy, had just lost what felt like my only opportunity with the twist of Jill's wrist!

After dinner, Robert and I went up to our rooms to get ready for the talent show that evening. I was going to play "Greensleeves" on my flute, which was an easy piece that I could play perfectly. After rehearsing the piece one last time, I left to find Robert.

He wasn't in his room, so I searched the halls, peeping into rooms through open doors. I found him sitting on the edge of a girl's bed, chatting with her. It was the beautiful girl he had asked me about earlier. As I came upon them that evening, the way he was looking into her eyes made me insecure. I wanted to be the only one he looked at that way. "Hey, Robert," I blurted out. "I've finished practicing and was just walking by when I saw you." It was a lame half-lie.

"Denise, this is Vanessa," Robert said, gesturing to the beautiful girl. "Vanessa, Denise."

Vanessa's roommate needed to change before the talent show, so Robert and I went out into the hallway and sat on the floor while we waited.

"So, do you like her?" I asked.

"Of course I like her. If I hated her, I wouldn't talk to her." Robert smiled impishly.

I said nothing as I stared at the opposite wall. My mind had gone blank, and I was struggling to hold back a torrent of emotions.

"Denise, I don't know what you're thinking if you don't talk to me. I'm sorry if I hurt you. I don't usually find two girls that make me feel this way at the same time," he said.

I stood up and, without speaking, walked back to my room without looking back. I was jealous, angry, and upset at myself for not being as beautiful as Vanessa, with her perfect olive skin and huge hazel eyes.

I went to the talent show still in this sour mood, but as I did in school, I blocked out my emotions and gave a good performance despite my melancholy. Afterward, Robert and I met in our family group, as scheduled. I had temporarily forgotten that he was in my family group and was my prayer partner. Since I was still mad at him, I sat across from our usual spot. He walked over and sat down beside me. He tickled me, but I continued staring straight ahead. Outside, rain was beginning to fall.

When our family group meeting ended, Robert took my hand and led me to his room. I followed as waves of both sadness and elation pulsed through my chest. As we walked into the darkness of his room, thunder crashed outside. Robert's face was illuminated for an instant then vanished into the darkness. We watched the lightning storm in silence for several long minutes. I hadn't realized how incredibly beautiful New York was until then. The lightning danced around skyscrapers, playing peek-a-boo. The buildings seemed to vanish into the night sky, only to momentarily reappear again and again. The awe and power of the storm made me feel that God was with us.

After a few minutes, Robert led me through the flashes of light and darkness to his bunk bed. With a gentle voice and a soft touch, he asked me to share what I was thinking. His concern finally pulled me out of the silence I had retreated into after being hurt that afternoon.

I knew how to retreat from pain; I had often done so when my parents verbally attacked me. I learned early on that any response other than silence would only lead to more abuse, angry words, and irrational consequences. Silence was my security blanket, and it was hard to let go of it. Robert, however, did not berate me. He actually heard my words.

As I told him how he had hurt me by giving his attention to another girl, I somehow got off track and started telling him my entire story. I wasn't used to having a sympathetic listener, and now, all the pain of my life I'd been holding back gushed out of me. I expected Robert to run, but he didn't. Instead, he simply asked questions, which made me feel safe for the first time in my life—safe to reveal, without fear of rejection, who I was and what I had been through. My chest was warm inside, and when he touched me, my skin became electrified. For a moment, I wondered if what I felt for him was love. All I knew for sure was that when he was with me, I wanted to live.

When Robert's roommate returned to their dorm room, we left and walked up the stairwell to the top floor, which we couldn't enter, as it was closed off. Sitting at the top of the stairs, we spent the next two hours talking.

At one point, Robert leaned in closer to me. I was afraid of what I felt for him, so I inched away. I was afraid that he might kiss me and that it would cause me to grow even closer to him. Undeterred, he moved closer again. "What are you afraid of?" he asked.

"What do you mean?" I asked innocently, as if I didn't know what was happening.

"You keep pushing yourself away from me as if I'm going to

hurt you. I'm not your parents. I would never do something like that to you. I don't think you're ugly. I think you're beautiful. Do me a favor, okay? The next time you look into a mirror, truthfully tell me that you're hideous and ugly. I'll bet you ten bucks you can't do it."

"Oh yeah? Do you even have ten bucks on you?" I couldn't deal with what he was saying, so I tried to turn it into a joke. If I really was beautiful, then what my parents and the kids at school had been saying for years was just too cruel to face. It was easier to see myself as ugly so I could avoid knowing how unjustly cruel they were. It was easier to believe they were telling the truth.

Robert didn't respond to my joke; he just stared back at me, his eyes completely serious. I was drowning in their intensity. Stumbling for my next words, I barely noticed how close his lips were to mine. I sank deeper into the teal sea of his eyes, my own chest rising and falling in rhythm with his breathing. I wanted him to kiss me more than I had ever wanted anything, yet I was so scared of how I would feel afterward, I hesitated.

He seemed to read my mind and pulled back slowly. "I bet you twenty," he whispered. Then he stood up and walked me back to my room.

The next day was our last in New York, and we were leaving around midday. Robert slept late that morning and missed breakfast, so I didn't see him until our last family group meeting. I was worried that I had driven him off and that exposing the dark corners of my life had been too much for him. I was worried that he thought less of me now that he had seen the ugliness within me. But when he finally arrived, he was his usual flirtatious self, which eased my concerns. Neither of us mentioned what had happened the previous evening. It was too intense to bring up.

Everyone had to make a bracelet for their prayer partner to remind them that someone was praying for them. Now, at our last meeting, it was time to give each other the bracelets. I handed mine to Robert and grinned as he slid it on. It was flawlessly symmetrical, with no loose strands or pulled pieces. It was a reflection of how I approached everything in life: desperately trying to make everything perfect.

"I know my bracelet sucks," Robert mumbled as he passed it to me. "It's not as good as yours, but here you go."

"It's great," I said. I joked, "I especially like the big knot here and the little one there." I slipped the bracelet on my wrist. It was a perfect fit. "I love it," I reassured him. He smiled down at the bracelet I had made for him.

With the day's whirlwind of activities following our meeting, we lost track of each other and only met up again on the sidewalk as we were leaving. Robert's church bus was in the opposite direction from where our youth leader had parked her car.

Will this be the last time I ever see him? I pushed the thought from my mind. *No. Somehow, we'll meet up again,* I thought to myself as we silently waved goodbye. Neither of us could think of just the right thing to say.

Because I knew my parents would flip out if I ever made a long-distance phone call, even if I paid for it when the bill came in, I hadn't even asked Robert for his phone number. He hadn't asked for mine, either. It didn't occur to me that maybe he wasn't as interested in keeping in touch as I was.

The tiny flame of love that had supported me during the week of the youth conference was still flickering as I rode home, but asking it to survive the onslaught of my daily life and with such a great separation was too much. It was like asking a match thrown into the snow to stay lit.

After returning from the conference, I sank back into depression. While I did have Robert's address and wrote to him, the letters weren't enough of a lifeline to keep me going, especially since he didn't write back. My connection with Robert soon became a thing of the past, and in my present situation, I was alone.

At home everything was still the same, but the fleeting moment of love exacerbated the raw feelings of pain and hopelessness I felt there. Nearly every day, my parents got into screaming matches about money. My mother could have worked outside the home to help alleviate the financial strain, but she did not. My suspicions that she had gotten pregnant with Gabrielle as an excuse to avoid getting a job—and all other responsibilities—were confirmed.

When my father came home from work each evening, he never asked her why the laundry wasn't washed, why the dishes weren't cleaned, or why she hadn't made dinner. With the exception of the laundry, I was held responsible for incomplete chores. We all knew that having a baby at home granted her special status in his eyes. It was her free ticket to a life of indolence.

Even though money was always tight and the family could have used more, when the opportunity arose for my father to receive additional training at work, which would have led to a raise, my mother refused to let him spend the extra hours after work. I was only fifteen, but I thought the training was a great idea and was surprised that he gave it up so easily. He could have argued that it was important for him to pursue it, but he didn't. I could only conclude that my mother's objections were just a convenient excuse for him and that he didn't actually want to exert himself. Instead of coming up with solutions for our family's financial straits, they preferred to scream at each other over what little remained at the end of the week.

I began to realize that there was something wrong with them or, more specifically, with their interactions within the family. My father was always interesting, funny, and nice to the random strangers he bumped into on the street or in the grocery store. He sometimes lingered in a conversation with someone he had just met ten minutes earlier, yet he only occasionally shared that pleasant, social side of himself with his own children. It's like he saw us as holding a lower status than everyone else, like we were less important, less intelligent, and less useful. I couldn't reconcile his behavior with that of my friends' parents who, with beaming faces, bragged and crooned over their children's every small accomplishment.

As summer waned, our lives took another turn for the worse. One day, my mother took Gabrielle, Amanda, and Helen to the playground on Rowley Street, which was a main artery in town. My mother, who was pushing Gabrielle in the oversized stroller my parents had purchased when Lillian was born, lost sight of Amanda, who liked to sprint around, sprite-like.

In her little-girl way, she ended up too far ahead of my mother, and at the crosswalk that led to the playground's entrance, she dashed into the street. My mother, who had not been paying attention, suddenly saw a car speeding toward her daughter. Reflexively, she screamed for Amanda to stop. This was a bad reaction, as it caused Amanda to actually stop and turn to face my mother. The car would have missed her if it weren't for that moment's hesitation. Instead, it struck her and sent her flying into the air.

What had to be only a few minutes later, I answered the phone at the house. A woman was asking for my mother. When I told her that my mother was out, she let me know that Amanda had been hit by a car. This woman explained that she had been at the scene of the accident and asked Amanda for her name and phone number so as to alert her mother. She was calling, she said, from a payphone near the park.

I was confused, since our mother had gone on the walk with the girls. Where was she? I told the woman I'd be there as soon as possible. Being the runner I was, I made it to the scene of the accident, nearly a mile away, in just over five minutes, my legs driven by adrenaline. *Oh my God, is Amanda going to be okay?* I thought as I approached the scene and saw an ambulance pull up.

A police officer was crouched beside Amanda, who was lying silently on the ground. He was yelling, "Where's this child's mother?"

A dozen people had gathered on both sidewalks. I scanned the crowd for my mother and spotted her standing only a few feet from Amanda, holding onto the stroller with a blank expression.

Seven-year-old Helen stood beside her, trembling and crying.

I had seen my mother like this so many times that I jumped right into action. "Mom, I'll watch the baby," I half-shouted, half-whispered. I was out of breath from my run. "Go to the policeman and tell him who you are."

My mother stepped forward and approached the policeman. "I'm her mom," she croaked as she approached Amanda.

I knew that, had I been there, the accident probably wouldn't have occurred. I would have told Amanda to wait for me at the crosswalk, and we would have crossed together. It was just a commonsense thing to say to a child, but my mother didn't think that way. This incident reminded me that my mother was incapable of protecting us and that I had to step up to take care of my sisters. I was exhausted by this need to be the mother in my family; it was too much. I wanted my own life. I wanted parents who could do their job.

Not knowing my sister's condition, I choked back tears as I watched the EMTs load Amanda into the ambulance. My mother climbed in after her. The crowd dispersed once the ambulance left, and Helen and I started walking home. Gabrielle was still sound asleep as I pushed the stroller.

Once we got a little further away from the scene of the accident, Helen wailed, "Mom was screaming, Niecy. It was horrible. I don't ever want to remember this."

"I'm so sorry, Helen," I said softly. "Did you get to see Amanda at all? Is she okay?"

"I don't know. She was just lying there. A lady was talking to her, and then Mom just stood there. No one knew she was our mom."

"I'm so sorry I wasn't there with you," I said.

We walked the rest of the way home in silence. I could not get over the feeling that I could have prevented this accident had I been there.

As it turned out, Amanda's leg had been broken at the femur's growth plate. When she came home from the hospital three days later, she wore a cast that stretched from hip to ankle. Her front teeth had been knocked loose. One was recovered a few feet away from her in the road. She had become extremely thin in the hospital, and the skin on her face was pulled tight against her high cheekbones. I couldn't believe how much weight she'd lost in such a short period of time. She looked like a dying angel, her huge hazel eyes shining against a pale snowy background.

As was typical, my parents placed all the blame for the accident on the driver of the car, who was just a teenager. They claimed that she should have seen Amanda, that she was driving too fast, and that somebody ought to do something about that dangerous road.

My father converted the pull-out couch in the living room into a bed so we wouldn't have to carry nine-year-old Amanda up and down the stairs each day. She only weighed about sixty pounds, but that was more than I could manage. We propped her up against a pillow so she could watch television. She was largely quiet this whole time. The only time we heard a sound from her was when she needed to use the bathroom, which my father and I would carry her to. He carried her body while I held up her cast so it wouldn't twist her hip. I brought her dinner in the living room after preparing it for the family. She never complained that it was cold, though I knew it was; I ate mine, which was already cold, immediately after bringing Amanda her plate. My sisters and I helped her bathe by holding her cast out of the tub while she washed herself down in six inches of water. The cast seemed to weigh as much as she did, and for weeks, she was helpless but incredibly appreciative of our assistance.

My father had good health insurance, but there were co-pays and deductibles, all of which prompted further screaming matches between my parents. Those of us who could escaped upstairs. Amanda was alone downstairs and had to endure the screaming. I wished we could carry her upstairs, but her weight was beyond all of us, and we simply couldn't bear to remain downstairs with her. In fact, the weight of everything that had happened that summer and before had become too much for me to carry.

I sank further into negative thoughts. I kept ruminating that I was ugly, useless, and a disappointment at best. Even things that had nothing to do with me, I attributed to being my fault. I was a burden to my parents and the world. After all, they had to pay for my food and medical expenses.

Who would even notice if I were dead?

I became angry at God for allowing me to be born as the person I was. I was drowning in a sea of pain and didn't want to continue this life. I wanted to be in heaven, where—as my religion teachers told me—I would be loved unconditionally just for being me.

During the summer of 1990, day by day and despite the reprieve of my interlude with Robert, I was falling apart inside and spiraling downward. I refused to cry out for help or let anyone take pity on me. I turned my face into a mask. Only my eyes told of my misery, and my parents were not the kind of people who looked into their children's eyes. Plus, I stared at the floor whenever I was around them.

Alone in my room in the evenings, I returned to cutting myself. It was only in slitting my wrists that I felt something akin to being alive. The deadening sensations I had to induce when I was around my parents could be reversed in the evenings as I slid a razor across my wrists. At last, I could feel alive again, if even just for a while. Soon, my wrists were covered in thin scabs, though neither of my parents noticed. To hide my secret activity, I became a girl who wore long-sleeved shirts. The scabs were my secret, a reminder that I had a choice: the choice to feel, to live, and even to die.

Chapter 14

The Dead Sea

Fall 1990

When school resumed in the fall of my sophomore year, challenging sports, fun activities, and even access to friends failed to make a difference in my mood; nothing lightened my spirit. I felt as alone and as worthless as I had during the summer. Keeping busy kept my mind off of my death wish for short periods, but then the gloom would return to settle over me even more firmly than before. It was practically smothering me. Every night I prayed for death. My obsession with checking out and my belief that death was the only viable choice filled every spare moment.

In my youthful, romantic imagination, I fantasized that people would remember me as young and maybe even beautiful. They would love the memory of me, a girl who had died so tragically. If I were dead, I could do no more wrong, and perhaps my parents would finally understand just how much I did for the family. Perhaps they might finally have a glimpse of how much pain I was in. Well, at least my father might. My mother would probably just blame me for being an inconvenience to her by dying.

By that point, I had sliced my wrist on several occasions, though it never resulted in more than a few large drops of blood and minor scabs. I continued indulging in the activity, but found that I was too chicken to go through with the final, deep slice that would end it all.

I felt myself coming apart, collapsing like a crumbling cement wall. I started having bizarre dreams that were even more frightening than what I'd experienced before. Now, in addition to being awakened nightly by demons chasing me down, I had nightmares that sometimes affected me for days.

In one, a black shadowy figure stood menacingly beside my bed, looking straight down at me as I slept. This figure scared me so much that I woke myself up to get away from the dream, but I was paralyzed, unable to open my eyes. I could still see the figure through my closed eyelids. Then I'd realize it wasn't a dream. I actually was awake and was trapped in a paralyzed state. The black shadow figure reached down to me, placed its hands on either side of my pillow, and brought its black vapory eyeless face within an inch of mine as I struggled to move and escape. I could feel the pillow depress beneath its formless weight, and a sense of doom swept through me. Whoever or whatever the figure was, it hated me and wanted to harm me. No, "harm" is not really a big enough word for what it wanted to do to me. It was worse than that. It wanted to torture me.

Eventually, I willed myself to move, and then the figure disappeared. It scared me so much that the fear kept me up the rest of the night and for many nights afterward.

This experience was so real, it continued to terrify me as I went about my day. I had no one to turn to. No one would believe me if I told them about the dream and certainly there was no one who could protect me. Where other teens might have a loving parent, trusted minister, or concerned teacher to turn to, I didn't feel I had any of these connections. I had too many secrets. Secrets that, if I told anyone, would lead to my sisters being taken from me, splitting us up permanently into separate homes.

Many things did not go well for me that fall at school. At the beginning of the cross-country season, I caught a bad cold that kept me from performing well the rest of the fall. The star-in-the-making of my freshman year had disappeared, and in her place was a girl who couldn't help her team. In addition, my grades were hurting. Instead of my usual nineties, I was slipping into eighties and even the seventies. I couldn't seem to pull myself out of my academic rut. To top things off, I was still convinced the guys at school thought I was ugly. I was sure I could hear their whispers as I passed in the halls. When I turned my head to see who they were laughing about, they stopped talking immediately.

Another girl might have taken these "failures" in stride, but for me, they only compounded the message I was receiving at home: I was a failure.

One night in late October, my parents indulged in another of their verbal attacks on me. These had become so frequent, I could no longer distinguish the contents of one ambush from another. Afterward, I sat on the edge of my bed, curled into a ball, rocking back and forth and staring at the floor. My mottled plush rug became a blurred field of brown; my vision and my mind seemed to be receding. I dug my long fingernails into the palms of my hands, but I felt nothing. Silence engulfed me, numbed me, and permeated me with an emptiness that pushed aside what little was left of my soul.

What's the point of living? I thought, my parents' stinging words still shrill in my mind. *This torture, this pain, will never end.*

Slowly, I unclenched my fists and stared at the bright-red crescent moons I had imprinted on my palms. The flies had returned earlier that spring and were now buzzing overhead, as they did every night, but their whir faded as I continued focusing on my hands. This fingernail imprint had not produced any kind of feeling response; I needed to cut myself to get the feeling I so craved.

I got up and walked toward the dresser, where I stored my diary with the razor blade tucked inside. I felt like I was floating through a dream. I reached down and pulled out my diary. I opened it and carefully drew the blade from its protective cardboard slip. The sharp metal appeared rusty due to the spots of dried blood.

I sat back down on my bed and turned the razor blade around and around in my hands. Then, with the middle finger of my right hand, I searched for my pulse on my left wrist. Even in my malaise,

I was so used to not making a mess for fear of reprisal that I walked to the sink in my room so I could bleed into it.

The numbness I felt was so profound, I was practically floating to the sink. Standing over it, I traced the outline of my artery ever so lightly, took a deep breath, and then pressed the corner of the blade into my skin. My flesh bent inward around the razor, preventing it from breaking the surface. I pushed in with greater strength and pulled the blade across my wrist.

The result was merely a scratch. I was disappointed it hadn't done more damage. I was ready to go all the way this time. I again forced the razor into my skin, twisting it to make it dig deeper. This produced only a tiny cut, but even a tiny cut will bleed. It bled too slowly, though, so I cut myself again. Warm, sticky, red liquid flowed slowly across the blade onto my fingers. My mind was blank.

Then, all at once, I became conscious of what I was doing. I wasn't just cutting myself to get some kind of feeling; I had taken a step to committing suicide. In fact, I had taken more than a step; I *was* committing suicide.

I've suffered long enough. It's time for my misery to end. The thought came so easily and surely that I continued to act upon it. It was time.

The small slit in my wrist was now oozing large drops of blood that fell onto the white porcelain. This time, I would go all the way. My miserable life would be over soon.

In the midst of this, I heard someone call my name.

The voice was not harsh; it couldn't be my parents. Instead of the hardness I was used to hearing, this voice had a gentle tone to it, yet it was also firm. I couldn't imagine who would be calling me.

This was not a good time to be distracted. I was on a mission. I swung my head around to see if someone was walking in on me, but no one was there.

"Great," I grumbled, "now I'm spooking myself out again."

With my thumb, I wiped aside the blood that was spreading across my wrist so as to see the purple veins clearly. I wanted to succeed at ending my life. I envisioned cutting myself so deeply that the blood would drain out and my body would collapse on the floor. And that would be the end of my wretched existence.

"Denise, put down the razor blade," an adult male voice whispered. It was urging and imploring, yet detached, like a teacher politely commanding his students' attention. His voice penetrated the silence of the room, though it was not audible. It seemed to be coming from within me.

Caught off guard and used to following orders, I placed the blade on the edge of the sink.

"Now turn on the faucet and rinse your wrist with cold water," the voice continued.

Even as he said this, I realized that living was not what I wanted. I picked up my razor again, ready to finish the job of ending my life. "Leave me alone," I snapped. The conversation was going on entirely inside my mind, but it was as real as any I'd ever had. "Who are you?"

"Put the razor down and rinse off your wrist."

"Shut up and go away."

"Put the razor down and rinse off your wrist," he repeated patiently and sternly, yet still detached. The voice was like the opposite of an echo. With a real echo, you hear your own voice coming back to you from the surrounding environment. This was someone else's voice coming from within.

Whoever I was communicating with was trying to help me. For some reason, someone or something beyond me, beyond what I was able to comprehend with my limited senses, wanted me to live.

This thought—that my life mattered to someone—was a new one, and it moved me. I put the razor down, turned on the water, and let it flow over my wrist and hand. The bleeding stopped. I put the razor away and then placed a Band-Aid over the cut to keep it from oozing on the sheets. I didn't want my parents to know what I had done. They would harangue me rather than commiserate with me.

Having done this, I was aware that the presence had left and that

I was alone in my room. It felt somehow colder and emptier than it had just a moment before. I had been so close to relief, yet here I was, still alive. I climbed into bed and prayed, as I did every night, for an end to my life. My prayer was an angry one. I chewed God out for giving me such a miserable life and for not giving me an "out."

In the midst of this prayer, the voice came back: "God doesn't want you to die."

"Who are you?" I snapped. "Why doesn't God want me to be with him up in heaven?"

The voice disappeared without giving me an answer.

I was shocked. I had been addressed by some intelligent being that was speaking directly into my mind, and he'd told me that God didn't want me to die. For the first time in my life, I felt like a parent I adored and respected had spoken to me in love. Me, worthy of love! What a new thought! Someone or something cared enough to talk me out of doing something I desperately wanted to do. He had reached out to me for my own good. I'd never experienced that before.

Drifting off to sleep, I pondered whether the entity was actually a manifestation of my subconscious, a schizophrenic response, a supernatural entity, or someone truly sent by God. My skepticism waned as I considered the fact that I had been hearing a voice calling my name for years. So had others. I had seen a ghost on the stairs and the watchers in the back of the church, and I had accepted them as parts of the spiritual dimension of life. As I wrapped my head around what had happened, I accepted that the voice must have been sent by God and that He did not want me to die.

My last thought, as I drifted off to sleep was, *Why don't You want me to die, God, when all I want is to be with You?*

As always, God did not answer me directly.

The next morning, I pushed away any thought of the previous night. It was like changing the subject of a conversation, but this conversation was within my own mind. This denial was the easiest way to keep up my facade and to appear "normal" at school.

Through all of the stress and anxiety I was experiencing, the only "person" I could turn to was God. The problem was that God was not a person, and I wanted a living breathing person in my life. In order to find that someone to connect to, I resumed writing to Robert regularly. To ease my pain, I told him the details and secrets of my life.

The previous summer, I had been afraid to scare him off by revealing too much. Apparently, that is what happened, because he never wrote back. Some part of me believed that if he were to write back, he would tell me that I was pathetic and crazy, and he'd ask me to stop sending him letters. That rejection would have been too much, so I was relieved when he did not reply. But the Methodist church and the people I met in it weren't ready to let me down so easily. They would still be there as a refuge even if Robert no longer played a part.

I turned to my Friday night church youth group to find acceptance. I looked forward to our weekly meetings, which actually gave me a reason to live after my failed suicide attempt. After our group meeting, I occasionally lingered at the church, finding a dark corner of the sanctuary to pray in. My prayers often turned to tears as I cried in the darkness of God's home. I prayed desperately through those dark nights of my soul. I prayed for an escape, for an end to my pain, for relief from the futility and fear of my life. I had little hope for change. I just couldn't envision a future that was any different than my past. My grades were falling, and since Princeton was now definitely impossible, so was my hope for any sort of a college education. I felt destined to live at home with my parents, forever their indentured servant.

I decided to go forward with my plans for an "out." Even though the voice had told me that God didn't want me to die, I made plans to kill myself on January 12, my sixteenth birthday. *Sweet sixteen, rest in peace*, I thought to myself. It was as romantic an idea as seeing

Robert again. What I didn't count on was the church spoiling my plans temporarily.

At the end of November, I went on a three-day Adventura weekend youth retreat. It was a local multidenominational retreat for teens living in the surrounding towns. We were told nothing about the weekend's activities in advance. When we arrived, all the clocks were covered with paper to make us appreciate time as something that can have quality, rather than just quantity. Out of habit, I was tempted to ask the people looking at their bare wrists how long it was until dinner.

Adult and youth members of the various churches gave speeches, and the head minister presiding over the retreat told the story of a friend of his who was a college professor. One year, a beautiful girl who never spoke to anyone sat in the back of the professor's class-room. Her eyes, shining with a delicate sadness, caught his attention. On occasion, when he caught her gaze during lectures, she smiled. A couple of months into the semester, the girl suddenly stopped coming to class. Noting her absence, he inquired into her disappearance. She had killed herself. Upon hearing this, the professor felt guilty about not preventing her death. He wondered if there was something he could have done to stop her.

The minister told us that the dead girl was like the Dead Sea: beautiful on the surface, but beneath her rippling blue eyes, she was empty. That sounded like me, except that the girl in the story was beautiful. I stared at the floor, hoping the minister wouldn't notice me and realize how like that girl I was.

During this retreat, we received cards, letters, and small gifts from Adventura members and parents, most of whom I didn't know. These cards contained hand-written scriptures and poems that claimed the donors loved me. Alone in my room and angered by their "lies," I threw the gifts on the floor and stomped on them. I kicked the mess under the bed, and then sat back down, weeping.

Later, I gathered the crumpled cards and gifts to dump into a brown paper bag. In doing so, I found a small package of Kleenex. An attached note told me that I would need them—later. Later?! I already needed them.

On the last day of Adventura, we gathered in the chapel to reflect on our weekend. I was actually relieved that I would soon be returning to my familiar life, as miserable as it was. At least at home and at school, I knew where I stood and wasn't thrown off by a bunch of people sending letters filled with unfounded and untrue statements of love. I knew everyone hated me, and I felt like I had been living a lie that weekend.

After the opening prayer, past attendees stood up and talked about how coming to Adventura had changed their lives. Soon, new members began to stand and confess their private thoughts. They poured out the pain of their lives, and I was shocked to learn these people were like me: stressed, lost, and confused. They, too, felt they weren't good enough or worthy of love. I was surprised that everyone was so openly sharing their darkest secrets and fears. I kept my eyes down, afraid that if my gaze fell upon the sobbing people around me, I would start crying, too.

I was sitting next to my new friend, Josh, whom I had met earlier that week. Suddenly, he stood up and walked to the podium. Josh told the story of how his best friend had been hit by a drunk driver and had to have brain surgery. He had to learn how to speak all over again. He talked about how much he prayed for his best friend and how he felt abandoned by God. But eventually, his friend recovered and he realized that God had been there helping all along. By the time he was done, he was crying. When he sat back down beside me, I took his hand in mine. A couple of other people spoke. Everyone around us was weeping and sniffling. It was worse than a funeral. We were all damaged and hurting, every single one of us.

Without realizing what was happening, I felt myself stand. I tried to sit back down, but I couldn't. It was like something beyond myself, like the voice that had told me to put down the razor, was compelling me to stand. I tried to turn, to run away, but Josh still held my hand. With no escape, I started crying hysterically. Until then, I had been one of about four people with dry eyes. I stood there, trying to say something, anything, but no one could understand me through my tears.

Josh grasped my hand more tightly, and then a sensation of peace cut through the haze of tears. I suddenly started speaking clearly and with a voice that sounded foreign to me as it echoed back to my ears. I felt God there with me, as He had been when the words, "I rebuke you, Satan," had come to me over a year earlier in my bedroom. But now, the words coming from my lips were my words. Before thirty-plus people, I admitted that I wanted to die, that I was empty and broken inside. Finally, I sat down, sobbing and spooked by my outburst. I had obviously been moved by the Holy Spirit I so desperately wanted to deny at that moment. Josh held me as I cried on his shoulder, telling me to let it all out.

After we dried our eyes and left the chapel, we entered the main meeting hall, where approximately one hundred people sat on folding chairs. Our parents—including my mother, who had received a ride from my youth leader—were waiting for us. I was surprised to see her. My youth leader must have convinced her to come.

We were asked to say a few final words to the gathered group. Anyone could come forward.

"Josh, will you come up with me?" I asked.

"Sure, let's go." He stood up first and draped his arm across my back, relaxing me and nudging me forward gently.

I was relieved to have a friend at my side to support me both physically and emotionally. I didn't know why I was compelled to go up there or what I was going to say; I just knew I had to.

I thanked everyone for their support and for the experience. In my nervousness, I stared at the floor in front of me as I spoke. Then, from somewhere deep within, an unfamiliar strength sprang forth within me. As I finally raised my eyes and looked out at the audience, my voice rang out, clear and strong, "There are live fish in the Dead Sea."

Recalling the minister's tale about the dead girl, the room roared to life with applause. I stepped down from the podium and noticed my mother smiling slightly. It was one of only a few moments in my life when she smiled at me. How could she not know that she had helped create the Dead Sea in my life?

But in that moment, there were indeed live fish within the dying sea of my soul.

Chapter 15

Intervening Messengers

Fall 1990

That night when I returned home, I settled down to do my homework for school the next day. I hadn't done it before going away for the weekend, and now I had to focus. I was upstairs, studying and writing, and my parents were watching television downstairs, when I heard my mother scream my name. I put my work aside and went downstairs to see what she wanted.

"Make some popcorn," she ordered.

"Popcorn? But I have homework for tomorrow."

"You've been gone for three days, doing nothing. I told you to fix us some popcorn."

It was only a short walk for her down the hall to the kitchen. All she was doing was watching television, while I was working on homework that needed to be done. Her frivolous demand was just another demonstration of her continued control over me.

"You're so lazy," she shouted. "You do nothing around here."

Nothing had changed. It seemed easier, as usual, to give in. As soon as I made her some popcorn, I ran to my room in tears. Those fish in the Dead Sea that had been so alive just a few hours ago had already drowned.

The next day, when I left for school, I was uneasy. Although most of the Adventura attendees went to different schools, a couple attended Gilbert. These students now knew my dark death-wish secret, which I had kept hidden for months. What if I ran into one of them? What would I say?

When I got to school, I headed to the band room for a few minutes of solitude before the rush of school started. I wasn't ready to face these people yet. Music was always a salve for my injured soul; practicing my flute took my mind off of everything. However, before I reached the band room, I ran into Steve, my friend from the band trip to Myrtle Beach who had been asking everyone on the bus whether they had thought about killing themselves. I must have looked worse than I realized, because he asked what was wrong. I started crying. I felt like an idiot.

"You want to talk?" he asked.

Steve and I talked through two classes. Luckily, he had been to Adventura the year before and knew what happened there. He reminded me that things always got worse before they got better. I hoped that wasn't true. However, it was not his words but his presence that helped me the most, even though it was difficult for me to accept that anyone actually cared about me.

His brother, my former crush, Brian, also stopped by the band room while I was talking to Steve. He asked me if I was all right. Steve covered for me and told him I was fine. His sweetness calmed me. I almost smiled.

Later, I wondered about the coincidence. I could have bumped into anyone, so why had I bumped into Steve and Brian? Now, years later, I suspect that someone who had been at Adventura with me that weekend had talked to Steve the night before, and he had been actively looking for me.

While I welcomed talking to Steve, I also desperately wanted to keep my feelings in. I did my best to only reveal what I felt was safe to share. But all my self-loathing started spilling out against my will. I couldn't restrain my words or emotions, although I desperately tried. I was like a glass that had been overfilled, and now, pain was pouring out.

Of course, anyone could have arguments with their parents and feel unworthy. I'd heard kids say things like this so many times, but

I also knew the parents of these kids, and I knew that these parents really loved their children and were trying their best. In my case, with my parents, we didn't have arguments like most families; we had one-way irrational verbal attacks. I still couldn't imagine that others could possibly understand my situation.

Even as my pain poured out, I kept my ever-present fear to myself. There were so many things I just couldn't explain without sounding utterly insane: a haunted house, a demonic attack, voices in the night trying to save my life. These were things that happened in horror movies, not to real people in real life. Surely, I would be institutionalized if anyone knew.

I allowed shame to speak its language: silence.

Two days later, despite the respite of my talk with Steve, I still wished for death. I couldn't accept that God wanted me to live, as the voice had revealed. I planned, once again, to end my life. I couldn't wait until my birthday. January felt so far away. I chose a date a few days later to go up to Devil's Jump-Off and leap from the cliff to my death. My head would splatter on the jagged rocks below, finally freeing me from my awful life.

Devil's Jump-Off offered a striking view of the valley that stretched for miles. It was a beautiful place to throw myself from to find my rest. However, when the appointed date arrived, I didn't make the trip. I worried that I wouldn't actually die, but would live on, paralyzed. In that case, I would be stuck with my parents for the remainder of my life. I was too afraid of that possibility to risk it. I needed a better plan.

I returned to cutting to try to end my life. Again I walked to the sink with my razor then watched with indifference as the blood pooled up on my wrist.

"Denise! Denise, stop," the voices pleaded again. There were two voices this time, one male and one female.

I ignored them as I watched the blood ooze from my wrist. I was numb. Dejection weighed my body down. My thoughts were vacant. I let my despair have its way.

Cut deeper, I told myself, contradicting the voices.

I sliced my wrist with the razor again, though I wasn't strong enough to cut deeply—or perhaps I just wasn't brave enough.

I felt no pain as the razor's edge scraped against my fair skin. I wanted to feel something, so I did it again. This time, I broke through the skin and felt the pain I sought. This pain, mild as it was, made me feel alive. The pain broke the pervasive numbness.

But it still wasn't enough. Feeling something for a brief moment wasn't enough. I wanted to end my misery above all else. I pushed the razor deeper. "This should do it," I whispered to myself. "I can't take any more of this life."

Blood flowed down my wrist in a thin stream. Soon, this wretched life would be over, and I would be dead.

I rubbed the warm blood between my fingertips then continued my cut. The thin blade turned red. I was desperate to be successful this time, but the cuts weren't producing enough blood. I couldn't push the razor deep enough, couldn't make it gush forth the release I craved. I had prayed again and again to die, but God never listened. He had not pulled me from this life.

"Denise! Denise, stop!" The voices broke my concentration. They were intervening again. I was irritated at their unwelcome intervention.

"Denise, put the razor down," they called out, but my depression and the intensity of my emotional pain pushed me to persevere. I had to succeed at my own self-destruction.

Leave me alone. I just want to die.

At that moment, something astonishing happened. A sensation similar to a mild electrical charge traveled from my back through all my limbs. The hair on my arms stood on end. Then, strangely, I was filled with warmth, as if I were being held and wrapped in a blanket, even though the room was chilly. I became calm, and for the first time in my life, I felt deep inside what I believed to be love.

As though from a distance, I watched myself turn on the faucet of the sink I was standing over. I thrust my bloody wrist under the cold water. Soon, the frigid water slowed the flow of blood. I dabbed the last drops with a tissue and crept into bed.

"God," I asked, "what are these voices? Why do they keep trying to stop me?"

I strained to hear something, anything, in the cold silence. The voices had been successful. Evidently, there was nothing more they needed to say.

A couple of weeks later, the kids from Adventura gathered at the Torrington Methodist church for a reunion. Some of the girls from another school had made T-shirts that proclaimed, "There are live fish in the Dead Sea." It felt wonderful to see them grasp onto what I had said and to find it hadn't sounded crazy to them. I didn't have the heart to reveal that the fish were floating belly up on the waves, that I was still struggling even more than before.

I was surprised to find that the members of Adventura had become a closer family to me in one weekend than many of my closest friends had over the years I'd known them. I was shocked at how comfortable I was around them, despite the fact that my cover had been stripped from me. I felt almost as safe with them as I had with Robert the summer before, whom I felt I could reveal everything to. Robert had given me a reason to live, and now, my new family gave me an outlet to relieve my tension. But it only lasted while I was in their presence. When I left them to return home, I went back to the toxic stress.

Throughout that fall and early winter, I wrote to Robert monthly. Whenever I was upset, the same voice that had told me to put down the razor the first time, which I had come to accept as some sort of spiritual counselor, now told me to write to him to "put things in perspective." Robert never answered my letters, but that didn't bother me. I felt better just by writing. Expressing my feelings to someone was a relief, even if that someone did not reply.

Although writing made me feel better momentarily, it wasn't

enough to squelch my desire to die or heal the enormous pain afflicting me. It was just an ointment placed on a wound that was still gushing blood. It wasn't enough to stop the hemorrhaging. For that, my entire life needed major surgery.

I felt like Alice in Wonderland falling down the rabbit hole and crashing into the sides in pitch blackness until the pain was unbearable. Yet, it wasn't actually pain I felt; it was more of a blankness that emptied me, pulling the very fibers of my life apart with its vacuum. I was no longer sure that there was anything left inside me.

I felt alone and isolated, even among others. Sure, I had fun with Kelly and Dawn, but they had no idea what was happening. I distanced myself from Steve, who I now realize would have been there for me. Even my Adventura friends couldn't rescue me. Perhaps because the emptiness was so familiar, I feared losing the comfort of it. I continued making plans to kill myself on my birthday. I gave up on slitting my wrists or throwing myself off Devil's Jump-Off, though. Instead, I turned my hopes to aspirin and Tylenol, the only medications in the house that offered the potential of a fatal overdose.

A few nights after deciding to try this different tactic, I had another nightmare. In it, I awoke in my room. Earlier in the dream-day, I had somehow learned that Brian had proclaimed his love to someone else. Now, without hope of ever gaining his love, my dream-self was preparing for death. At 1 a.m., the house was still, and I sat on the edge of my bed, holding back tears and writing a letter to Brian with directions to Luxaya and a request that he meet me there in the morning. Then I folded the paper in half and walked to the closet to fetch a Renaissance-style dress I had bought at the thrift store. The lace bodice pricked at my skin as I slipped into it. Enjoying the sensation of the soft plush carpet under my feet, I remained barefoot and dug my toes into the soft pile.

Quietly, my dream-self tiptoed down the stairs, note in hand, and into the darkness. The cool, wet pavement felt soothing to my bare feet, and a warm mist swirled around me. It touched my skin with gentle kisses, bringing peace to my heart. The slender rays from the streetlights sparkled off the glistening leaves above my head. The stillness was broken only by the wind rustling the trees.

I ran through the patches of shadow to Steve and Brian's house two miles away. Dashing unseen down back roads, I stepped on an occasional pebble, sending waves of pain shooting through my foot and up into my leg, but I did not falter. The wind wafted the damp smell of predawn earth across my path, and I inhaled a deep lungful of cool, dewy air. The mist had not yet soaked through my hair, which was still dry against my back.

Because I was in dream-time, I arrived at Steve and Brian's house quickly. The porch light illuminated their door as I raised my hand to knock, but at the last minute, instead of knocking, I kissed the door with tears in my eyes, slid the note under it, and turned away toward Luxaya. My dress felt warm and damp against my legs. My feet hurt from treading down the sidewalks barefoot, but the pain was comforting, like an old friend.

Then I was suddenly at Luxaya. Beside my log there was a rope with a noose attached. I knew it was mine and that I had left it there to hang myself. After tying the rope to one of the branches of the dying tree, I stood on my log and placed the noose around my neck. The rope scraped at my skin. Then, with a hard shove, I kicked the log out from under me. For several minutes, I hung in the air, gargling, wheezing, struggling, and kicking against my sudden fear and the heaviness of my weight against the rope. Then my body relaxed.

Instantly, I was floating above my dream-self and looking down at my limp body. I felt no warmth, pain, or even sorrow. I was at peace, a peace that was both familiar and infinite.

Although it was late at night, a bright light behind me lit the area. I sensed another being floating alongside me. I identified it as an angel, but I didn't turn to look directly at it. I understood that it was there to guide me, but I was still fixated on the scene below me.

I was still hovering over my body when I became aware of hurried footsteps rustling along the path. Looking down, I saw it was Steve who had come to find me, instead of Brian. I watched my worried friend scramble up the rock, where he discovered my dangling body with its ashen face and purple feet.

"No, no, *no!*" he screamed. "Why did you do this? No!" He reached up and touched my leg tentatively, then pulled his hand back with a jerk, obviously feeling something unexpected. He gasped, turned, and ran back through the woods, alternately wailing and hyperventilating, as I stared down at him indifferently.

At this point, I startled awake. My suicide dream had seemed so incredibly real. Hot salty tears slipped from my cheeks, and a shudder of nausea passed through me. I felt as if I had actually experienced Steve's reaction to finding my body. God had just shown me what would happen if I chose that particular path. No matter how I ended my life, someone would have to find me and experience the anguish I had seen on dream-Steve's face. I wouldn't, couldn't, let my friends or sisters go through that. For a while, I stopped plotting my death.

A month later, in December, I had another nightmare, but this one was very different. There was a man in our basement. His hair was gray and wiry, and it sprang from his head like Albert Einstein's, but dirtier and more disheveled. He had a short, boxy stature and a crooked nose that deviated to the side. He had somehow broken into our house, although there was no obvious entry point in the basement. There was a hatchet beside him, and when he picked it up, he grinned evilly. His teeth were broken and decayed, making them shark-like. He appeared to be only half-human, as if he were crossbred with a stumpy troll. He swung the hatchet over his shoulder and made his way up the stairs, still flashing his rotting smile. In my dream, I suddenly realized he was heading for my parents' room. He intended to kill them.

I woke with a start and bolted out of bed to save my parents. By the time I realized it was only a dream, I had made it to the bottom of the front stairs, having leapt down them in five long strides. As I slowly realized what was going on, it dawned on me that I wouldn't have stood a chance against a madman with a weapon.

Spooked and shaking, I decided to get a glass of milk since I was near the kitchen. I was surprised by my reaction. I'd never imagined I would dash into harm's way to save my parents, yet here I was. After pouring my milk, I went to the back stairs so I didn't wake anyone by walking up the creaky front staircase.

Just as I was about to take my first step, I noticed a large black shadow on the stairs ahead of me. It had a nondescript rounded form approximately twice the size of a human. It was darker than the surrounding darkness and vaporously smoky. Terror washed over me. I froze in my tracks. This was not a shadow; it was the physical manifestation of the evil half-man from my nightmare. I recognized it through its intentions toward me and my family. The figure emanated the same intense hatred, complete lack of empathy, and desire to torture others as the evil entity in my dream.

Still frozen in place, I blinked a couple of times, trying to focus. The form became slightly denser and continued moving up the stairs like an amoeba. It was not walking on the steps, but rather gliding along the wall. I continued to stand there, mouth agape, until it turned the corner at the top of the staircase and headed toward Mariah's room.

Once it had vanished into the upstairs hallway, I bolted back into the kitchen, leaving my milk on the table. In a flash, I was back in my bed by way of the front stairs, not caring if I woke the whole house. I pulled my blankets over my head and grabbed hold of my Bible, which I kept under my pillow. I repeated the Lord's Prayer at least a dozen times before I was able to fall asleep again.

The next morning, I felt guilty for not checking on Mariah the night before to see if she was okay. She seemed normal enough, though, or as normal as she could be. I didn't mention my encounter to anyone. I was terrified and didn't want to scare my sisters, whom I tried so hard to protect.

Chapter 16

Voice in the Chaos

Fall 1990–Summer 1991

In the ensuing days and weeks, I was sure I had somehow released the black spirit that had floated up the stairs. I suspected it was the same spirit I had unleashed through the Ouija board well over a year before. The realization that it was still somewhere in the house haunting us terrified me and filled me with guilt for exposing my sisters to something so sinister.

But this wasn't the only challenge I had to contend with during my sophomore year. Mariah, who was now thirteen, routinely erupted into fits of rage. Anything and everything set her off. She continued striking out physically at whoever was closest to her. She had likely learned these reactions from observing our mother. Like Mom, Mariah sometimes ran outside screaming at the top of her lungs, eliciting neighbors to call the police. Out in the yard or on the sidewalk, she shouted that my father had beaten her. The bruises that dotted her body were actually self-inflicted; she sometimes hit herself when she was angry or frustrated.

My father and I were always the ones to wait for the police to show up. He would enlist me to be his corroborator, the third person in the he-said, she-said rebuttal. Never one to involve herself with solving family problems, my mother would hide out in her bedroom. My sisters would sneak upstairs to sit quietly in front of the television with the volume set really low to avoid attracting our parents' attention.

Not knowing when the police would show up or how the encounter would play out was strangely stressful, and I often felt like vomiting as the seconds ticked by. There was no reason for this nervousness, as I was not the focus of the police visit. After all, it was my father they were coming to speak to. Yet I felt so responsible for my family, primarily for my other sisters, that any threat to our family felt like a threat to me. I would do anything, endure anything, to keep my sisters together and to prevent us from being separated in foster care, a fate that seemed likely if my father were arrested.

Eventually, there would be a knock on the door, and my father would send me to answer. Some of the officers barged in as soon as I opened the door, accusing my father of crimes Mariah alleged he had committed (but had not). Others were polite, remaining outside until invited in, and treated both my father and me with respect.

Even after witnessing her fits for many years, it seemed downright unbelievable that Mariah would hurt herself and then scream that my father had beaten her. I always told the police the truth, complete with all the absurd details. Almost always, after taking a good look at Mariah, they believed me and left within thirty minutes.

In time, we started seeing the same two or three officers again and again. My father, in a state of frustration, began singing "La Bamba" to them once they arrived. It had been on the radio and he latched onto it randomly. The song's title—he didn't know any of the other lyrics—spilled from his lips over and over again, accompanied by the occasional disturbing chuckle. Then he would laugh and say, "Go ahead and arrest me. It would be better than living here."

Neither the officers nor I knew how to respond to that. These familiar officers started ignoring my father and walking right past him to take my statement.

Shortly after my sister's outbursts began and my father starting singing "La Bamba" to the police, he began seeing a therapist twice a month after work. At the time, I thought he did this voluntarily to help him cope with stress. I was happy that he was finally doing something positive for himself and the family. But looking back, I realize my father would never have spent the time or money to speak with anyone outside the home unless forced to. I suspect he was required to appear in court at some point for being uncooperative with the officers and was required to get counseling. If anything, the counseling made our lives worse. My father had a way of twisting what the counselor said against my sisters and me.

My parents' endless crazy behavior, Mariah's outbursts, and my belief that I had released an evil entity, mixed with a dose of teenage hormonal angst, pushed me further into depression. One night late that November, I took ten Tylenol tablets. I didn't even bother to walk across the room to get water. After only ten pills, I found I couldn't swallow any more. The tablets dried my throat and kept sticking there. I sat on my bed, wondering if I had ingested enough to kill myself. I decided to get a glass of water to help me finish the job.

Before I could summon the willpower to move, a woman's voice, soft yet firm, interrupted my thoughts: "Denise."

"What?" I retorted, annoyed.

"Do you really want to die?" she asked. It seemed more like she was telling me I didn't want to.

"Of course I do," I shot back. "I wouldn't be sitting here swallowing pills if I didn't."

She repeated the question: "Do you really want to die?"

"I can't live this life anymore," I said, pleading. I desperately wanted a reprieve from my pain and fear. "I can't bear this. It's never-ending." That's when it struck me that I was not speaking out loud. "Who are you? Why are you trying to stop me?"

The woman's voice answered, "I'm a messenger of God."

"What?" I asked as the Latin word *angelus*, meaning messenger, flickered into my head. "Does that mean you're an angel?"

"Some people call us that."

"If you're an angel, tell me why God keeps trying to keep me alive. What's the point? Why doesn't He just fix my life? I feel like I'm being tortured."

The woman did not reply, but I realized an unusual calm permeated the room. All my tension, paralyzing fear, and overwhelming sadness had evaporated. How had that happened without my noticing it? This experience halted my protests. I was surprised and bewildered that God had sent a representative, an angel messenger, to convince me not to kill myself for a third time. Why would He do that? After all, I wanted to be in heaven with Him. Wouldn't my death just speed up the process of getting me to heaven? Or was I missing something? Was there something going on I didn't understand?

I went to the sink, gagged myself, and threw up the ten pills I'd already taken.

As November turned into December, I found the experience of the messenger continued to alleviate the tension in my life. I was less miserable. I got into my life more. As they often did, my friends proved to be a much-needed distraction. Dawn took me to the teen dance club once a month. We would have gone every week if our parents allowed it. Dawn had a way of getting me out of my head. She brought me along on little adventures where I didn't have to think and could simply exist in the moment. And for those small moments, I was happy.

But as the days progressed, my misery crept back in bit by bit, and I found myself entertaining thoughts of suicide again. These thoughts were not overwhelming as they had been, though. Even though my sixteenth birthday, a day on which I had once planned to commit suicide, was approaching, I was able to manage these self-destructive thoughts.

The Adventura group planned a get-together for late December. I called Steve and asked him to give me a ride, since I knew he was attending. When Steve's mom pulled into the driveway, Brian, who had gone to Adventura two years earlier, stepped out and helped me into the car. He was wearing cologne, and I inhaled it deeply while attempting not to look obvious. My chest filled with a warm, full sensation as his soft, musky scent wafted around me.

At the reunion, Brian stood next to me in the prayer circle. We were all holding hands, so it was only natural that he took mine, but he actually squeezed my hand—and not once, three times! It was as if the world had blurred out around me, and only his warm grip was in focus. After the reunion gathering, we went out for ice cream, and Brian sat across from me. We made eye contact twice. I thought I had finally gone to heaven.

On our way home, I sat between Steve and Brian once again. Brian started out leaning against the door, but he slowly inched toward me. As our shoulders touched, my skin erupted with goose bumps.

I thought about all the times I had kissed his yearbook picture. I wondered if he had kept the tab I'd left in his locker. Was it the same one he had thrown in my direction the following summer? Would I ever tell him about the feelings stirring in my heart?

If only for one wonderful evening, the accustomed—and now growing—melancholy was alleviated. After this, I began to focus on my appearance more, particularly my smile. I filed down my long pointy canines with a fingernail file. I used Q-tips dipped in bleach to whiten my teeth. I had one slightly crooked tooth that I tried to push into place by putting pressure on it with a spoon. Eventually, the tip of the crooked tooth broke off from the force I was applying to it. My gums bled and burned from the bleach. Eventually, the pain convinced me to stop my whitening regimen. Fortunately, my father had full dental coverage for the family. I was delighted when the dentist restored my chipped tooth to make it appear straighter. I believed that if I could make myself prettier, someone would love and adore me, maybe even Brian, but my homegrown attempts at dentistry did little to improve how I felt about myself or impact how I felt others perceived me.

As my sixteenth birthday approached, the thought of suicide grew stronger again. Although the angel had told me that God didn't want me to die, I could not discern that God had actually done anything to help me to deal with my daily life. I was frustrated that God wanted me to live, yet left me in the same predicament. I had been looking forward to my death for months. And now, my hunger for it and for an end to my misery was stronger than my hunger to follow the expressed will of God.

On my sixteenth birthday, January 12, 1991, I was in a good mood. This was uncommon at the time, given my pervasive unhappiness. I turned sixteen on a Saturday, a day when I was less busy than other days. Even my parents' demands lessened on the weekend. Uncharacteristically, I was on top of the world, perhaps because my friends called to wish me a happy birthday. As evening approached, my good mood pushed away thoughts of carrying out my suicide plan. There didn't seem to be a need.

The morning after my birthday, however, my good mood was completely gone. In its place was a deep disappointment that I was still alive and that I had broken my promise to myself. I was angrier at myself than I'd ever been, and my desire to die dominated my thoughts all that Sunday and the next few days at school.

One night later that spring, when track season was underway and I was swamped with homework, my mother called me downstairs. As usual, she wanted me to do something she could have easily done herself: "I need you to fold the clothes in the TV room."

"I'm not doing it tonight. I'm busy with homework. Ask one of the other girls," I whined in exasperation.

She never asked my sisters to help with any of the housework and, busy as I was with schoolwork, I'd had enough. My sisters were old enough to pitch in and capable of helping. Why was I alone expected to do the work of eight people? I was tired of being used by my mother, of being the object of her abuse. She was always so unreasonable, as if no one else in the house had any needs. She was like a selfish child. *She's like Mariah*, I thought.

I stormed upstairs and locked myself in my room. I needed to study, but I was so angry, I wasn't sure I could pick up my homework again right away.

My father followed me upstairs and started banging on the door. "Denise, get down here and do what your mother says."

"*No!*" I said firmly. The "no" was uncharacteristic for me. It had been formulating for a very long time. Given the unreasonable nature of my mother, who was home all day and did very little cooking or cleaning herself, I had finally erupted into a rebellion.

"What is wrong with you?" my father demanded. "We told you to get down here now." He was in the habit of saying "we" to back up my mother.

When I didn't respond, he walked down the hall and descended the back stairs. They creaked under his weight. I suspected he was going to retrieve the key to my room. Remembering how he had once followed me upstairs, pulled me out of my hiding place next to the refrigerator, and beat me with a broomstick, I stood bravely at the deadbolt, holding the latch in place.

I just wanted to be left alone. I rarely acted this willfully and wasn't entirely sure why I was taking a stand on this particular evening. That evening, I was just too exhausted.

My father came back upstairs. When he inserted the key, nothing happened because I was holding the deadbolt in place. He wiggled the key, shook the door handle, and tried again. When that didn't work, he started yelling, "Denise, open the door and obey your mother."

I remained completely silent on the opposite side of the door, clenching the latch tightly with reddened fingers. Eventually, he gave up, called down to my mother that he couldn't get the key to work, and went back downstairs.

Later, after I had calmed down and had done a good bit of home-work, all while listening for heavy footfalls on the stairs, I turned the radio on. By then, I knew my father would not be coming, and I didn't have to worry about being surprised by him. Soon, my favorite song came on the radio, and my thoughts turned to Robert. I had placed the bracelet he had made for me into my pocket that morning. As I reached into my jeans to retrieve it, I found nothing. The bracelet was gone. I had lost it!

I burst into tears.

That bracelet, my only tangible reminder of Robert, was more important to me than anything else I owned. Robert was the first person I'd loved who had loved me back. He had held my hand, listened to me, and talked with me honestly. That relationship had given me hope and helped me get through the fall and winter. And now, the evening of my defiance, I discovered I had lost my only tangible reminder of that time. Now there was nothing to assure me that I had not made it up.

Less than a week later, I discovered that the wings had fallen off the angel pin on my backpack. I took this as an ominous sign that my little angel, whom I imagined was watching over me, had abandoned me. I tucked the angel away in the back of the jewelry box my grandmother had given me on my birthday several years earlier.

These two losses occurred during track season. A year earlier, I had been the third-highest point-scorer on the team. But this season was different. I started off with a cold, and a growth spurt that had turned me into a girl with wide hips and shoulders. I was trying my best to overcome the limitations of my new figure and my illness, but I found it was difficult to breathe during my runs. Now, I was lucky if I completed a race. My teammates were no longer cheering me, only encouraging me to keep going.

I would frequently collapse a few feet from the finish line, hyperventilating. I was nervous about what was happening to me, and it was scaring—and probably irritating—my track coach. One day, after I had a particularly bad attack, I sensed he'd had enough. The next day, he suspended me from the team until I had a doctor examine me to find out what was wrong. Half the team approached me in school to tell me how purple my face had been at the meet the day before.

A few days later, my father took me to the pediatrician, despite my mother's protests that I would cost them the twenty-dollar co-pay. The doctor thought I might have exercise-induced asthma and gave me an inhaler. I was back on the team.

Unfortunately, the inhaler's effects were minimal. My coach was afraid that I had a heart condition, and he suspended me again until I saw a cardiologist. Perhaps because of his upbringing by his physician father, my father took the coach's advice and took me to a cardiologist. I was grateful that he went out of his way in this instance, in spite of my mother's opposition.

After various tests, the cardiologist found that I had a mild tricuspid regurgitation (a leaky heart valve), but that didn't explain any of my symptoms. They decided to try an exercise stress test. After twenty minutes of running on the treadmill, I was at one hundred percent of my oxygen capacity. The treadmill's speed continued to increase, and three minutes later, I tore the mask off of my face, hyperventilating at one hundred and ten percent of my oxygen capacity. The doctor concluded that I was pushing my body further than it was capable of performing, and it was causing my breathing problems. For years, I had relied on my strong willpower to survive. Now, in trying to get approval from my teammates, I had exhausted my body, and it was no longer performing as I insisted it should.

My mother had fits about all the tests I'd had to undergo. All those twenty-dollar co-pays quickly piled up. In addition, my father's health insurance plan had renewed for the year, and his yearly deductible had reset. She screeched at me daily to quit track because of the cost, but it was a moot point, since I wasn't allowed to run anyway.

During one visit, the cardiologist told my father that he would accept whatever Dad's insurance paid and waive the co-payment. I was nearly as delighted with the news as my father. We hadn't asked him for a break, but it was apparent that we were struggling financially. He could see my father's threadbare pants and the patches on the knees that I had hand-sewn for him. My father wore his poverty like a badge of honor, as if he were a silent beggar, advertising that he accepted charitable donations. Dad could have picked up a new pair of pants at the Salvation Army for just a few dollars, but he refused to throw anything away, preferring instead to have me rehabilitate his clothing. His filthy white sneakers were in even worse shape than his pants. He had glued the front of the soles back on, and a small, frayed hole had developed over his big toe on his right shoe. His socks also had holes in the toes, exposing his thickened yellowed toenail. From this, the doctor must have surmised how much a single bill impacted our lives.

When we got home that day, my father told my mother the good news. Instead of celebrating the doctor's generosity and feeling relief that I would now be assured care, she yelled at me for not cleaning the table. Although I had recently revolted, I didn't dare point out that she hadn't asked me to clean the table. I had just walked in the door. Without complaining, I went to work picking through the mounds of garbage, careful not to throw out anything she might perceive as valuable—such as the partially eaten candy bars or old mail circulars.

Even as I struggled with my health, Mariah's behavior was worsening, and try as we might, we couldn't control her. She started fights with my sisters even when they were minding their own business. If my parents tried to send her to her room, she started yelling, running through the house, and bucking and kicking like a wild animal. At such times, the only way to keep her from injuring my sisters or destroying the house was to lock her outside. When Mariah wasn't outside, it was left to Lillian and me to control her—as if we, not my mother and father, were the parents. My father feared being arrested, and my mother did nothing more than screech at her wild daughter.

Unfortunately, Mariah was now my height and nearly fifty pounds heavier than me and had become too big for me to pin down or hold. When she became violent with the younger girls, all I could do was beat her off of them. Lillian helped me occasionally, but it was still difficult to control her. We would push Mariah away, trying to create space between her and the younger girls. Usually, after being separated from her victims, she would storm off to a different room in the house or outside. However, at least once a month, she wouldn't give up, and we had to escalate our efforts.

In such moments, Lillian—who was petite compared to Mariah—would jump on Mariah's back, grab hold of her hair, and ride her like a bull in an attempt to subdue her. Alternately, I would come up behind her and punch her in the back of the head to get her attention away from the little girls or whatever she was hell-bent on destroying at the moment. She would then turn on me, and we would scratch and bite each other. I tried not to hurt her badly, but I often bruised my knuckles in my attempt to stop her rampages. This brutality stopped her, at least for a few minutes, from hurting ten-year-old Amanda, eight-year-old Helen, and her favorite target, two-year-old Gabrielle.

Not wanting to hurt Mariah, I tried bribing her, but this was increasingly useless. She frequently stole money, usually mine, whenever she wanted to buy something at the convenience store. Sometimes, I'd grab a knife to threaten her. I had no intention of hurting her, but I wanted to protect myself and my sisters. Wielding a knife was effective at getting Mariah to settle down, but only for a few months. One day, as I was wielding a chef's knife, she grabbed a carving knife, and we started lunging at each other. Fortunately, she was slow and clumsy, and it was easy to kick the knife out of her hand. This scared her into submission. It scared me, too, but I tried hard to appear in control.

I often felt nauseous after resorting to such measures, but Mariah had no higher intellectual functioning. She could not be reasoned with. There was an uncontrollable rage and wildness in her eyes, and it was clear that she was acting on a purely aggressive impulse that came from some angry, frightened core deep within. I was afraid that she might kill one of my sisters and then, once she had calmed down, ask why they were dead.

After a fight, she sometimes locked herself in one of the rooms, and my father would demand that I get her out since she broke everything in her path. It was my job to calm her down before she caused too much damage. I spent hours halfheartedly trying to coax her out of the room by talking to her through the door, but I really didn't want her to leave whichever room she had chosen to hide out in. We were all safer with two hundred pounds of mahogany between her and the rest of us. I also knew better than to try to explain this to our father.

A couple of weeks before school let out for the summer, I was pulled out of class one day to be questioned by a state social worker. After a brief introduction, he jumped straight to the point of his visit: "Does your father ever hit or physically harm you or your sisters?"

I had heard stories of siblings being split apart by the child protective system and getting moved from home to home until they were simply left on their own to fend for themselves at eighteen, so I was wary of social workers. Being split up and lost in the system seemed like a worse fate than the abuse and chaos we lived with under our parents and Mariah. I wanted to keep my sisters together at home, even though I knew the high emotional cost for all of us.

"No," I answered, only partially lying. It had been at least a couple of years since he had hit anyone. In fact, my mother was more physically abusive. She would slap at Mariah and occasionally me, but was so weak it didn't hurt. However, the social worker hadn't asked about her.

"Are you sure that he has not struck or otherwise harmed anyone in the family?"

"Yeah."

"Can you tell me about your sister, Mariah?"

That was easy. "She's crazy. The things she accuses my dad of, she's actually the one doing. She attacks the little ones. Sometimes, I have to protect them from her."

"I've heard about that. How's life at home otherwise?"

"Fine," I replied in the dismissive tone teenagers are renowned for.

The nondescript man, whose name I had already forgotten, looked at me as if I had been wasting his time. "That will be all. You can return to class."

I had followed my intuition in responding to the social worker. I knew that telling the truth about my parents would result in us girls being taken away from them. Something about being separating from my sisters didn't feel right, and I felt that by hiding the truth, I was protecting them. With the exception of Mariah, my sisters and I were a team. Lillian and I looked after the younger girls, and we all supported one another, no matter how violent the storm. Lillian, Amanda, Helen, baby Gabby, and I rarely fought with one another. We were all just trying to survive the chaos. We were each other's protectors and champions. We needed each other. We were a band of sisters. The thought of being separated from them was unbearable.

When summer came, a brief respite from Mariah's torments unexpectedly materialized via an argument between Amanda and Mariah. Mariah responded by beating the younger, smaller girl. I stepped in and began pounding Mariah's back with my fists to stop her. Enraged, Mariah punched out the window in the kitchen door. Glass shards skittered across the room.

Mariah fled out the door she had damaged and made her way down Main Street to the apartment of her boyfriend, a guy in his early twenties whom she had met a couple of weeks earlier. We were suspicious of this "relationship" but felt powerless to keep her from him. The whole way, she was screaming that my father had beaten her and broken her arm. Blood was slowly oozing from cuts on her hand. Her boyfriend brought her to the hospital, claiming she was his wife so she could be seen.

Since the police were constantly picking Mariah up from Main Street and bringing her in for evaluation of her wounds, the emergency room doctors knew her by name. When they questioned her about her new marital status, she went into a screeching frenzy. They sedated her and held her there until that evening, when the doctor wrote out the papers admitting her to the Institute of Living, a renowned mental-health center not far from where we lived. She was then brought to the institute by ambulance.

Mariah remained there for three weeks. My father spoke with the doctors and visited her nearly every day after work. One of the nurses reported to my father that after kicking and biting her psychiatrist on the first day of her stay, Mariah had been tied to a bed by three big men who told her they would release her when she calmed down. Three days and many sedatives later, she finally quieted down enough to be untied. The doctors then worked with her extensively, treating her with medications and electroconvulsive therapy. My father hoped to keep her there for a couple of months so her therapy would be comprehensive, but when his mental-health insurance benefit ran out, he couldn't afford it.

The Saturday before Mariah came home, my father, most likely at the doctors' suggestion, brought the entire family to visit her. My mother threw a fit and refused to go to the "loony bin," so she stayed home with baby Gabby. The rest of us went to see if Mariah was sane yet. I hoped the doctors had given her a drug that had magically cured her.

We arrived at the hospital and drove past its handsome one-hundred-year-old brick buildings to a newer facility in the back. I expected to walk through cold white halls. Instead, we entered what looked like a hotel lobby. Dried flower arrangements sat on dainty wooden tables, with gigantic paintings of deceased psychiatrists displayed above them. The room was painted in soft, warm colors, with an overstuffed, pastel-blue couch in one corner.

We rode the elevator to the third floor. Mariah was in the upstairs lobby, which was also free of the expected sterility, waiting for us. Each of us in turn quietly said, "Hi," not sure how Mariah would respond.

"Go home! I don't want you here," she responded to us.

"We came to see how you were doing," I replied cautiously.

"I'm doing bad. Go away." Mariah turned from us as if to bolt, but then she seemed to decide against that.

Mariah had not improved as much as we'd hoped. None of us returned to visit her again, except my father.

A few days later, she came home in much the same condition as before, except now there was documented proof of her mental disorders.

I wanted to know what Mariah was suffering from. If I did, perhaps I could better understand what she was experiencing and manage her outbursts. When I asked, my father told me that she fit into eight DSM IV classifications, but he wouldn't tell me what any of her diagnoses were. He claimed the doctors had specifically told him not to share her diagnoses for fear of her being stigmatized.

This was just fine for my father, who was a man of secrets. He was more likely to come up with a legitimate-sounding excuse than to say the truth out loud. I often suspected he believed that if he just pretended something didn't exist or wasn't happening, then it would actually cease to be and would no longer be a problem. Denial was his protection. I thought he was ridiculous to deny the obvious.

Even decades later in life, my father claimed to have forgotten what Mariah suffered from. "Old age has set in," he chuckled, but I didn't find his evasion funny in the least. I was tired of being denied the truth. The only people in the family who benefited from these secrets were my parents.

While he blamed the country, the state, and his insurance company for not helping Mariah more, I now believe my father's denial of the severity of her condition was why Mariah didn't receive adequate mental-health care.

Since prodding the information out of my dad wasn't working, I started looking up her symptoms in my psychology book from school. I didn't get very far. She didn't seem to fit neatly into any category but had a myriad of traits from several types of mental illnesses.

I also wondered what my mother suffered from. If Mariah had been diagnosed with eight mental disorders, then my mother must have been suffering from at least a few herself. But according to my parents, they were normal. It was the rest of the world that was "crazy." I wanted them to admit to their shortcomings and perhaps even get some help, but I knew they were too deep in their denial. Help would never come for them or for us.

Chapter 17

Walking through the Valley of the Shadow of Death

Summer 1991

In the summer of 1991, shortly after Mariah was released from the mental-health institute, I once again attended the Methodist youth conference where I'd met Robert the year before. Naturally, I wondered if Robert would be attending again, too.

For weeks leading up to the trip, I kept myself busy trying to get in shape. I wanted to look my best in case Robert was there. I kept my caloric intake under one thousand calories a day. Each day, I went to the YMCA, put the stationary bike on the highest setting, and "rode" ten miles, burning close to a thousand calories. I was pushing myself as hard as I did for track. When I hit puberty, I had developed a small fat roll below my belly button, and it became my mission to shrink my gut so I would look good for Robert. I wanted to look like the girls in the magazines I bought at the convenience store, but my awkward body was angular and wide where I should be slender and slim. I was flat where I should have had curves—something akin to a starving Viking with a little belly.

After a couple weeks of this training routine, my hair started falling out in small clumps. I was constantly nauseated and woke up exhausted, even after nine hours of sleep. If I bumped into anything, I bruised. I convinced myself that I'd caught a virus and that my strict regimen would eventually make me feel better.

This year's conference was held at Camp Quinipet on Shelter Island, just off of Long Island. A couple of friends from my church youth group drove us down to the ferry. The hour-long ferry ride passed quickly, and our connecting bus was waiting for us when we arrived. As soon as I climbed aboard, several girls asked me if I was Robert's girlfriend from the previous year.

"No... Well, sort of," I responded, surprised that people thought he was my boyfriend.

I asked if he was coming this year, and some of his friends from home told me Robert decided to stay behind for a summer pre-calculus course so he could take calculus his senior year. I was deeply disappointed at this news.

At camp, my roommates were three extremely thin girls, all friends from the same school. I was the only person in the room that weighed over a hundred pounds, although just barely. Rebecca and I became fast friends. She came from a poor family, like me, and had a genius little brother whom she was very protective of. She also told me she was a recovering anorexic.

The first night at camp, after everyone else fell asleep, she told me that she had become so thin from anorexia that she'd had a heart attack. She nearly went into full organ failure in the hospital. It was a miracle she'd survived at all, and now, it was her mission to rescue her friend, Christine, from a similar fate.

Christine was Austrian-American and was the second girl in our room. Her mother had won a couple of beauty pageants in her youth, and Christine constantly talked about how she wanted to be just like her mother. She took diet pills, which she ate like candy, swallowing two or three at a time, several times a day. She claimed they were sustenance in themselves. "Models aren't fat like me," she would constantly say. I wondered if she could see, as I could, the bones in her arms or the dark shadows under her eyes.

Of course, at this point, I didn't look much better myself, and I too was blind to these physical changes in myself.

Still, I liked Christine. She was genuine and sweet and clearly experiencing some sort of emotional turmoil. I had a feeling that, if we had the time and she was willing to open up to me, we could relate to each other.

The third girl in our room, Claire, was the only one I didn't get along with. She and I disliked each other the moment we introduced ourselves. Like Christine, her parents had emigrated from Austria, and her father was a master chef who cooked for movie stars. She carried herself arrogantly, walking with an exaggeratedly straight posture, chin high, looking downward at me over her high cheekbones. I couldn't have cared less about her "important" lineage, and she picked up on my disdain.

On the third day of camp, I received a phone call from my father. I was surprised to hear from him or anyone in the family and, looking back, I wonder if perhaps the therapist that he was seeing made the suggestion.

It was a fairly typical exchange for a teenager:

"Did you have any trouble getting to camp?"

"No."

"Are you having a good time?"

"Yes."

"Did you bring everything you need?"

"Yup."

But then, right before we said goodbye, he said, "I love you."

Not knowing how to respond in the moment, I replied, "Well, say hi to everyone for me. Bye, Dad."

That was the first time he'd ever told me that he loved me. I was caught off guard, completely unable to repeat his words back. I didn't really know what I thought of him. Did I love my father? I didn't know. My feelings toward him would have been best described as guarded.

The moment was so intense, I retreated to the safety of my room and the book I'd brought.

As I sat on my bunk bed reading, Rebecca walked in. She went over to the dresser, grabbed Christine's whole container of diet pills, and stuffed it into a pocket in her long, flowing skirt.

"Don't tell Christine that I took these," she said. "I'm going to bury them in the woods behind the cabin. I don't want her to end up in the hospital for three months like I did. I almost died."

"Don't worry. I won't say a word."

Before Rebecca could leave and carry out her plan, Christine walked in. She went over to the dresser, presumably to take some more diet pills. When she realized they were gone, she tore through her drawer, bed, and suitcase. "Where did my pills go?" she wailed. "Rebecca, have you seen them?"

"No. You shouldn't leave things like that out in plain sight. Somebody probably stole them."

"Denise, have you seen them?"

"No. No one else came in while I was here. But I just got here a few minutes ago." It was a half-lie.

"What am I going to do? I need those pills. I'm not thin enough. No one understands. I *need* them! What am I going to do if they're gone?" Her anxiety caused her voice to tremble and her pitch to rise. She started digging through her belongings, as well as everyone else's, including mine, but I said nothing and did not move to stop her. I watched her despair in silence. I could feel how lonely and lost she was. She didn't realize that she had friends there, friends that were protecting and helping her. Even I, who barely knew her, understood her. I could see myself reflected in Christine's pain. So could Rebecca as she took Christine in her arms and motioned for me to leave the room.

As I exited, I had the sudden realization that I too had an eating disorder. Perhaps because I could see myself in Christine's pain, the thought dawned on me. I had believed I was only getting in shape.

Later that night, I took a moonlit stroll alone along the pebbled beach after our evening program. I climbed the rocks that stretched out into the sound and reached down into the water. Tiny glowing sea creatures swirled around my index finger as the salty breezes caressed my body. Slowly, the agitating fragments of my thoughts settled like the sand, and I became an extension of the calm waters. I felt God with me, comforting me.

The next day, I began eating regular meals again. A day later, I returned home.

Of course, nothing had changed at home, and the pain I felt there was now even more acute and piercing after my brief reprieve. I'd had a tantalizing glimpse of freedom, but nothing more. I felt trapped and I couldn't envision my life actually changing for the better. I felt as if I was being teased instead of being shown what was possible.

In late July, a week after camp ended, I was home alone in my bedroom. My parents had gone out to get groceries with my sisters, but I'd elected to stay behind. I wanted to be alone. I'd spent the first half of the summer looking forward to seeing Robert again, but he hadn't come to camp. That evening, the vast emptiness of my disappointment swallowed me. My unfulfilled expectations of a romantic reconnection had left a bottomless black hole in my heart. I had to escape this feeling, which was even worse than the daily fear and pain I endured. I could not withstand the nothingness.

I took out the bottle of Tylenol that I kept in the small cabinet above the refrigerator in my bedroom, sat back down on my bed, and opened it. A mass of pills rolled out onto the pink satin-and-lace comforter I had carefully picked out as my birthday present seven months earlier.

My mind was blank. I felt nothing but a compulsion to swallow the pills. I rolled them under my palm, spreading them across the comforter. Then I picked up a few. The first five pills slipped down my throat with ease. Since I again lacked the motivation to get a glass of water, the rest felt stuck in my throat. It felt like I was swallowing small, rough pebbles. I took a pill for each year I had lived through. After ingesting sixteen pills, I sat on the edge of my bed, waiting to die and hoping that sixteen was enough to do the job.

Death approached slowly. Becoming impatient, I decided to walk to Luxaya. I hadn't been there since the storm the previous year, but it seemed like the ideal place to lay my body to rest. Plus, if I didn't die from the pills by sunrise, Devil's Jump-Off cliff was a short hike away.

Yet as I walked toward my once-beloved secret spot in the woods near my high school, my feet would not obey me. I walked right past the road that led to the woods. It was almost as if invisible hands were holding my shoulders, guiding me straight ahead. When I reached the end of the short street that continued past the turnoff for Luxaya, an ominous building loomed before me.

My feet had brought me to the hospital, but I still wanted to die. I turned back toward Luxaya but stopped, frozen in my tracks, as if my feet refused to carry me back. Instead, I crouched down in the darkness behind some hedges. I willed myself to stay put and not advance any further toward the hospital. The roar of cars drifted to me through the trees. They never stopped—just like the pain that was my life.

Let me die, God, I prayed. But instead of dying, I stood up.

I can't do this anymore, I implored, believing that He would finally let me take my life if I could just convince Him of its futility.

But rather than convincing Him, it seemed that my prayer was just empowering Him to lead me to His own outcome. I started walking toward the hospital. *No, God, please. Let me die.*

But steady feet carried my thin, shaking body through the emergency room doors. I stood in the waiting area for a few minutes, trying to figure out what exactly I was doing there. Eventually, the receptionist came over and asked if I was hurt. I looked at her and started crying.

Through my sobs, I blurted out my name and that I had swallowed sixteen pills. I was immediately brought into the emergency room. A nurse asked me for my parents' names and phone number and gave me Ipecac, which caused me to throw up more than I ever had in my life.

As my head bobbed in and out of a garbage bag, a doctor began talking to me. He asked me why I'd swallowed the pills. I told him that I didn't know, and he didn't press for more information.

After calling my parents, the nurse asked if I wanted to call a friend as well, but I didn't want to bother anyone this late at night. Plus, I didn't want any of my friends to know what I had done. Other than Steve, none of them knew about my attempts at ending my life. There would be too many questions that I wouldn't or couldn't answer, and we would just end up sitting in awkward silence.

A few minutes later, my father arrived at the emergency room with Helen. Seeing him, I felt keenly embarrassed. I was always the strong one at home, and I felt emotionally exposed now in the hospital. My father attempted to cheer me up with a series of random bad jokes as the nurse drew blood from my arm so they could determine if it was indeed Tylenol, as I said, or something else that I had swallowed.

I had arrived at the emergency room around nine, and it was close to eleven when I was handed a bottle of liquid charcoal to drink with a straw. "You'll want to throw this up, but try to keep it down. Otherwise, you'll have to drink another bottle," the doctor said.

I eyed the bottle in my hand suspiciously.

"It's meant to soak up any Tylenol left in your stomach and safely remove it from your body."

After my first sip, I was determined to keep it all down, just so I wouldn't have to repeat the experience. It tasted exactly as I would expect charcoal to taste, like grainy dirt. My lips and teeth were coated with the black grit. I forced myself to swallow the muddy liquid in large gulps.

A few minutes later, the nurse took another blood sample, which confirmed that the levels of Tylenol in my system had started to drop.

The doctor returned and said, "You'll just have to stay here for another hour or two. You'll be fine."

As he opened his mouth to say more, noises in the hallway distracted him. A woman in labor had been rushed to the emergency room. The hospital was no longer equipped for births, but her baby was on its way.

I looked out of my room to the pregnant woman lying on a stretcher just outside. She was young and pretty, even as screams of pain escaped her pursed lips. Her husband was running around her, first holding one hand, then the other. I knew that neither parent was contemplating the idea that someday their baby might wish it had never been born.

Minutes before I left the emergency room with my father and sister, I heard the mewling of an infant. It was like something out of a surrealist painting: behind one curtain was a teenager trying to end her life, while behind the next was a newly born baby with ecstatic parents. Had my parents once been delighted at my birth? Perhaps for a moment, I contemplated, but that was a very long time ago.

The next morning, when I entered the kitchen, my mother was standing near the table. "You took all of my Tylenol last night. You could have at least bought your own." Her voice was shrill and just one octave below a shriek.

"The Tylenol was mine," I snapped back.

"Then where did mine go? The bottle was full yesterday," she howled.

"You probably lost it. I bet it's in the back of the cabinet somewhere."

"I hate you. You're not good for anything. I wish you were never born. You're... you're useless."

Although I hadn't expected my mother to come to the hospital with my father the night before, I was surprised that her main concern now was her missing Tylenol. I dug through the cabinet dramatically and found her lost bottle of pills in a coffee mug. I threw it at her and stomped back up to my room.

That night, we fought again, this time about the dishes—our usual argument. "Denise, get down here and wash ninety-three dishes," she screeched up the front staircase. She always gave an exact number, usually an odd one.

"I still don't feel well. Why can't someone else wash them for once?" I shouted back down to her.

"Because I told you to wash the dishes."

I made my way downstairs to the kitchen. "I'll wash them for ten minutes," I said. The chore typically took over half an hour.

"I told you ninety-three!"

I am not your slave, I thought to myself, but instead of vocalizing this thought, I ran outside into the driveway. My mother followed. "Go on, leave! You never help anyway. I wish you had died last night. The funeral would have been far cheaper than the hospital bills!"

"No, it wouldn't," I shouted back, as if my words could actually convince her otherwise.

"I'd have buried you in the backyard in a garbage bag," she screamed.

While my mother had often shouted terrible things at me, in the wake of my suicide attempt, this was possibly one of the worst. I ran down the street, crying and irrationally envisioning my burial in a garbage bag. I knew my mother was like a child who said anything that entered her mind, and I had learned to distance myself from her words over the years, but this was still deeply upsetting.

Since I had no idea where to go, I made my way back home thirty minutes later and snuck up the back stairs to my room. I saw that the kitchen was empty, the dishes not done.

Later that night, I couldn't fall asleep and didn't want to stay at home in my room, which was as creepy as ever with its dark door-less closet and randomly moving objects. I went out again to take a walk and made my way down the road I had taken just the day before. Amber light filtered through the leaves of the trees lining the sidewalks, casting a dim glow on the pavement. I didn't know where I was going. I just kept walking.

Eventually, I made it to the high school. Just past the student parking lot, there was an old field that was occasionally used by some of the sports teams, but for the most part, it was forgotten. I walked into the center of that grassy moonlit rectangle.

At that moment, I felt like there was a thin veil between this world and the next, like a sheer cotton curtain. If you got close enough to it and stared long enough, you could make out the movement of light and shadow on the other side, but none of the images were clear. For most people, it billows away from them, remaining just out of reach. But some people exist along a tear in the fabric, and once in a while, they find themselves accidentally stumbling through it. I had often felt that I was such a person, and this was such a night.

I stood there in the moist grass, wondering why I had come to this particular spot. The air was cool and fresh. I inhaled deeply while gazing up into the night sky. The thousands of stars above me seemed so far away, yet they were so clear. I felt the beauty of the night all around me.

"Why, God?" I asked the night sky. "Why did You save me?" I had no doubt in my mind that God had intervened the night before and yet again prevented my self-induced demise. I'd had no intention of walking to the hospital. It was almost as if I had been carried there.

I noticed that the air around me on the field was still, yet the surrounding trees were rustling, as if a light breeze was blowing through them.

"Why don't You want me to be with You? Why do You keep saving me, yet leaving me here?" I wailed up into the clear heavens then fell to my knees sobbing.

I was devastated and angry with God. I felt as if God were saying, "I love you, but you can't be here with Me." I felt somehow rejected by Him.

The trees stirred even more. I sensed something ominous moving behind them, yet I was safe and protected here. The air around me remained still, like it was cradling me. I could feel God there with me, listening.

"Why won't You let me die? I'm worthless. What good could I possibly be to anyone? Why do You keep me here only to suffer?" I sputtered through my tears. I thought I saw a dark shadow dart between the trees. It made me shudder, but I didn't move. Warm tears streamed down my cheeks, running alongside my nose and to my upper lip. I tasted the warm, salty liquid.

"Why am I going through this?" I cried. "I give up, God. I give up. This life is Yours. I'll do whatever You want me to do. I can't live this way anymore. Please, God, please help me through all this. Tell me what I'm supposed to do. Tell me why You keep me here. My life is in Your hands. I turn it over to You. I just want to be with You, and if You want me to live, then I need You to carry me through it."

I looked up at the stars again. Tears dripped down my cheeks and onto my jeans. Warmth spread through my chest from somewhere deep within. It was unexpected and comforting. I felt as if I was protected and something—or someone—was watching over me. I sensed a shift in the atmosphere around me, something like a spiritual shudder, and intuited that it meant something was finally starting to work on my behalf. At the time, it didn't dawn on me that God had already been protecting me from both myself and others.

I stood up and wiped the tears from my face with the back of my hand. My knees were soaked from the dew that had settled on the grass. The moon bathed me in its warm light, and I stood still for a moment, soaking it in. I felt as if all the cells in my body were singing. I had never felt so close to God. I sensed that I was at a turning point and that God was going to intervene somehow. I knew something was going to change. I could feel it within my soul.

"Okay, God, my life is in Your hands now," I repeated. "Do with it what You think is best. If You can lead me through this chaos, I'll do whatever You ask, because I can't keep living like this. Show me the way, Your way, and I will follow You. I promise." I meant it with every fiber of my being.

Suddenly, the surrounding woods howled with movement, as if something menacing was about to jump out at me, like in my nightmares, and it shook me from my reverie. I darted back to the empty parking lot and the comfort of the streetlights. Slowly, I made my way back home, breathing in the crisp, cool air in long, deep inhalations.

Although I had been dead and rotting inside for months, something living did indeed remain in my hollow shell of skin—a single fish swimming in the Dead Sea. God's fish. I felt it at last. I had felt God within, but the hollowness I had lived with for so long was comfortable and secure. It was hard to let it go.

My thoughts of death subsided slowly in the coming days, but pulling myself out of the depths of despair was a difficult task. With every passing week, I pushed back thoughts of suicide by reprimanding myself for such a selfish and pitiful desire. I reminded myself that my death would only hurt the people I loved the most: my sisters. That night, I had made the decision to endure, but I still had no idea who I was or where I was headed. And yet, for the first time, I knew I was headed to something better. I just didn't realize that road would be a very long one.

SECTION III

RESURRECTION

Chapter 18

Creeping Transformation

Fall 1991–Spring 1992

After such a profound encounter, I expected my external world to immediately change for the better. But as week followed week, nothing changed. Still, I believed that God would work a great miracle in my life soon and would whisk me away from my misery.

I continued to pray every day and attend church every week, but life did not improve. Even so, I knew now that God was with me. I felt His presence like I might feel that of someone sitting beside me in the dark to keep me company. That night in the field, I had made the decision to endure, but I had no idea how to get beyond simply enduring. Still, for the first time in a long time, I knew I was moving toward something better.

I kept my experience in the field to myself. I was afraid my friends would tell me I was crazy and reject me, and I felt I needed to be strong for my sisters. I didn't want to burden them with another crazy family member. Even with my church friends, who would have been supportive, I still failed to open up. I felt it was the best way to protect everyone.

The fall of my junior year was much the same as the one before it, with the same routines and stresses. I struggled through the cross-country season and performed poorly. I just wasn't a good runner anymore. I wasn't built the same, and I was constantly afraid of hyperventilating and collapsing, as I had the previous year.

When winter came, I caught the flu, as I did every year. For days,

I vomited and had no appetite. One evening, feeling somewhat better, I pulled myself out of bed and walked to the mirror. When I looked at myself, I saw I had wasted away. I had lost all of the weight I'd gained back after my bout of anorexia, plus another five pounds. Conscious of my protruding ribs, I decided I needed to actively work on regaining some weight.

The next day, I felt well enough to return to school. As I walked through the halls with Dawn, I noticed posters on the walls for an upcoming weightlifting club meeting.

"Hey, Dawn, let's join weightlifting," I said impulsively.

"But there's only guys in weightlifting."

"Exactly," I said. "All the more reason to join!" I grinned at her.

"I don't know." She really didn't seem all that interested.

"Come on, I don't want to go alone," I begged.

"Okay. I'll meet you at your locker after school."

That afternoon, Dawn and I showed up at the weightlifting meeting early. When Coach Maddison arrived, he took one look at us and shook his head. "What are you two doing here?" he asked.

"We came to lift," I replied.

"Weightlifting is extremely tough. It takes a lot of determination and dedication. I had a girl try it a couple years ago, and she quit after two days. She couldn't handle it. Are you prepared to arrive here on time every day and not miss a day unless you're dead?"

"Yeah, I can handle it," I said. I was used to hard work.

Dawn, however, stared silently at the floor. Coach Maddison didn't even acknowledge her presence.

Throughout that first meeting, the guys eyed us suspiciously. They probably felt that girls would be a hindrance to the club, but I was determined and somewhat oblivious in my excitement to get in shape so that I wouldn't look like a scrawny freak anymore.

The next afternoon, I searched for Dawn to join me again, but she was nowhere to be found. So much for having a lifting buddy!

Aware of being an intruder in a boys' club, I stayed in the back of the room during our stretches, trying to remain inconspicuous. Though I rarely spoke, I showed up every day, and my hard work started to pay off. I began to transform from a stick figure into a lean, fit young woman. I began to actually like what I saw in the mirror, which was a welcome relief from hating my body. Plus, the exercise helped me remain healthy for the rest of the winter.

Shortly after weightlifting began in November, my school's drama department held auditions for the musical *Godspell,* an energetic dramatization of several parables from the Gospel of Matthew in the Bible. Since I was a poor singer, I was convinced I couldn't possibly land a part and declined to audition, but Dawn and Kelly decided to. A few days before tryouts, Dawn asked me to come along as moral support.

The day of the audition, I arrived late, and all of the auditioning students were already on stage, creating scenarios and acting them out. When it was time for the individual vocal auditions, only three people, including Kelly, volunteered. Once they had finished, the director looked out into the auditorium, where we were all sitting, and asked for more volunteers. When no one approached the stage, she asked again.

I began badgering Dawn and some of the girls around me to sing, but when they didn't budge, I jumped out of my seat and shouted, "I sing worse than anyone in this room, so I'm going to get up there and sing. That way, no one can claim they're the worst singer here. Then you'll have no excuse for not coming up." I ran up to the stage and sang "Mary Had a Little Lamb" at the top of my lungs.

Two weeks later, the cast list was posted. I had landed the supporting role of Gilmer, a feisty, comical character that fit me perfectly. I was shocked.

Dawn was offered a spot in the chorus, and while she never said she was angry with me, I had a feeling she was. She could easily have felt I'd stolen a part that could have gone to her. I was only supposed to be there to support Dawn, not capture one of the speaking roles.

As scheduling problems between other school activities and the musical arose, many students gave up their parts, and the chorus members began to move into the vacated roles. Every time Dawn heard that someone couldn't continue their role because of other obligations, she ran to the choir room to read the revised cast list. After a couple of weeks, she was the only chorus member left without a role. Since a chorus can't really comprise a single person, the director asked Dawn to be a shadow. She wore black and appeared in the death scene, in addition to working backstage.

Godspell filled part of the void in me. Between weightlifting, working three or four nights a week washing dishes at the Italian restaurant down the street, attending church youth group, and rehearsing for the musical, my life felt full and rich. I felt like I was part of a greater community that accepted me in all my different aspects. Plus, it was wonderful to be out of the house so much.

I owed much of my newfound freedom to Amanda. At eleven years old, she had taken over making dinner and helped our mother with the dishes and all the other random chores that I was missing when I wasn't home. The reprieve she provided helped me escape my parents' tirades and reduced the amount of time I spent in the house. This was vital for my emotional state because, even after more than two years, I was still afraid of the house.

Objects in my bedroom continued to move on their own, and the radio, which I played quietly at night to break up the silence, changed stations mysteriously. At least the flies had finally died out after I used every means available to kill them. Despite all my prayers and sleeping with my Bible, I still experienced weekly nightmares in which demons pounced on me as I ran through the darkness. I felt that something sinister still resided in my room.

I had given up on having a "normal" home life, so I avoided being at home as much as I could. It certainly made my life easier.

As my sisters and I had grown older, we'd started taking showers instead of baths. I snuck in showers late at night after everyone else was asleep, since the once-a-week bathing rule was still in effect. Despite having three bathrooms in the house, only one had a working shower, which was unfortunately directly at the foot of the attic stairs across from Mariah's room. That back hallway still spooked all of us, and we felt a sinister presence back there, particularly after dark. It was the same feeling one would get while walking down a dark alley in a seedy part of town late at night.

We all stayed in the shower just long enough to lather up and rinse our hair. I would shave my legs so quickly, I often nicked myself. Blood ran down my leg and onto my foot as I scrambled back to my bedroom with my wet hair dripping down the back of the towel wrapped tightly around me. We all had the uncomfortable feeling that an invisible voyeur was in there, spying on us.

The lights would flicker whenever we started the shower, contributing to the ominous feeling. I assumed it was due to a short in the wiring caused by the steam, despite running the vent fan. But then, one day, my sisters and I were talking about the light when Lillian said, "All you have to do is say, 'Shower ghost, stop that!' and the light will stop flickering."

The next evening, I tootk her advice and whispered loudly, "Shower ghost, stop that!" The light stopped flickering immediately and stayed on.

Our father did eventually check the wiring and replaced the light bulb in there, but despite his best efforts, the light continued flickering on and off unless we addressed the shower ghost directly. It worked every time.

* * *

It helped that the rush I experienced after working out kept me from sliding back into depression. I felt wonderful after working out, and I had energy for the first time in months. However, I was still very weak, and only a few of the guys were patient enough to spot me when I lifted. No one was impressed as I tried in vain to bench press the forty-five-pound bar. Even the coach just shook his head and turned away to help the guys.

Aaron, a sophomore, spotted me most of the time. We never spoke outside of the weight room, but while we were lifting, Aaron was always at my side, as if he were protecting me. I assumed that the coach had assigned him to me or that he felt bad for me because none of the other guys wanted to spot me. Still, after a couple months of constantly being next to his huge, strong, sweating body, I was smitten, even though I was sure he didn't find me attractive.

Late one night, as I tossed and turned, unable to sleep, I began contemplating the idea that no one could ever possibly think of me as more than a friend, in particular Aaron. Suddenly, through the darkness, the female voice who had intervened when I was cutting myself months before said, "He loves you."

I hated it when the messengers told me things I didn't want to hear. In this case, it was something I couldn't possibly believe was true. "Shut up," I snapped. "Stop teasing me, you—you voices."

"He loves you. You will see."

I didn't believe her.

A couple of weeks later, we had our *Godspell* dress rehearsal and performances. The musical was a hit. The auditorium was packed for every performance, and the standing ovations filled me with a feeling of acceptance I'd never known.

Once the play was over, though, the feeling of completeness disappeared. I was home more often, and that made me easy prey for my mother. I felt directionless again. Despite placing my life in God's hands, I still hadn't seen the types of changes in my life that I'd expected. Yes, life had improved, but I still felt like I was stumbling through darkness, like I continued to do in my nightmares. I used my activities to compensate for my lack of purpose and create an appearance of success that I desperately clung to and appreciated, even as I couldn't shake my sense of worthlessness. Something was still missing. Part of the void was still present, even as the scars on my wrists were fading.

The reprieve Amanda had provided me came to an end. I once again became my mother's gofer the moment I walked through the door after school. Since most of her requests continued to be frivolous, I felt like she was trying to prevent me from getting my homework done, as if she didn't actually want me to succeed.

One evening, after I finished the dishes, she ordered me to clear the kitchen table of the mounds of garbage and unsorted mail. This debris had been there for months, but suddenly, she insisted it be cleaned right away.

"Mom, I need to study!" I protested. "Can't I do it this weekend?"

"I told you to do it now!" she screeched.

"It's already 8:30. It'll take hours to go through everything, and I have homework."

"I don't care. I told you I want it done now!" she screamed, then reached out and slapped me across the face.

It wasn't a hard strike, but before I knew what I was doing, my own hand shot out and slapped her face in response. She stared at me in shock. I had never hit her before, but I'd had enough of being bullied. I turned and walked out of the room, leaving her standing in the kitchen, stunned. For a moment, I was proud of myself for standing up to her. Then I realized that retaliation would soon come and raced upstairs.

To my amazement, none came that night.

The next day, when I proudly told Lillian about the altercation, she squealed, "How could you hit Mom? That's our mom. You don't hit Mom!"

I was surprised at her reaction. I'd assumed she would be proud of me—in awe, even. "I was defending myself! She hit me first. Why aren't you backing me up?"

"Are you crazy? You hit Mom. What's wrong with you?"

"Am I supposed to just let her beat me?" I snapped before storming out of her room. I had never felt so alone and dejected. I would have given my life for my sisters, yet Lillian was siding with the woman who had emotionally and physically abused me, as well as her and the other girls, for years.

Looking back, I realize that Lillian simply didn't see all the abuse I was enduring. When she was home, which was infrequent, she was in her room, not fully aware of what I was going through downstairs. However, we were both right. Lillian saw our mother as someone who needed to be protected—a nearly blind woman with wild, tangled hair, who never wore a bra and reeked of body odor. I, on the other hand, saw a snarling, biting, wild animal backing me into a corner. I needed to protect myself, even if that meant fighting back. But at that time, I couldn't understand Lillian's response. I was angry at her and felt abandoned by her, my sister of all people.

I could feel the black hole of emptiness widening and intensifying again. I desperately wanted to fill it, and soon I had the opportunity to do just that by adding another new activity to my schedule.

Coach Harding, one of the football coaches who also helped with the weightlifting team, approached me at practice one afternoon. "So, Denise, are you going to play football with us this fall?"

"What? I'll get smeared!" I responded wide-eyed.

"You could be a wide receiver."

"What's a wide receiver?" I asked.

"Well, if you join the team, you'll certainly learn." He laughed good-naturedly. "Come to spring training, give it a try, and see what you think."

"Okay, sure. I'll give it a shot," I heard myself say. *What am I doing?*

Half an hour later, while I was spotting Tim on the circuit, I heard Coach Maddison exclaim from across the room, "What? You're kidding, right?" Both coaches were looking in my direction. Apparently, they had different opinions about inviting a girl onto the team, even if it was just the JV team.

I went to sleep that night wondering if I'd made the right decision in agreeing to go to spring football training. "Dear God," I prayed aloud, "am I going to regret this? I never seem to know if I'm making the right choices." I paused as I pondered all the ways I felt I was making poor decisions, and then added, "I don't even have a boyfriend. I must be doing something wrong with my life."

"Denise," one of the now-familiar messengers said clearly, "don't worry about not being in a relationship yet. Aaron loves you. You'll have a boyfriend when you're ready."

It was like listening to someone else's well-intentioned but ultimately clueless parents. *Yeah, right! I'll never have a boyfriend. Besides, Aaron barely knows me. We never even talk,* I thought back in response.

"Aaron loves you. You'll see. Be patient."

You're lying just to make me feel better.

"Wait. You will see."

A few days later, trusting God's messengers against my better judgment, I gathered enough nerve to risk rejection by asking Aaron on a date. After weightlifting practice, I half-chased him down the stairs and caught him just before he ducked into the boys' locker room.

"Would you like to go out for pizza or something on Friday?" I asked, unable to believe my nerve. Was I actually asking a boy out on a date?

"Sorry, I have to babysit my sister Friday."

"Uhh, how about Saturday then?" I asked, not deterred.

"My cousin has a graduation party I have to go to that day," he said. "But I'd like to go another time."

"Oh, that's okay. I was just wondering," I muttered, my courage failing. I was certain he was lying to spare my feelings. I was convinced that the angel had been wrong.

As I fell asleep that night, I asked God why His messengers would tell me that Aaron loved me when it was apparent he didn't even want to go out for pizza with me.

"He is telling the truth," the messenger from the previous week replied. "He wants to go out with you." For some reason, convincing me that Aaron loved me was important enough for God's angels to answer my repeated teenage-girl requests.

Although I wanted to believe the messengers, I avoided Aaron at school the next day. As soon as the school day ended, he approached me in the hall near my locker. "Hey, Denise! You know, weightlifting doesn't start for another half hour. Would you like to hang out or something until it's time to go?"

"Sure." I was delighted that he had approached me.

We talked about nothing and everything on the outside steps of the weight room, which was little more than a gigantic detached shed with carpeting. When it was time, we walked into the weight room as if we hadn't spoken at all. When it was my turn on the machines, another classmate, Allen, walked over to spot me.

"I already told her that I was spotting her," Aaron said, stepping close. "Go spot Doug. He needs someone." When Allen walked away, Aaron smiled. Perhaps the angels really did know what they were talking about.

Not long after that, spring football training started. It was intense but exhilarating. By the time it was over, I was covered in bruises. But, like the cutting I used to indulge in, the bruises made me feel alive. Football allowed me to be fearless, throwing my body in front of large, young men who were speeding down the field and trying my best to stop them. I enjoyed the complexity of the plays and the mental determination required. It was a challenge I was ready to take on. By the time Coach Harding asked me if I wanted to join the team, I had already decided to play.

At our school, anyone could join a sports team, and if there wasn't a female equivalent team, girls were allowed on the boys teams. Extra players sat on the bench during games and moved up the roster as their skills improved. All that was required was that you show up to every practice, game, and team event and do your best.

Over the summer, we had weightlifting practice three days a week, with two sessions each day to choose from: one in the morning and another in the afternoon. Since I was still working at the Italian restaurant down the street from my house in the evenings, I lifted in the morning. Aaron, who was a lineman on the team, came at the same time. After we finished lifting for the day, we would sit on the bleachers or the lawn in front of the school and talk.

Aaron asked me out on a date for the Fourth of July. Within a week, we kissed for the first time behind the school. I was now seventeen and heading into my senior year of high school. His kiss was electrifying and his soft lips tasted like honey, making my entire body shudder. I was hungry for more. When he told me that he loved me a couple of weeks later, I believed him. And when I told him that I loved him, I meant it.

A few days after this, I rode my bike to his house. Just down the road was a stream a short distance into the woods. Aaron and I headed to an outcropping of large, flat boulders alongside the stream bed and sat on the largest rock as butterflies flitted past us in the bright sunlight. The rough granite warmed my hands and bare legs as I leaned back on it. I turned my face up to the sun and closed my eyes. It shone brightly through my pale pink eyelids. Dragonflies flew around us as helicopter seedpods twirled down from nearby maples. The sun reflected off the water like thousands of small diamonds. The moment was magical, like a romantic dream come to life. We spent the early afternoon there, kissing as Aaron fumbled with the buttons of my shirt. Carefully, he slid his hand under my spandex shorts. As his fingers inched further down, I pulled his head to my lips, afraid of and exhilarated by what might happen next.

That night, he called me, and we talked about contraceptives and what we would do if I got pregnant. The conversation was so intense, I nearly started crying. We had been dating for only a month and we both knew how easy it would have been that day to "go all the way." His voice came through the phone sounding shaky and uncertain. I wanted to hold him, to touch him, to tell him that everything would turn out fine, even as I worried about the outcome myself.

After that conversation, we backed off over the next couple of weeks, opting to talk and kiss instead of fooling around. Although the passion between us was strong, he seemed to be distancing himself from me. His grandmother was dying, and it upset him a great deal. I begged him to talk to me about it, thinking I could help. He explained that she was all he had left of his father, who had died when he was an infant. Then he changed the subject.

I helplessly tried to hold onto Aaron, but he was slipping away from me. One day, when I called him, we talked for about ten minutes before he said he had to go clean his room. This became a frequent excuse to end our calls, and he rarely called me back after finishing the so-called chore. It irritated me that he kept using the same lame, obvious excuse. I thought I was at least worth a creative lie, or maybe even the truth.

Near the end of summer, after begging Aaron to speak to me, we snuck up the back stairs to my room to talk more privately. The house was quiet since my sisters had left to go "on an adventure" on their bikes, and my mother was reading a book in the rocking chair in the hall.

After talking for a while, we began kissing. Before I could clearly think about what we were doing or what I wanted from our relationship, he was sliding on a condom, and our two bodies merged into one. All the horror stories I'd heard at school about picnic tables and the backseats of cars vanished for those few moments when I couldn't distinguish where I ended and he began.

We barely spoke afterward, and he left quickly.

When I woke up the next morning, I wondered if I should tell my friends. A part of me wanted to call them immediately and blurt out the news, while another part wanted to keep it to myself. I worried about what they would think and decided to keep it to myself. Aaron and I talked about it and continued speaking daily for the next couple of weeks. He gave me his jacket in exchange for my class ring, which he wore on a heavy gold chain around his neck.

Then, as my senior year started, we both got busier with school and saw each other less often.

One day in mid-September, he calmly told me that he had to attend his grandmother's funeral, as if death were an everyday event. I understood that this was a particularly difficult event for him. Aaron handled his grief by withdrawing.

The less he spoke to me, the more I spiraled into my usual negativity. I doubted my self-worth. In an attempt to rescue our relationship, I kept having sex with him, desperately hoping it would be enough to make everything all right. But my desperate clinging to him only drove him further away.

In early October, he wrote me a note saying he wanted to see other girls. I tried to call him, but he didn't answer. Instead, our friend Tony came up to me after practice a few days later with a message: "Aaron told me to tell you that he's dating Jennifer again." He walked away from me, shaking his head.

Chapter 19

Toughing It Out

Spring–Winter 1992

While Aaron and I had been together, my parents' craziness had receded into the background of my consciousness, but now their destructive force came to the fore again. I quickly started to spiral back down into depression. I was still starving for the love and intimacy I didn't receive at home and was desperate to have someone who would be there for me. Of course, it was unrealistic to look to a teenage boy to rescue me from my life, but I was young and naive. After all, my father had swooped into my mother's life when she was only nineteen. If I had thought it through, I wouldn't have wanted my parents' relationship, but I was not mature enough to make these distinctions yet.

When the heavenly messenger told me that Aaron loved me and that I should be patient, I'd had hope for a better future, but now I found myself questioning why she had said such a thing. I knew that Aaron had loved me—I had felt his love—at least as much as any adolescent boy can love his girlfriend, but I needed more than he could give. I needed a parent—a real one—and a therapist. I needed to heal. Aaron could not possibly provide these things.

Not long after my relationship with Aaron ended, Dawn told me about a guy named Jason whom she was going to hook up with our friend Joan. She told me about how he played guitar and was a little bit of a "bad boy." He sounded interesting, and I half-jokingly asked if she would give me his number instead.

"You two wouldn't be right for each other," Dawn said. "He's a better fit for Joan."

"Okay, but if she doesn't like him, I'd love to have his number."

It was a casual request, and the thought of Jason and his phone number quickly escaped my mind, as I was still hung up on Aaron. I wanted to restore the peace I had known all too briefly with him, and I somehow managed to convince myself that I could win him back and make my life endurable again.

Meanwhile, I tried, with mixed results, to get a respite from the pain of losing Aaron and the absence of his emotional support by concentrating on football. Of course, this was difficult, since Aaron was also on the team. I was a terrible player to begin with, and with this distraction, I played even worse.

I was a receiver, but I wasn't good at catching the ball. It often bounced off my helmet and shoulder pads. Twice, the ball got stuck in my face mask. A couple of my teammates who refused to hit me lifted me in the air instead and held me there as I laughed in embarrassment.

But for every player who shied away from hitting me, there was another who wanted to beat me into quitting. It enraged them that none of their tactics of harassment made me leave. Apparently, working out with them in the weight room was one thing, but being on the football team was beyond what they could accept, even though I was only a JV player who received virtually no game time.

Still, despite my lack of coordination and skill, the distraction of Aaron's presence, and the harassment of other players, I enjoyed playing. It made me feel alive. For the first time in my life, I was allowed to fight back, to stand back up after being flattened and say, in my mind, "You can hit me, but you can't keep me down."

Even though I struggled to keep up with the guys, I developed what I thought was a great defensive technique as free safety. After the player carrying the ball knocked me over, I would grab onto his leg and let him drag me along the ground until one of the other defensive backs tackled him. The stronger receivers were able to drag me two or three yards before they were tackled. Everyone but the freshmen who were my size hated this strategy.

The guys who wanted me off the team got some measure of revenge the day one of them sacked me from behind during drills. For a couple of seconds, I lay on the ground, unable to move, gasping for air. When I staggered to my feet, my vision was gray and hazy. I stumbled back down the field, barely missing the line of blurry players. I opened my mouth to swear, but all that came out was, "Fu, fu, fug." Coach Harding, who was running drills, pulled me out for the remainder of practice. For the next six weeks, a sharp pain shot through my chest whenever I took a deep breath.

Around this time, a reporter came to interview me about being the first girl in Connecticut to play on a previously all-male football team. I felt awkward answering his questions and gave short, simple answers. I think he was hoping for something inspirational, perhaps a story of a girl who had tossed a football around with her father in the backyard as a child. He appeared disappointed when I explained that I had joined the team because I was a member of the weightlifting club.

Of course, my reasons were more complicated than that. I had to prove to myself that I was capable, valuable, and special, despite what my parents had been telling me. Even though I was a terrible player and football might not have been the best medium in which to prove myself, it did allow me to channel my self-destructive behaviors into something marginally healthier. But I couldn't tell the reporter any of this.

When the reporter noticed my bruises, he asked how I endured the hits.

"I don't know. Just tough, I guess," I said simply. But I knew that was a lie. I was still suffering from loneliness and a sense of worthlessness. I was in emotional pain from losing Aaron; any toughness I displayed on the football field was only an emotional front so that no one else would see how weak and desperate I was.

That desperation to reconnect to Aaron surfaced on the bus ride to our rival school on the opposite side of the state, who we played against every other year. Eventually, I fell asleep on his shoulder. I was back in heaven again, and all the angst of the previous weeks dissolved. I had received what I'd been praying for.

A few days later, we had sex again. Afterwards, I asked Aaron, "What are we?" He responded by saying that we were friends. My heart sank. I didn't want to be friends. I wanted to be more. I wanted to be loved. Within days, he stopped returning my calls.

At this point, my true friends had had more than enough of our relationship. They told me again and again that I was obsessed with Aaron and needed to move on and forget him. I knew they were right, but I desperately wanted to be loved and clung to the hope that he would once again return my affections.

In fact, at this point, my friends' loyalties were divided between Aaron and me. When he was around but not speaking to me, I became weepy, morose, and generally unpleasant to be around. Aaron was always warm, funny, good-looking—a great person to have at parties. He was in theater with many of my friends, including Dawn and Kelly. Since I had not landed a role in the fall play after auditioning, I was no longer part of that circuit. Dawn and Kelly started inviting him to their parties, since he was so much fun to be around. They knew we weren't having an easy time together and didn't want our bad feelings spilling out into their good time, so I was omitted from the guest lists for these gatherings. I was even shut out of their birthday parties, which I had been invited to for over ten years. Soon, they stopped inviting me out with them entirely.

I sank further into myself and drifted away from people in general. Now I was isolated not only from Aaron but from Dawn and Kelly, too. Without Aaron and my friends, I didn't know where to turn for help getting out of this emotional mess. Even my church youth group had broken up since the majority of the teens were a year older than me and had graduated. I didn't have my license, so I was unable to get to the Aventura group meetings.

One afternoon, when Dawn and I bumped into each other in the school bathroom, I made a blatant attempt at receiving her sympathy after watching Aaron pass by the door. "Dawn, I don't know what to do. I can't stand seeing him in the halls," I cried.

"Get over him. Who cares?" she snapped back.

Shocked at her callousness, I ran from her, dashed out into the hall through the throngs of students, and made my way out the school's side door. I kept running and didn't stop until I was in the student parking lot within sight of the field where I'd begged God to help me and to take control of my life. Seeing the field stopped me in my tracks. *Where am I going?* I thought.

I turned my face upward toward the bright sun, closed my eyes, and took a deep breath. I was aware that further isolation was a very dangerous thing for me, but I felt powerless to control my downward spiral.

What am I doing wrong, God? I wondered. *Why is my life getting worse, rather than better?* If I hadn't already hit bottom before, how much further down could it possibly be?

The next day, neither Dawn nor I spoke a word to each other, even though we had several classes together. We each wanted an apology from the other, but neither would give it. Kelly quickly filled in as mediator, trying to explain each side to the other. Dawn felt I was being juvenile and unfair, since she believed I would get better simply by forgetting Aaron. I wanted some sympathy, not another piece of my life dismissed and tossed aside. I wanted some kind of acknowledgement that I was hurting. And what I really wanted was to have Aaron and my friends back. Neither Dawn nor I apologized, and I simply gave up on pursuing my friendships with Dawn and Kelly.

How was I to ease my pain now that I'd lost all my friends? I was in a state of despair and began contemplating taking aspirin to end it all when an angel came to me.

"God loves you, and He wants you to live," the female voice said gently yet firmly one night after my standoff with Dawn.

"I just don't get it. Why would He care so much about me living? I told Him that He was in charge, and look at where I am. He hasn't taken over at all. I'm still not what I want to be. I'm still nothing," I cried into my pillow.

"You're beautiful. That's what you are."

"No, I'm not. Why are you lying to me?" I felt so dark, ugly, and empty inside, like a shriveled prune with an empty, rotten pit. I couldn't imagine myself looking any different on the outside.

The angel did not respond. I was angry at God and His messengers for making me feel guilty about wanting to kill myself. However, I could feel the messenger's love and sincerity. It seeped into me like warm sunshine after a month of overcast skies. She was so matter-of-fact, so sure. A part of me trapped deep inside knew she was telling the truth.

Because Aaron and my friends had abandoned me and because I was still young and didn't want to accept responsibility for my own life, I blamed them for my misery's resurgence. But as time passed and I contemplated the past few months, I realized *I* was the one responsible for my destructive actions. Not Aaron, not my friends, not my family, and not God—*me!*

I was the one not having fun. I was the one swallowing pills. I was the one covered in bruises. I was the one that hated my life. I had somehow chosen, or even created, this existence, and I was the only one who could change it.

My life was a road that I alone had to travel, but perhaps God could help by throwing me a lifeline. I knew He was there, looking out for me. After all, if that weren't the case, why was He sending me all these angelic messengers to tell me that He loved me and didn't want me to die? Why had He guided my feet to the hospital the night I swallowed all those pills? Why had He comforted and protected me that night on the field?

Of course, this realization, however spot-on, didn't stop me from feeling like I was shattering. I didn't know how to integrate this new realization into my life to improve my emotional well-being. If anything, I was slipping deeper into the darkness again, and my world was spinning out of control. While I believed that God didn't want me to die, I couldn't make the pain go away.

Still, something fundamental in me had changed with this realization. I removed the aspirin bottle from my nightstand. God had let me know that He was with me, yet the responsibility for changing my life lay with me.

My life is a journey only I can take, I repeated to myself over and over again.

It set me on the path to improve my own existence. I started working on changing myself versus waiting for God to send someone to me. Somehow, I was going to live. I knew God was there; I could sense Him in the darkness of my room as I wept bitterly. He watched over me like a caring parent listening outside my door. I could feel that He worried about me and waited patiently for me to open up and let Him in.

* * *

My father had a black leather biker jacket that he'd worn as a young man. As hoarders do, he'd held onto it after gaining weight, even though he hadn't worn it in more than twenty years. Something about it spoke to me. When I asked him if I could have it, I assumed he wouldn't trust me with it, and I expected resistance. Yet the day I asked, he was in his "loving dad" mode and was happy to give me his jacket. I was delighted.

The jacket hung so loosely over my thin frame, it looked like I was swimming in it, but I loved it. As winter came on, I walked to school in it every day, relishing the jacket's weight draped over my shoulders. It was like a suit of armor. It screamed, "Don't mess with me. Don't talk to me. If you do, I will hurt you."

Surprisingly, students at school actually heard the jacket's warning. They parted before me as I walked down the halls in it. On weekends, when the weather permitted, I wore it as I rode my ten-speed bike around town, since I wasn't allowed to drive. I felt like a badass, completely impervious to the ridiculousness of a tall, thin, blond girl in a gigantic leather biker jacket riding around on a ten-speed.

One afternoon, as I was biking down the wide sidewalk flanking Main Street, one of the messenger's voices popped into my head. "Stop. Your front tire is going to fall off," he said with a sense of urgency.

That's ridiculous, I thought back as I kept riding, not even considering that I should listen to the voice.

Within five minutes, I hit a curb while crossing the street. My tire caught the cement, the fork of my bike where it attaches to the rim of the tire bounced off the rim, and my tire rolled away from me. I flipped over the handlebars and somehow surprisingly landed upright on my hands and knees. They were scuffed, but that was the extent of my injuries.

With a jolt, I realized that I should have listened to the messenger who had warned me just minutes earlier. This was important proof to me that the messengers weren't just a hallucination or delusion brought on by mental illness and that they were trying to protect and assist me. I already knew this, but a small sliver of doubt had persisted. Now, this warning of a future event left me no choice but to believe.

Neither the messengers nor the jacket were enough to separate me from my comfortable misery. I was no longer afraid that the world would see my misery and judge me for it, so I stopped running from it. I went from coping back to not coping, from being emotionally strong to being weak again. I stopped caring about anything and anyone other than my sisters. My senior-year grades continued to fall. I hadn't even signed up for Latin that year, a decision I came to regret, since my Latin teacher had been one of my favorites, and I had been a Junior Classical League member for the past three years.

I stayed up until 1 or 2 a.m. every night, tolerating the random noises and moving objects in my room while writing poetry and drawing. I hoped that when I did fall asleep, I would be too exhausted to dream. If I didn't dream, I couldn't have nightmares. The problem with this solution was that I often ended up sleeping through my classes. I may have been alive, but I was not living.

Aaron came by my house to wish me a happy birthday on January 12th. I invited him upstairs "to talk." I wish I could say that we "made love" in my room that afternoon, but the truth was that it was more of a desperate clinging. I imagined that was what it's like to be an addict, to keep making bad choices out of desperation, even when I knew better.

Then, to make matters infinitely worse, I missed my period later that month.

Chapter 20

Seeking Prince Charming, Again

Winter 1992–Summer 1993

Missing my period terrified me, and I plummeted further into anguish. I had never skipped a month before and was convinced I was pregnant, but at that time of older technology, it would be another three weeks before I could get an accurate reading on an at-home pregnancy test. Afraid of this terrifying reality, I didn't tell Aaron—or anyone else—about the missed period.

I needed to escape from the looming specter of pregnancy, so I joined another all-male sport: wrestling. I was looking for the kind of emotional release that playing football had given me, and joining the wrestling team allowed me to run as hard and as fast as I could away from depression and myself.

Aaron was also on the wrestling team. Looking back, I should have walked away from the sport to put distance between myself and Aaron, but I was self-destructive, and I believe a part of me still hoped for reconciliation. Plus, the busier I was, the less time I had to think and the less I hated myself. This approach worked well until I crumbled under the burden of my schedule.

At this point, I rarely spoke to any of my former friends, except for Paul and another mutual friend, Scott, both of whom sat with me at lunch. Neither gave a damn about Aaron, who hadn't spoken to me since our birthday tryst. I also befriended some of the potheads, who were warm and funny. They couldn't have cared less about a breakup—or about anything, for that matter. Their marginality fit well with my current mental status, like outcasts who couldn't have cared less. I was still spiraling downward despite my efforts to rise above my emotional chaos. As I did this, my classmates were submitting their applications to their favorite colleges and taking road trips with their parents to visit the campuses. My father was oddly silent on the subject. We both knew there was no chance of a full-ride scholarship to Princeton in my future, which meant college was now out of the question.

When I went to the required session with my guidance counselor at school, he explained that the total cost for a public college like the University of Connecticut, including room, board, books, and fees, was just under twenty thousand dollars a year. Furthermore, the maximum loan and scholarship amount any student could personally get at UCONN was fifteen thousand dollars, unless they were on a full sports scholarship. This would require a minimum annual contribution of over five thousand dollars from me or my family, and where was I going to get that? This was at a time just prior to new student loan legislation being passed that would allow students to sign their own loans for the full cost of their tuition. My father had made it clear that he wasn't about to pay anything himself or sign his name to any loans. The guidance counselor recommended that I live at home and attend the local community college, and while his logic was sound, there was no way I was going to choose to remain with my parents.

With this in mind, and still weighing my options regarding a potential pregnancy, I called the Army recruitment office. The Army recruiter was pushing a crane-operator position, but I was interested in health care. When I explained this, he told me that there was an available position as a dental lab technician. When he started explaining the various benefits I would receive in the military and mentioned the GI Bill, which would help pay for my education, I was sold. The Army seemed like the answer to getting me out of the house and financing a college education.

The next day, the recruiter came to my house to interview me. When I opened the door, the pungent stench of cat urine wafted out from behind me. I was embarrassed and didn't want to let him enter, but I was desperate to enlist, so I led him into the kitchen. The table was smeared with grime from a month's worth of dinners and was piled high with the usual junk mail, discarded wrappers, crumpled paper towels, and half-eaten boxes of candy. The floor was littered with torn paper grocery bags full of winter clothing that we'd out-grown, abandoned toys, and empty two-liter soda bottles. In one of the corners, the cats had created their own litter box in the piles of debris. I expected the recruiter to pause or gasp when he saw this mess, but he did neither. Later in life, I realized that he had likely seen similar neglect and disorder in the course of his duties and had the emotional intelligence not to draw attention to a situation that a teenager would have no real control over.

I directed him to Mariah's chair, which was closest to the door, and he immediately sat down with his folder full of paperwork and started asking questions from his checklist. Though I was nervous and anxious, I answered his questions as honestly as I could.

His last question was, "So, do you still want to enlist?"

"Yes!"

"Okay, then. I'll make the arrangements for your physical exam, and since you don't have a driver's license, I'll drive you up to Springfield for your exam and paperwork."

Physical exam?! I should have thought of that. I internally groaned. I still wasn't sure whether I was pregnant, and I was worried that being pregnant would prevent me from enlisting. I spent hours each night praying that I wasn't and pondering what I would do if I were. Abortion seemed like my best option.

I was also worried that I might fail the Army's physical due to a recent wrestling injury. A couple of weeks earlier, as we'd been prac-ticing holds, I'd heard a crunching sound and felt my right shoulder pop out of its socket. I'd glanced down at my arm; it had looked disturbingly pushed back. I asked Scott, my lunch buddy who was on the team, to grab my hand and pull. He looked at me with an expression of half-fear and half-concern, but he reluctantly agreed. I twisted my torso until my arm loudly cracked back into place. It was a painful maneuver, but it helped me regain some mobility. Scott squirmed when he felt the joint give, but I continued practicing despite the pain.

Since the season was more than half over, I tried to tough it out and show them I could do it. But with one arm injured, I often ended up flailing around on the mat, like a bass tossed on shore. I became known as "the fish," and the guys frequently threw themselves onto the mat, imitating my thrashing and laughing.

After joining the wrestling team, I'd initially thought that seeing Aaron every day at practice would make it harder to get over him, but as the taunting from my teammates became more severe, I no longer noticed him. He never stuck up for me or asked about my arm. His complete lack of support helped me start getting over him.

When I was far enough past my missed period to get an accurate reading on a pregnancy test, I took one at home. The negative result relieved my worries. I had been living in secrecy and near-terror for more than three weeks. It had been traumatic. Now, I could finally leave that fear behind me.

At this point, my senior year was well past half over. Lillian was sixteen; Mariah, fifteen; Amanda, twelve; Helen, ten; and Gabrielle, four. Except for Mariah, my sisters were all growing up to be strong, intelligent, and socially well-adjusted young women. I prided myself on having raised the little ones well—or at least as well as I could. Amanda and Helen now got themselves up in the morning, did their homework on their own, shared the responsibility of helping Gabrielle, and even took turns helping me prepare dinner. I was proud of them.

As they matured and took on more responsibilities, I was able to shift my energies from caring for the family to caring for myself. Since my mother kept complaining about how much I ate, I began buying my own food. When my father still refused to allow me to use the washing machine, I walked the mile to the laundromat, carrying my clothes in a black thirty-gallon garbage bag. The few times I tested the water with him and asked for permission to use the washer, he launched into a tirade about how he was sure I would break it and how he didn't have the money to repair it. According to him, he was the only responsible person in the house.

After that, I decided that walking the mile through the snow, looking like a bum, was better than listening to another angry lecture about how we were all incompetent. The extra effort was worth it to get the musty smell of spaghetti sauce out of my clothing, and it gave me the opportunity to start washing my bed sheets, which hadn't been laundered in years. Plus, now that I was eighteen, my mother had started charging me rent. Granted, it was only ten bucks a week, but I got the hint: I was not welcome in her house. Thankfully, I was still working at the Italian restaurant down the street, which helped me afford all these extra expenses.

My mother appeared to have given up trying to force me to bend to her every whim, but being charged rent—even though I was still in high school—felt like being kicked out of the family. In some ways, it was worse than her previous abuse. She would ignore me and never made eye contact, even when I was in the room. It was as if I had been erased. At least when she was screeching at me, I knew she saw me.

I still wanted a "normal" mother, but I knew that wasn't possible. It was clear that she suffered from some sort of mental illness, although it was different from what Mariah had been diagnosed with, whatever that happened to be. I was still angry at my mother for having so many children that she couldn't care for and for making poor decisions, even as I was making poor decisions of my own.

Mariah, now over 170 pounds, had become uncontrollable. She spent her time walking up and down Main Street, snorting and kicking her right foot up and back at her butt. I suspected that she wanted to be anywhere but at home; enduring the elements was preferable to being subjected to my parents' emotional instability—the same instability she exhibited. The Connecticut Department of Youth Services told my father that if she continued wandering around downtown late at night, they were going to place her in a foster home. To prevent this, my father started cooperating with the police whenever they brought her back to the house. It was the first time I heard my father have a civil conversation with them. I was also surprised that, despite her violent tendencies, he tried to keep Mariah at home. I wasn't sure if it was due to misplaced pride, a sense of responsibility, or the fear that the authorities might take all the children.

My father was unable to control Mariah's outbursts and didn't restrain her for fear that she would run to the police, so he let her come and go as she pleased. Plus, having her out of the house was a reprieve, like being in the eye of a hurricane. When she was home, I continued to protect my other sisters from her whenever I could. Mariah chose Gabrielle as her preferred target, regularly tormenting her by pushing her onto her back and then sitting on her chest so she couldn't breathe.

I was at work the day my father drove Mariah, Amanda, Helen, and Gabrielle to the grocery store to pick up a couple of items. On the trip home, Mariah went into a rage because Gabrielle had poked her. She grabbed Gabrielle by the throat and began choking and shaking her. Helen and Amanda stared in horror, stunned and frozen in place. My father stopped the car, reached past my sisters, and pulled Mariah away from Gabrielle. Able to breathe and cry again, Gabrielle huddled in Amanda's lap.

Later that night, Helen recounted the story to me. Her eyes filled with guilty tears over her inability to rescue Gabrielle, as if she herself had some terrible character flaw. If Mariah had been around at that moment, I would have threatened her with terrible consequences if she ever repeated the incident. This would have made me feel better about being at work that day, but it probably wouldn't have prevented a reoccurrence. Instead, I went to the grocery store to pick up a few items for myself.

When I got to the store, my friend Joan was working the register. I happened to remember the name of the mystery guy that Dawn was trying to hook her up with and asked her if she'd called Jason yet. As usual, her reply was, "I'm not interested. I don't want to go out with a seventeen-year-old. That's too young for me."

"I'd love his phone number, then," I said.

I had asked for his number a couple of times before and this time she answered, "Okay! I actually have it with me." She handed me a small, neatly folded piece of paper with nothing but a number carefully written on it.

"Thanks," I yelled back as I hurried toward the door.

I decided to call Jason the next day, an hour before the recruitment officer took me to my Army physical. I still couldn't believe I finally had the phone number of someone who didn't know anything about me or my family, and I was intrigued by the prospect of meeting someone new and having a fresh start. My finger spun around the rotary dial, trembling in anticipation. The phone began ringing on the other end.

Nuts. What do I say? I wondered. I was so excited to have finally received his number, I hadn't given any thought to the actual conversation.

"Hello?" an impatient male voice answered.

"Oh, hi! Is this Jason?"

"Yup."

"My name's Denise. You don't know me or anything, but I got your number from Joan, who got it from Dawn, who got it from Mark, who's your best friend, right? I heard you play guitar. What can you play?" I asked brightly, disguising my panic at calling someone I had never met.

"Yeah, I was expecting a call from Joan a while ago. To answer your other question, I can play some pieces by Metallica and Led Zeppelin," he said with considerably more pep in his voice.

We talked for another half hour after that, and our conversation was interesting enough for me to call again a few days later.

"Hi," I said in a high-pitched, bouncy voice when Jason answered the phone. I stepped out onto the porch for some privacy, pinning the twisted, knotted, ten-foot-long phone cord between the door and its frame. However, I quickly retreated inside due to the late-February snow blowing in my face.

"I've been waiting for your call," he said, his voice warm. "How'd the physical go? Do you know where you're going yet?"

By then, the recruiter had confirmed I would get the position of dental lab technician, as I had requested, and that I was to be assigned to a base in California, a state that I'd always wanted to visit.

Jason was helping at the YMCA down the street from my house, and a few days later we were able to meet there in person. It was a fortunate coincidence, since neither of us drove yet. He looked like a rock star, with his long hair pulled back in a sleek ponytail. I was hooked.

Within a few weeks, I was regularly staying up until three in the morning, talking to Jason. We talked about our families, our aspirations, and anything else that came to mind. When the conversation died, he would play "Stairway to Heaven" for me on his guitar. While listening to his soothing voice, I would curl up on one of the kitchen chairs and cover myself with sweaters to warm myself against the cold that penetrated the room. We even occasionally fell asleep while still on the phone and would have to wake one another up without creating too much noise.

At one point, Jason told me that he was sixteen—a year and half younger than me. This surprised me, since Joan had told me that he was seventeen, but at that point, his age didn't matter. Talking with Jason until late at night was like being drunk. There was a sort of euphoria to it. We were both struggling adolescents who used each other to lift ourselves out of depression, and we were just glad to have one another. We were both trying to figure out our place in the world.

Talking to Jason helped dissipate the anxiety produced by my home life. The craziness there had caused all sorts of problems outside of it—just as a problem with one part of the body can throw the rest of it off. Now I had Jason to balance home. He provided the support and feeling of being cared for that Aaron had once given me. It was like a drug to me, and I gave up everything else in my life to pursue it.

Because I was on the phone with Jason every night into the early-morning hours, I was regularly two or three hours late to school. I spent most of my time at school in the library, catching up on homework. When I did go to class, everyone was surprised to see me.

One afternoon, my English teacher approached me in the hall to point out that I had skipped his class every day for three weeks. I found an easy excuse to slip away from him, and he didn't pursue the issue further, although I did start attending class again for fear that he might fail me. I didn't realize until years later that he was attempting to reach out to me. If I hadn't avoided him, he may have been able to help me navigate the emotional storm I was traversing, but I was skeptical of adults. In my opinion, they were too preoccupied with their own lives to help a "raggy" like me.

After years of fantasizing about an Ivy League education, here I was skipping class and joining the Army. I knew there was nothing wrong with the Army, but it wasn't the path I'd thought I was destined for.

I was surprised that neither of my parents yelled at me about staying on the phone all night or about being absent from school. Stable parents certainly would have taken issue with such behavior. Instead, my mother was still conspicuously silent around me, and my father just seemed relieved that I had found a way to pay for my education. It was an out for both of us: I wasn't pressuring him financially, and I wouldn't have to continue living at home.

Though I had desperately craved this freedom from their tyranny for years, their lack of acknowledgement only deepened my depression and anxiety. I was like a child's toy that had been kicked under the couch and forgotten. I wanted parents who would say, "We love you. How was your day?" That was not going to happen.

What did happen was that Jason's voice became my world, and my voice, his. We were alike in many ways, both of us having grown up poor and taken care of ourselves to a certain extent. He felt abandoned both by his parents' divorce and by his mother sinking into a prolonged depression that left him fending for himself. At last, I had found someone who understood me and spoke the language of my soul.

He must have felt the quick, close connection, too, and he clearly didn't want to lose it. He frequently tried to convince me to stay in town after graduating, but I was still intent on joining the Army and leaving.

One day in late March, he asked, "What are we?"

I'd been wondering the same thing. Obviously, we were more than friends, but exactly how much more, I wasn't sure. We hadn't had any intimate contact yet, but we did have the type of emotional bond that I would have expected from physical closeness. "I don't know," I said honestly.

"Okay, then. Do you want to go out?"

"Yeah, sure." The exchange felt a little silly, but it at least formalized our commitment to one another.

On Saturdays and Sundays, I now worked from five in the morning to one in the afternoon at Dunkin' Donuts. The new job came with more hours and higher pay than I'd gotten in my previous job as a dishwasher and pizza prepper. When my shift ended, I would sneak in a quick shower—still conscientious of my mother's one-shower-a-week rule—and then ride my bike the eight miles to Jason's house, even though I was already exhausted.

The heavily wooded scenery along the roads was broken up by

marshes and ponds. Then, after a steep, mile-long incline, there was a picturesque reservoir within a ring of lush green hilltops at the trailing edge of the Berkshire Mountains. The hills reached out for miles and faded into the horizon.

When I arrived at his house, I always found Jason waiting for me. We would take care of small repairs around his house or go grocery shopping with his mother. Other times, we'd take a walk or go on a bike ride—as if I needed more exercise!

We often rode to one of the nearby undeveloped cul-de-sacs. There were a lot of them around there. We'd stand in the turn circle, entangled in each other's arms as we watched the sun set, letting the breezes tickle our faces while raspberry-and-apricot-colored clouds spilled across the sky. Then came the stars, and with them, Jason's warm kisses. I melted into him. He was my prince who had come to save and protect me.

While the hours I spent with Jason were wonderful, time at home ticked by slowly. I started taking driver's education classes after school that April without my parents' permission or knowledge. While my father had forbidden us from getting our licenses because he didn't want to pay for the extra insurance, I saw all my classmates getting their licenses and felt that it was time to prepare myself for adult-hood, despite what I perceived as my parents' efforts to hinder my maturation.

Nearly every night, my father ranted at me about not driving: "Don't you dare forget that you're not allowed to live here anymore if you get your license. If you don't like it, there's the door. Leave!" He would forcefully point toward the back door with its brown streaks and duct-taped window that Mariah had shattered so long ago.

When I didn't respond, he'd continue, "You kids are killing me. Any day now, I'm going to have a heart attack and die. And then where will you all be? On the street, that's where, because you can't support yourselves. Just yesterday, I had heart palpitations, and they're getting worse every day. It's not like any of you can hold down a job.

Nobody can do anything around here but me, and it's killing me. Where will you cunts be then? Huh? Answer me! Where will you be then?"

I didn't bother to answer. My father didn't actually want an answer. He just wanted to yell, to bend us down under the weight of his fury, to push us beneath him in the pecking order of the world. So I stood there, straight-backed but looking down at the table, as his voice bellowed through the house like the warning whistle of a great steamboat about to crash into us all. Though I acted as if his tirades didn't bother me, and I didn't believe what he said, his words pierced through my ears, shot down my spine, and sent cold shivers of dread into my heart. Why was I always singled out as the recipient of his rage?

Despite his warnings against driving, I decided to get my license anyway and just not tell him. I knew his ravings were not idle threats and that he would keep his word, but I had already enlisted in the Army and would be leaving home in October. Being able to drive seemed like a vital skill I would soon need. To cover up the fact that I was taking driver's ed after school, I told my parents that I was on the yearbook committee. Amazingly, I passed my driving test after only two hours in parking lots with Jason and his mom and another six on the road with my instructor.

Graduation that June held little importance for me. Although my entire family, Jason, and his mom attended to cheer for me as I walked across the stage, I had mentally left high school months earlier. I had given up on my education and was ready to begin the next chapter of my life.

Chapter 21

An Unexpected Blessing

Fall 1993

O ctober of 1993 approached too quickly for both Jason and me. Afraid we would lose touch and perhaps never see each other again, I started having second thoughts about joining the military, while Jason became moody and went through spells of anger and depression.

But in spite of my apprehension about losing him, I stuck with my plan to join the Army. Now that my sisters were older and caught up in their own social lives, they barely seemed to notice my absence. Lillian, Amanda, and Helen were old enough to hold their own and mature enough to take care of each other and little Gabrielle. They would be fine without me. There was little I or anyone else could do for Mariah. Besides, my parents had always focused most of their anger on me.

When October arrived, I packed a few essentials, said a tearful goodbye to Jason and my sisters, and began my journey to boot camp in South Carolina. My sisters were happy for me. They saw the Army as a positive next step. My father, who had managed to avoid the draft by being underweight during his years as a hippy, had mixed feelings about my joining the military. He was relieved I had found a way to pay for college on my own but was worried that I might get deployed to a war zone. My mother had no comment at all. It was as if this was happening to a girl she didn't know and not her own daughter.

The journey south began with a ride north. My recruiter drove me up to the Military Entrance Processing Service (MEPS) building in Springfield, Massachusetts, for a final medical checkup. Since our plane was scheduled to leave early the next morning, the military put us up in a hotel overnight. That evening, as I lay in bed, one of the angel messengers came to me. I hadn't heard from any of them since they had warned me about my bike tire, so I was startled to hear the voice in the darkness again. "It's over, Denise. It's over," he whispered gently.

"What's over?" I asked, but there was no reply.

I immediately assumed the messenger meant my relationship with Jason was over, and that worried me. Determined not to let the relationship end, I began writing a lengthy letter to Jason, but fell asleep writing it.

The next morning, the other recruits and I were woken at 4 a.m. and herded into a van that took us to the MEPS building. After waiting a couple of hours for my turn, I was ushered into an office to go over my medical files one last time with an Army physician before leaving for basic training.

Everything went well until the doctor commented, "It says here that you have a mild tricuspid regurgitation."

"A what?"

"A tricuspid regurgitation. They found it when they did an EKG a couple years ago. It means the tricuspid valve in your heart leaks back a little blood after it contracts. It's nothing to worry about. It'll probably never bother you."

I had completely forgotten about the cardiologist's findings from back when I was running track. "But is it going to be an issue for me as far as the Army's concerned?" I asked. In my heart, I already knew it was going to be a problem. This was what my angel messenger had been talking about the night before, not Jason. My heart sank before the Army physician could even reply.

"We always double-check everything before sending you off to boot camp. I'm just going to make some calls to make sure you have clearance. I don't expect it to be an issue, but they require us to look into it. We should get an answer in half an hour."

Two and a half hours later, instead of flying to South Carolina for basic training, I was in a car with my recruiter, returning home. "This almost never happens, especially since you already passed your physical," the recruiter said in an attempt to console me.

"I guess I'll think of something else to do," I replied quietly. I was deeply disappointed to be returning home when I thought I had said goodbye to it for good. Of course, I didn't tell him that. Instead, I said, "I joined to earn money for college. Now I don't know how I'll afford school."

"There are ways. You just have to look for them," he said consolingly. "You know what I do? Every morning, when I get up and look at the paper, I turn to the obituaries first and thank God that I'm alive."

That's nice, I thought sarcastically, remembering how many mornings I'd awoken wishing I were dead instead of having to face another day of my life. Aloud, I sighed, "Yeah, that's a good idea."

As we drove home, I suddenly remembered my license and how I wasn't allowed to live at home if I had one. If I went home now, it was only a matter of time before my father found out and kicked me out. I didn't want to deal with that drama. I wanted a normal life that included having a license and going to college. My palms grew sweaty as I worried about what I would do next.

I had already said goodbye to my old life, and I didn't want to return to it. A few months earlier, Kelly's dad had offered to let me stay with them if I ever needed a place to go. I considered calling Kelly when I got back to town, but quickly rejected it. Between the rift that had formed between us after Aaron broke up with me and just becoming caught up in our own lives, we hadn't been speaking regularly anymore. I didn't feel comfortable calling her with such a huge request, even if she was my only option at the moment.

As we approached the Connecticut border, I still hadn't decided what to do next. To give me time to think, I asked the recruiter to drop me off a quarter-mile from Jason's house. His place was on the way into town, so the recruiter wouldn't have to take a detour; in fact, it would save him some time. I reasoned that going to Jason's and hanging out there for a few hours would give me time to think and come up with a plan.

After letting me out, the recruiter waited for me as I walked up the hill with my bag. He was probably waiting for me to change my mind and get back in. Crimson and yellow leaves from the surrounding woods fell around me, swirling at my ankles in the crisp fall breeze.

I stopped for a moment, unsure if I really should continue on to Jason's or just get back in the car with the recruiter and return to the well-known, albeit chaotic, rhythm of my parents' house. I took a deep breath, then turned and waved goodbye to my recruiter, who was still pulled over on Route 218. I'd made my decision. With that, I turned down the narrow side road that led to Jason's house, disappearing behind the crest of the hill. As I stood alone, surrounded by the woods that day, I chose a new path for myself.

It was still early when I arrived at Jason's place, and no one was home. I sat on the steps, waiting, my mind churning. The Army had been my one opportunity to break away from my parents and the emotional turmoil they wrought. I couldn't bear the thought of returning home.

"What am I going to do?" I worried aloud.

Should I just go home, look for a job, and find an apartment? Could I ask Jason and his mom to let me stay with them for a while? How would my relationship with Jason change if I lived with him every day? Was I ready for that? Should I just go ahead and call Kelly?

I prayed, *Dear God, please help me. I don't know what I'm supposed to do now. Where am I supposed to go? I've handed my life over to You, but now I feel so lost. How do I get out of this mess I'm in? You spoke to me and told me that it's over. I realize You meant my military path, but what's next? I need You.*

I need You to tell me what to do. Please, God, please, help me, show me, lead me. I just don't know what to do.

I continued praying like that until Jason's school bus pulled up at the end of the driveway. When he spotted me sitting on the steps to his house, I didn't have to tell him that I'd been discharged. He knew. Before I could say anything, he said, "Stay with me."

Once we got inside, I told him what had happened and shared my disappointment at being back in town and having to deal with my parents.

I had been planning on asking him and his mother, Susan, if I could stay with them, but he beat me to the suggestion. When Susan got home an hour later, she echoed the offer, saying, "You can stay here. There's a little bed in the kitchen you can sleep on." They both knew about my home life and how difficult it was.

And that's what I did.

After a few days, I called my parents' house. My father answered the phone, and I told him that I hadn't been inducted into the Army after all due to my heart condition and that I was back in town. I didn't tell him why I hadn't come home and just said I was staying with Jason. For his part, my father didn't inquire if I was all right or ask me to come home. I didn't really expect him to. I gave him Jason's number and asked him to let my sisters know where I was and to give them my new phone number. When I heard them chattering in the background and asked to speak with them, he replied sternly, "I'll tell them where you are."

I'm sure he never actually told them where I was or how to reach me because after the call, a full month went by without any contact with my family. Though my parents had Jason's number, they never once called me, nor did I hear from Lillian, Amanda, or Helen, who I'm sure would have checked in with me if they'd known how to reach me. I should have sent my sisters a letter, but I assumed, erroneously, that they knew how to reach me and were simply mad at me for not returning home to them. This separation made me feel like I really had left for a faraway state, even though I was just a few miles away.

I settled into life at Jason's place. He was in his junior year of high school and was occupied with schoolwork and activities, while I was not. For the first time, the dynamics of our lives were different.

Of course, I continued to be disappointed over losing my chance to finance my college education through the military. My recruiter had said there were other ways to pay for college, and I wanted to believe him, but for now, it was a moot point: it was October, and classes at the local community college had already started. More pertinent was the question of what I was going to do now.

Susan solved that problem by offering me a job with her on the morning shift at McDonald's where she was a manager, and I accepted. I wasn't afraid of work; if anything, I worked too hard, which was one reason my mother had so easily taken advantage of me. Plus, I needed to make some money. Susan and Jason were already living pretty close to the edge, and I knew I needed to pitch in.

Susan and I left the house at four o'clock each morning so we would have everything prepped and ready for the store's 5 a.m. opening. The work was palatable, and I was grateful to Susan for making room for me on her shift. It wasn't easy, but it was better than the alternative of returning to my parents' house.

Even though I didn't consider Jason and his mom to be poor, they were far from affluent. In fact, Jason's house was mostly unfinished. All the floors were particle-board subfloors covered with a few well-worn, soot-stained area rugs. Most of the shelving consisted of flimsy wire units on wheels packed with random small items in cheap plastic containers. An entire section of the house, which was meant to be an enclosed sunroom, consisted only of framing. Large sheets of painter's plastic were tacked to the beams to keep the rain from ruining the particle-board flooring of the sunroom. There were tears in the plastic, and water splashed in during violent storms, soaking the boxes of rusting, sun-faded memorabilia of Susan's life before her divorce from Jason's father.

My parents' home was also badly in need of repair, so this new living environment with all its rough edges was somewhat familiar to me. Another girl might have chafed under its primitive condition, but I didn't.

The small makeshift bed in the kitchen was another matter, and I missed my far more comfortable bed in my old bedroom. This "bed" was really just a bench seat measuring five feet in length and consisting of a sheet of plywood on a two-by-four frame barely eighteen inches off the ground. The "mattress" was a two-inch-thick piece of foam with a twin bed sheet tucked around it. At night, it took me a while to adjust my bony shoulder into a position I could actually tolerate in order to sleep. I still kept my Bible, which I had packed in my bag to take to boot camp, close by in case I had a nightmare.

Shortly after I settled in each night, the cats would slink over and jump up on me. They often slept on my head or nested in my hair, which I didn't mind because they kept me warm. The house was heated by a wood stove at the edge of the kitchen and two space heaters: one in Jason's room and one in Susan's. Around two in the morning, the wood stove inevitably burned out, causing the temperature to plummet in my part of the house. By the time I awoke at 3:30 a.m. to get ready for work, the house's internal temperature had usually dropped to fifty degrees. When I rose from bed, my nose was often cold and pink, my head and face were covered in cat hair, and I had a headache.

Since we lived high up in the Berkshires, there was no municipal water or sewer available. There was a well, but it frequently ran dry. To conserve water, we showered only once or twice a week, and then, just for three minutes. Any water that would otherwise have gone to waste—such as the cold water that came out of the showerhead at the beginning of a shower—was collected in a bucket. This bucket was then placed beside the toilet so we could use the water to flush the toilet. There was no sense in wasting three gallons of water from the well just to flush. We washed our clothes at the laundromat and brought them home to dry, to save both the water and the two dollars. There were times when we arrived home late and forgot to put the clothes in the dryer. By the next morning, a sour smell in the kitchen would alert us to our oversight.

Despite these problems, Susan and Jason's house offered a sense of calm I had never experienced before. Even with others present in adjacent rooms, there was a feeling of comfortable solitude in the house, rather than the anxiety I had grown up with. A quiet melancholy mixed with delicate beauty, like a lovely fading flower, infused the home. A discarded past—the result of Susan's divorce—had not yet been cleaned out of the place, and it lingered. Yet the atmosphere within seemed to spring from the surrounding forest, as if the trees themselves had taken over and whispered through the airy rooms. I could feel myself starting to heal there.

It was no longer necessary to be on guard at every moment, fearful of unreasonable eruptions and brutal name-calling. There were no mysterious moving objects, swarming flies, dark shadows on the stairs, or self-closing doors. At Susan's house, I began to relax. I felt safe. I felt love and acceptance.

Jason and I continued to be boyfriend and girlfriend, but as we lived together in his mother's home and were subject to Susan's rules, we began to slip into a brother/sister relationship. After all, Jason was still in high school, while I was technically an adult. We continued to cuddle, but the magic of the previous summer was waning. It was as if I had been adopted by Susan, and although I didn't realize it at the time, my relationship with Susan profoundly affected my relationship with Jason. Increasingly, it was my relationship with Susan that dominated my life. I was experiencing what a "real" mother was like. I finally found a real live person that I could have conversations with, whom I could emulate.

In late November, I had an early-morning dental appointment. I had forgotten that I'd made it six months earlier, but since I was back in the area and I loved my dentist—who somehow magically remembered random details of my life—I decided to try to make it. The dentist's office was only a couple blocks from my parents' house, which made it an easy walk from there. I took the day off of work and asked Susan to drop me off at my parents' house, which was only a couple of miles away from the McDonald's we worked at. I intended to wait there until the office opened.

I hadn't seen my parents since leaving for the military, and the idea of being at their house again made me a bit apprehensive. In preparation, I called a few days before my visit to let my father know that I wanted to drop by and maybe even catch my sisters as they were getting up. I loved the idea of surprising them with an early-morning hug. He seemed fine with it at the time, and we had a brief cordial conversation about what I was up to.

I arrived at 4 a.m. Although my father always locked the doors at night, the duct-tape patch over the back-door window that Mariah had broken no longer stuck to the corner closest to the lock. All I had to do was reach in under the duct tape to unlock it. I was sitting on the living room couch when my father, who was also an early riser, came in around five-thirty.

"Hi," he said, as if he had just seen me the previous evening, and not weeks earlier. He had prematurely aged over the past few years. Now forty-five, he had gained a considerable amount of weight, and portions of his long, bushy hair and beard had turned bright white, causing him to resemble a young, tired Santa Claus.

"Hi, Dad." I tried to sound cheerful but felt a little nervous, as I always did in my father's company.

"It's nice to see someone else up this early. How's work?"

"Fine. Morning shift sucks, though." We chatted for a bit, and he gave no sign of missing me or of being worried about me.

At one point, I explained that Susan had driven me: "I'll head out for my appointment in a couple of hours. If Susan hadn't needed the car for later, I would have driven."

"What do you mean?" he shot back. I realized instantly that I had made a mistake. We were back to the old days, the days I hadn't experienced while living with Jason and Susan. "You have a license?"

"Yeah," I answered gingerly.

"Did you get your license while you were living here? I told you a million times you aren't allowed to have a license! Why do you kids do this to me? What address is on it?" My father's voice bellowed louder with each question.

"I don't remember," I spat out, startled and lying.

"It better not be mine! You better go to the DMV and change it right this moment."

"But they're not even open," I pointed out. I knew better than to answer him as he entered into a rage, but it was early and I wasn't thinking.

Instantly, his face blazed red. "I don't care. If the DMV takes away the registration on my vehicle because you're not insured, I won't be able to pass inspection again. I'll be fired from work, and it'll be your fault when we go on welfare, lose the house, and have to sleep in the street."

"But..."

He raised his hand to strike me, but before he could pull it all the way back, I jumped off the couch and vanished into the early-morning November darkness. Hot tears warmed my cheeks, yet I was chilled to my soul. I hadn't emotionally prepared myself to be run out of the house so quickly on my first visit back, especially since my previous call had given me no indication of any impending strife.

The darkness sheltered me as I searched for a haven to hide in until the sun rose. I walked toward my dentist's office, assuming I could wait somewhere nearby until my appointment, not thinking clearly in my panic. I suddenly realized what a mess I must look and didn't want to be seen with my face wet and swollen and my eyes red. My nose had started running, and the thin liquid crystallized on my upper lip. Shivering too much to take my hands out of my pockets, I simply licked at the mucus.

That's when I spotted the Second Congregational Church a few hundred yards down the road. "God, please let it be open," I sniffled.

Much to my relief, the front door was unlocked, and it was warm inside. I headed for the sanctuary. The sun had just begun to rise, scattering shards of color from the stained glass and lighting the surrounding walls with abstract designs. Still too upset to sit, I paced around the sanctuary and eventually found myself entering a room with a large table and a dozen chairs, which I surmised was used for Bible study classes.

While inspecting the room, I came to an uneasy halt. Hanging on the wall before me was a large picture of Jesus, but a younger version of my father stared back at me from within the picture frame. The resemblance was uncanny. If Jesus' eyes had been animated, they would have looked exactly like my father's. I turned away in disgust. How could I see the face of my father in a man like Jesus? In my parents' home, my father reigned like a god, so perhaps the similarity was not that far-fetched, but it felt wrong, nonetheless. My father was an angry, merciless god, the complete opposite of the true God that kept saving me from my own demise.

On the bright side, my curiosity about the resemblance gave me something to contemplate other than the recent onslaught I'd experienced at home. I stared at the picture, attempting to discern some significance from it. I needed something positive to think about so I could pull myself together before stepping back out into the daylight. I reached out to touch the old dusty wooden frame and remembered that, when my father came up with a truly awful pun, his eyes sparkled. It was the only hint of life left on his beaten face.

I felt torn between "honoring thy father" and admitting to myself the truth of who he was as a man and as a father. I began to feel pity for him; pity was easier to manage at that moment than anger or frustration. Facing down the emotional impact of admitting that a monster resided within my father was more than I was capable of at that moment, and there certainly was a lot to pity.

This was a man whose brother had a professional, well-paying job as a librarian, whose father had been a physician, and whose grandfather had been an Episcopal bishop. Yet in spite of this background, which must have led him to believe he would continue to live his life in relative comfort, he was a poor man. His shoes had become so worn, he placed cardboard in the bottoms to cover the holes in his soles, but he allowed his right big toe to remain exposed through the hole in the top. His socks had long since worn away there, offering him no protection. The stains on his shirts and the patches in his pants, which I had sewn for him, had been there for years. The scars on his back from the severe acne he'd had as a teenager were visible through his threadbare shirts. But he *chose* this existence. He had the money to purchase clothing at the thrift store, but he didn't. He kept his aging wardrobe—like the dusty frame before me—never thinking to swap it out. He let the debris accumulate rather than going through the effort of replacing his worn-out belongings.

Was the gap between the promise of his early life and the reality he had created for himself the reason behind his screaming and rage? Or had the rage led to the life he had?

Even as my father was unsuccessful materially, he also was less than successful on the family front. All six of his children were constantly defending themselves from him. I felt like he believed we were his property and needed to be dealt with if we didn't adhere to his expectations.

Did he actually believe that if I had my driver's license, the family would end up living on the streets? I knew his logic was faulty and way over the top. I kept searching for something logical in his argument, but I gave up. I couldn't find anything.

But why did he have to look like Jesus, the one person I respected above all others, the most tangible part of the Trinity? Was there good in my father that I wasn't able to see, or was Jesus more of a faulty, struggling human than I'd envisioned Him being?

Attempting to figure out the psychology behind my father's

motivations and the connection I had made between him and Jesus was only making me cry more, rather than calming me down. I turned my gaze away from the image and toward the wall that was glowing in rainbow colors from the stained glass window. I willed myself to think of something good about my father in order to pull myself together before my appointment.

The first thing that came to mind was planting roses and day-lilies with him each spring. We'd planted flowers in the yard until we'd run out of room. I particularly loved the roses, which I quickly learned how to hold without getting pricked. They bloomed prolifically throughout the summer, creating a bright spot in our lives that we looked forward to every year.

Finally calm, I went to my appointment as scheduled.

Decades later, I came to appreciate the yin and yang of that moment, the juxtaposition between my heavenly Father and my earthly one. It was more about the contrast between them than about their similarities, for one cannot fully grasp the brilliance of light without first being enveloped in darkness.

I soon put the incident with my father behind me and continued my new life. It was not a bad life for me: I had a job, and I was living in a supportive family environment. I felt respected and appreciated.

During those first months with Jason and Susan, I gradually realized that I had been suffering from chronic depression for years. This understanding came to me as if I were waking from a deep sleep. I found that having someone to talk to without fear of punishment or rejection kept the darkness from creeping into my thoughts. As it turned out, I now had two people to help me on my journey to health: one who still loved me unconditionally, even as I could feel our relationship transforming, and the other who was like a lighthouse guiding me forward into womanhood. I changed from being a generally melancholy person to a perky one. After years of self-loathing, this change in my circumstances and lifestyle was working miracles.

I had been the emotional equivalent of a feral cat, assuming that

emotional emaciation was the norm, until Susan and Jason's uncon-
ditional love and acceptance helped me begin to heal. My mangy,
depressed emotional coat was growing back thick, strong, and full
of luster. I no longer thought about suicide, and I wasn't afraid of
things in the dark anymore. Though I still had much to learn and a
long way to go, I was making progress.

Chapter 22

God's Entreaty

Winter 1993–Fall 1994

As the weather grew colder, I became desperate for my sweaters and my heavy winter coat. The few items of clothing I had packed for basic training two months earlier and the couple of outfits I had purchased at Goodwill since moving in with Jason and Susan were all fall pieces and weren't heavy enough to withstand a New England winter.

When I called my parents' house to see if I could come by to get my clothing, my mother replied unemotionally, "I guess so."

"Great, I'll be there in an hour." I hung up before she had the chance to change her mind.

My sisters were delighted to see me and helped gather my belongings into a couple of garbage bags while my mother hung out in the kitchen and didn't speak to me. I had been worried that my sisters might be mad at me for not coming back home to them, but instead, they told me they understood and were glad to see that I was happy.

Before I left in October, I had suggested to Lillian that she move into my room and that Helen could take over her room. She had taken me up on the idea. My room had more privacy since her room had become a second living room of sorts for all of us kids. Lillian had carefully pushed my things against the far wall of the closet and added her own items in the space she had made. I had already stored any nonessentials in the attic, but many of my daily wear items were still present. I appreciated how Lillian had cared for my belongings, despite my not returning for them earlier.

The next weekend at Jason's house, I was organizing the things I had quickly stuffed into trash bags, when I came across a pin of a small golden person. *My angel!* I thought as I twirled the wingless angel pin between my fingers. *My angel became a person. It wasn't a fallen angel after all. It was always an angel, but now in human form.* I smiled at my epiphany and thought of my sisters: little angels here on Earth.

Susan and I took turns cooking dinner at night. Susan often ate something small for herself, so I would cook spaghetti with marinara sauce for Jason and myself—the same meal I had once cooked for my sisters. Jason, still in high school, didn't contribute to the preparation, cleanup, or cost.

I was starting to feel like a second mother to Jason. I knew it was my own doing. I was taking care of him the way I used to take care of my sisters. Being of service to others was ingrained in me, but I understood that playing this role with a boyfriend would not be good in the long run. I wanted a fifty-fifty partnership.

Jason and I were rarely intimate outside of cuddling on the couch while watching television. It was endearing, and Jason was good to me, but I felt unfulfilled. I longed for a "romantic" relationship, but there were so many reasons to stay as we were: we never fought, and he never yelled at me or blamed me for anything. Of course, I wouldn't allow arguments to pop up; I always immediately acquiesced, as I was terrified of conflict.

I should have talked to him about this change between us, but I didn't. I feared losing him by "rocking the boat," and losing him would threaten my living situation. The fact was, I enjoyed living with him and Susan. I relished the peace and I loved Jason and Susan. I didn't want to return to the chaos of my parents' house and the demons that lurked there.

January was my first opportunity to obtain some college credits. I knew that working the morning shift at a fast-food restaurant was not my destiny, and I yearned to be something more. It was time to move my life forward.

I signed up for a single course that semester: typing. Even though I had some basic typing skills, I thought it was the most practical option. If I continued my education, typing would be helpful for writing reports, and if I decided to stay in the workforce, I could at least land a job as a receptionist. It was a good first step.

Since I now had to get myself to night classes at the local community college and to work during the day, I needed a vehicle. At this point, I had about fifty dollars in cash, and the spring semester was starting in less than two weeks. Jason and I found a white Nissan pickup truck with 105,000 miles on it owned by a farmer a couple of miles away. With its abundant rust, the Nissan resembled a spotted cow, but it was under ten years old, so I didn't have to have it inspected before registering it. Since the truck was selling for $300, I was $250 short. Susan covered the difference, and it was the best gift I'd ever received. The truck had a standard transmission, and Susan taught both Jason and me how to drive it.

I loved my little truck and proudly drove it to my parents' house to show my sisters a few days after registering it. I couldn't wait to show off my "new" vehicle. This was a triumph for me, since my father was still adamantly opposed to any of the kids in the house getting their license, even though Lillian was seventeen and a responsible teenager.

When I arrived, I hollered up the stairs, "Hey, Lillian, Amanda, Helen—come outside! Come look at my new truck!"

They all came clomping down the stairs with little four-year-old Gabby in tow.

"What do you think?" I asked proudly.

"When you drove it in, we thought we heard a motorcycle pulling into the driveway," Helen interjected.

"Well, the muffler is rusted out, so it's a little loud."

"Did you name it?" Lillian asked.

"Yeah, Trucky."

"More like the Beast!" laughed Helen.

"Yeah, Trucky the Beast!" Lillian was tickled by the new name.

Trucky the Beast turned out to be as reliable as the sun. It started every morning without fail, no matter what happened to it. Not long after purchasing it, the muffler fell off. I watched it skid off into the grass on the side of the road. I kept going. A few weeks after that, the exhaust pipe leading to the missing muffler broke off and rolled onto the dirt shoulder. I kept going. It wasn't long before the catalytic converter also bailed. As soon as I was sure that it too had made its way out of traffic, I kept driving. I loved Trucky the Beast! No matter what happened to it, it remained dependable.

As the weather warmed into spring and I acclimated to my new schedule, I suddenly remembered that my Aunt Clara had been sending me savings bonds for my birthday for several years. When they arrived each year, my father immediately stowed them "somewhere safe" in the strictly off-limits formal dining room, which he had taken over as a makeshift office. Any piece of paper that may have had a purpose at some point in his life was either stacked in a haphazard, two-foot-high pile on the eight-person dining room table or stuffed into the drawers of the tall china cabinet. Additional piles of paper leaned precariously atop the chairs, the two organs, and the red velvet bay window seats. My father always kept the sliding pocket doors closed so none of us or the cats would go in and disturb his "paperwork."

My aunt, who had believed in me all those years ago, had said she wanted to see me succeed in life and had sent me these bonds to help pay for college, even though I only saw her twice a year on Christmas Eve and for a preholiday outing to the mall. Since I was now attending college, I asked my father to gather up the bonds so I could cash them in for my education, knowing full well I would never be able to find them on my own.

When I told Jason about my plans, his eyes lit up. "Didn't you say your courses were free due to your low income since you're going to a community college?"

"Yeah, but not my books and supplies," I replied not yet knowing where the conversation was going.

"But since you're working, you can afford them anyway. You know… if *I* had a car, I could get a job, too. Plus, I wouldn't have to get up so early to catch the bus to school."

I was reluctant to spend the money my aunt had saved for my college education on a vehicle for my boyfriend, but I felt an over-whelming sense of obligation, since Susan had purchased Trucky the Beast for me and was allowing me to live with them rent-free. She hadn't had to take me in; most mothers wouldn't have. Plus, she was providing me with so much more than a roof over my head; she had become my role model and guide. Giving Jason the money to buy a vehicle seemed like one way I could repay her for the $250 and her kindness.

I liked living with Jason and Susan; they treated me better than anyone ever had in my life, and I ultimately accepted this as part of the price I paid for a peaceful life. After all, earning $4.25 an hour at McDonald's, even when working full time, wasn't enough to support the cost of an apartment and a vehicle. I would need another part-time job if I wanted to live on my own.

Jason soon found a Ford Thunderbird selling for one thousand dollars. That was an unfathomable sum of money for me to spend on a vehicle, especially since it was two-thirds of what my aunt had saved for me. But Jason was not to be deterred, and he eventually talked me into purchasing the Thunderbird for him.

During those first winter months, the three of us spoke late into the evening in front of the wood stove. We left the front panel open so we could watch the logs burn down to a warm glow. I told them about my experiences growing up, and they listened, mesmerized and understanding. They accepted me in a way I'd never been accepted before. To them, I was not a "raggy"; I was special. I loved them for that.

I could feel myself becoming emotionally stronger and less likely to break down in tears. My dark thoughts had vanished. I was becoming a healthier, better balanced person, and I wasn't about to screw that up. Where else would I find that?

That following summer, I started working at a munitions factory on a production line. It paid nearly twice what I'd been making at McDonald's, and we all appreciated the extra money. After a month, I was offered a permanent full-time position on third shift for thirteen dollars an hour, which was as good as winning the lottery. However, my intuition kept nudging me to turn it down to focus on school.

When I told Jason about wanting to pursue my education rather than working third shift, he looked at me in shock. He couldn't understand how I could turn down that much money to go to college. But Susan, by not charging me rent, had afforded me the opportunity to pursue the dreams I had deferred. Maybe, just maybe, I could become someone—maybe even a doctor.

I turned down the full-time position, despite Jason's arguments. It pained me that he couldn't envision me pursuing a better future than third-shift linework. I felt that he thought I wasn't smart enough or capable of achieving more. I began to feel that he was trying to hold me back.

The fall semester of 1994, I took three classes at Northwestern Community College, one of which was an English class. To make college possible, I scheduled these three courses for the evening and took a new job during the day. Although this meant fifteen-hour-long days three days a week, I was delighted to be back in school and earning enough for groceries, gas, and insurance. During my nearly two hours on the road each day, I studied using flash cards that I held up in front of me on top of the steering wheel while singing aloud to my U2 and Pink Floyd cassette tapes and praying. I talked to God a lot, asking Him to help me with school, assist me with making the right life decisions, and watch over my friends and family.

A month into the semester, I had an extremely vivid dream. I was standing next to my bed in Jason's house when a man appeared beside me. He had intense blue eyes, and his thick, curly chestnut-colored hair spilled over his shoulders. I got the feeling that I'd met him somewhere years before and knew him quite well, but I couldn't figure out who he was. He extended his left hand toward me, and I grasped it with my right as I turned to stand beside him. As I did so, an overwhelming feeling of warmth and love flowed through me, like I was immersed in a toasty bubble bath. Without asking, I realized that God, or perhaps the light that is an extension of God, was flowing directly through him into me.

As I realized that he was some sort of angel, we passed effort-lessly into a flash of blinding white light and then into a room. We were floating invisibly in a corner of the ceiling, looking down, like the watchers that had stood in the back of my church when I was young. At this point in the dream, I felt nothing—no sensations, no emotions, no warmth. I was there only to observe.

As I gazed down onto the room, I noticed how pretty and well-organized it was. Sunlight streamed through the gossamer cur-tains that covered two large windows. Books were aligned neatly on their shelves. A fourteen-year-old girl sat on her neatly made bed. The bedspread, tucked tightly into her mattress, was eggshell white with pink-and-beige detailing. Her stuffed animals were lined up symmetrically on her pillows. She had long, straight blond hair. For a moment, I thought I was seeing an image of my younger self, but when I focused on her delicate face, I quickly realized it was someone else. She was beautiful. She was crying; large teardrops fell on an open book lying on the bed in front of her. I realized that something she had read in the book had brought her to tears, but I was immediately whisked away into another room before I could do anything about it.

This room was darker. It was night, and only a small table lamp provided light. Again, we were floating near a corner of the ceiling, invisible. Clothing was strewn across the floor, and a blanket and single pillow were crumpled up on the bed. An older teenage girl with long brown hair was sitting on a pile of clothes next to her bed. Her hands covered her face, and her hair tumbled around her fingers. A book lay partially open on a piece of clothing a few feet in front of her. I sensed it had been thrown there. She was sobbing. Again, I realized she had read something in the book that had brought her to tears.

Instantly, we were in a third room, floating in the same position on the ceiling. A yellowed, flush-mount globe ceiling light filled with dried insect carcasses lit the room dimly. This room was dirty and small. A mattress lying directly on the floor took up a large portion of the room. It was bare, without a blanket or even a sheet. A Hispanic girl sat on a corner of the bed. Her black hair was loosely tied back in a disheveled ponytail. The girl was bent over a book, wiping tears from her cheeks as she continued reading.

A moment later, we were back beside my bed, and my guide turned to face me. His face was incredibly stunning, appearing lit from within by a warm, glowing light similar to sunlight. He was smiling slightly, but mostly with his eyes. He looked at me as if he were in love with me, which surprised me. Then, without moving his lips, he clearly said, "You can save them."

In a crushing wave of emotion, I realized I had written the book these girls had been reading. Their thoughts and feelings washed over me. All three were planning to end their lives. They felt like outcasts, like freaks. They had secrets they felt like they couldn't reveal to anyone. Their sadness and self-hatred was overwhelming. Although they all felt broken and ugly inside, I could sense their dazzling, intact souls shining through like an aura. They just couldn't see what I could: that they were beautiful deep within, not ugly and deformed as they perceived themselves to be.

I woke up sweating and shaking, but I was filled with a sense of purpose. God Himself had asked me to do something: write a book!

But I couldn't possibly do that. God wanted me to write about my secrets, about the life I'd had up to that point. There was no way I was going to do that. For most of my life, I had kept my experiences a secret to protect my family and to protect myself. Besides, I didn't know how to write a book. It seemed an impossible request, and I promptly rejected the idea, calling myself silly for thinking up such a notion.

However, several days later, I still couldn't shake the overwhelming feelings of those dream girls' despair. I started scribbling notes in my diary and on random sheets of paper, just to relieve the pain I felt for the girls.

I wrote a couple pages as one of my English assignments. My English professor turned it back to me with an 'A,' but with no notes, which was unusual for him. I desperately wanted to find out what he thought and started to fret again that the whole idea was ridiculous.

A few days later, I caught up with him in the hall. "What do you think about the start of my book?" I asked.

I wasn't prepared for his look of surprise. "Book? I think you should wait until you're older, much older... to gain perspective," he said, then turned from me, obviously dismissive and not wanting to be bothered with continuing the conversation. I could tell he didn't want to get pulled into some sort of drama.

More negative thoughts surfaced: *Everyone will think I'm a lunatic. It will negatively impact my future if people find out about my past. Everyone will think that I made it up and that I'm looking for attention. What am I thinking?*

But still, I couldn't shake my dream. It haunted me. My heart was burdened, and that burden was only alleviated by writing. I continued.

I recalled that Kelly's dad restored old computers as a side business, so I saved for months to scrape together two hundred dollars to use as a down payment on a used computer. When I told him that I wanted to write a book, he let me take a computer home with me that day.

It took another three months to pay off the five-hundred-dollar investment, but I knew I was on the right path. The burden I felt started to lift as I worked on the manuscript. What I didn't realize at the time was that I hadn't yet experienced the most significant part of my own story. That part of my journey was still five years away.

Chapter 23

Burgeoning Adulthood

Fall 1994-1995

In the fall of 1994, Jason's brother, Matthew, and his wife, Jennifer, moved into the house so they could start saving money for a down payment on a place of their own nearby. Susan's house was only 1400 square feet, and to accommodate them, she gave up her bedroom and moved into what would have been the small dining room, had the house been finished.

I was grateful to be moved into Jason's room, since he had an electric space heater in his room. It also provided us with more privacy, though that didn't increase our intimacy, as I had expected it would. This was a bit of a disappointment, but it was preferable to sleeping in the kitchen. I kept my Bible on the nightstand as my security blanket to help ward off the nightmares of being chased by demons that I still had once or twice a week. It seemed that part of my life managed to follow me, if only in my dreams.

Jason, perhaps used to being the man in the house, wasn't fully onboard with this new situation, and he diffused his angst through overly aggressive driving.

A few months after purchasing the T-bird, we were out cruising around town one night when we came across his best friend, Steve, driving his girlfriend's Mustang. Like me, the other girl was in the passenger seat. It was late in November, and a light snowfall had melted on the roadways earlier in the day. By evening, the temperature had fallen back below freezing, creating patches of black ice on the pavement. Seeing his friend, Jason reached across me and rolled down my window, letting in the frigid air. "Hey, Steve," he shouted, "what do you think about finding out which is faster, the T-bird or the Mustang?"

"The Mustang will smear you," Steve whooped back.

"Not a chance," Jason prodded. "Let's find out! I'll race you down Route 8. The first one to make it to exit 45 wins."

"You're on!"

"No, wait, I don't want to be in a race," I said, panicking, as I rolled my window up again to stay warm.

"Stop being a wuss, Denise. You know I'm an awesome driver, and there's no one out on the roads now anyway," Jason said irrationally, as if he were the one reasoning with me.

Route 8 wasn't far, and we were already at the entrance before I could contest further. Jason stopped the car in one lane and rolled my window down again as Steve pulled up in the one next to us, his Nine Inch Nails tape blasting at full volume. "We go on the count of one," Jason shouted out the window. "Three, two, one!"

Jason smashed the accelerator to the floor. The T-bird lurched forward, but Steve already had the lead by a few feet. Within seconds, the odometer read ninety miles per hour. At this speed, the car drifted slightly within the lane. My heart was beating so loudly, I no longer noticed the intense music blaring through the sixteen-inch subwoofer speakers. By the time we hit one hundred miles per hour, we were bearing down on another vehicle in the right lane, and Jason was still accelerating. Because the other car was traveling at the speed limit, it appeared to be parked. Fortunately, we were in the left lane, but Steve was in the right. He swerved onto the narrow shoulder to avoid the other car, still accelerating. As we rushed past the unsuspecting vehicle, which quickly blurred into the darkness, I felt the pull of the vacuum that had been created between us, and we veered to the right.

I held my breath as Jason screamed, "Woo hoo!" at the top of his lungs. I was bracing my arms against the dashboard. When I glanced at the odometer again, it read 120 miles per hour. Despite driving in the shoulder, Steve had nudged even further ahead of us.

Steve made it to the exit first, and Jason hit the brakes hard as we pulled up right behind him. I was grateful that the tires didn't lock up in the tight turn at the exit ramp and that we hadn't hit any black ice along the way. Either would have caused us to slide sideways into the nearby trees to our death. *Thank you, God*, I thought, taking a deep breath.

At the light at the bottom of the exit ramp, Jason pulled up alongside Steve and shouted out my window, "That was freaking amazing!"

"I smoked you, man! Mustangs rule," Steve shouted back as he lurched forward again when the light changed.

I remained silent, still shaking and angry at Jason for placing me in such a dangerous situation when I'd asked him not to. His testosterone-driven attempt to impress his friend had put another small wedge between us, and he was completely oblivious to it.

Around this time, I learned that my parents had handed Mariah over to the state foster-care system. Her uncontrollable outbursts had continued, and she'd accused our father of raping her. He hadn't so much as touched, struck, or even hugged her in years, but while I was gone, she had been raped by a man a few streets away from their house. She had since taken that terrible experience and projected it onto our father, who finally buckled under the toll of her emotional bludgeoning and placed her in foster care.

Mariah went to live in Waterbury with a widowed Italian woman who tried to teach her how to cook. However, one evening, after a disagreement, Mariah threatened the woman with a knife. The woman threw her out into the night. Still only seventeen, Mariah vanished. The state foster-care officials said they couldn't locate her, though I suspected they didn't put in much effort. My father was incensed at this news. The state had led her into a situation that was obviously worse than what she had with my parents.

For months, none of us were certain whether she was alive. Then, one evening, she called my parents from Waterbury to tell them that she was okay and living with her boyfriend.

I was so busy with my own life, I didn't spend much time thinking about Mariah and her struggles. Between working part time and taking a full course load at the community college, I had little time to think at all.

A few months after my twentieth birthday, in the spring of 1995, as Jason's senior year of high school and my current semester came to an end, I found a job cleaning houses that had flexible hours that I could work around my classes. That fall, as I entered my third full semester, I was busier than I'd ever been in my life. My days started at 7:30 in the morning, and I often didn't arrive home until 10:30 at night.

Lillian, who had also recently graduated from high school, was still living at our parents' house and had started taking a full course load at the community college like me. It took me nearly two years, but I finally convinced my father to allow Lillian to get her own license and her own car so that she could drive to the college. Lillian took an elective painting class with me, and this turned out to be my all-time favorite course. Lillian and I shared our paints and helped each other clean up after our three-hour session ended. It gave us the opportunity to reconnect.

Because of my hectic schedule, I saw Jason less and less. He had decided to become an auto mechanic and had signed up for classes at a nearby automotive technical college. My own future was now clearly linked to a college education, and I wanted him to go to a standard four-year college, not that there was anything wrong with being a mechanic.

However, I questioned our future financial stability if he and I were to get married eventually. A mechanic earned what my father did, and I was not interested in repeating that struggle. I wanted Jason to strive for more, but whenever I brought it up, he said, "Maybe I'll own my own shop someday, and you can help me run it." I felt that this future scenario of his was selling me short.

My dreams were elsewhere. I wasn't interested in answering phones at a mom-and-pop shop. I had not forgotten my youthful dreams of being a doctor, even if they still seemed out of reach. At this point, I valued my education more than anything in my life, as I intuitively knew it was my path to achieving those dreams. The goal of becoming an educated woman drove all of my decisions, even if it meant sacrificing everything else. I could feel that our trajectories in life were diverging, but I still wasn't about to bail on the best person in my life thus far. I had nothing to move on to yet.

Jason started working at a gas station in the evenings after his classes. When I did see him, usually on the weekends, he was working on restoring one of his cars. All of his income from the gas station went into buying dilapidated cars and car parts. He was always happy to show me what he was working on, but I had only a passing interest in it. That was fine with me because it gave me time to write. I no longer needed to be with him as I once had. When we did spend time together, it was always with a group of our friends. Still, Jason continued to provide me a sense of security, of home, and of a loving family. Security is only the second rung on Maslow's hierarchy of needs, but I had never experienced security before, and I wasn't about to risk losing it.

Chapter 24

Revelation

Fall 1995–Fall 1997

O n Christmas Eve, Jason and I drove to my Aunt Clara's house. My entire family—sisters, parents, and grandmother—had gathered there. When I told my aunt that I had left the house cleaning company I was working for and had started a small house cleaning business with my friend Amy, she asked if she could hire me to help my grandmother, who was having trouble taking care of her home. I was grateful for the extra income from my aunt and the opportunity to spend some time with my grandmother.

Grammy had a great sense of humor and endless stories about her previous husbands and the handsome young man who drove her to her doctor's appointments. She adored her little dog and fed him the meals that were delivered to her daily through Meals on Wheels. She ate ice cream for lunch instead. I considered lecturing her about her food choices, but she was so delighted to be able to feed the dog Salisbury steak, I could never bring myself to do it.

She had painted as a hobby in her younger years, and when I expressed interest in seeing some of her oil paintings, she instructed me on how to find them in her spare bedroom, which she was no longer able to enter due to the piles of boxes stored there. I could see where my mother's hoarding had started. Getting to know Grammy as a real person with a past, desires, and artistic talent was an unexpected gift.

One day, while I was scrubbing the kitchen, I asked my

grandmother a question that had weighed heavily on me all my life: "Hey, Grammy, why do you think Mom doesn't like me? Did I do something wrong? Dad told me that I cried a lot as a baby. Do you think that had something to do with it?"

"Oh, I don't think you did anything wrong. She just doesn't know how to show you that she cares," Grammy said simply.

"Then why does she always tell me that she hates me?"

"She doesn't mean it."

Why was my grandmother giving me platitudes when I was so clearly asking her to help me with my pain? "Then why would she say it? Why would any mother say that to their kid?"

"She just doesn't know how to express herself."

My grandmother's responses were frustrating. I felt like I was being condescended to rather than being treated like the serious young adult I was.

"But that doesn't make it okay to tell me that she hates me," I said, tiring of what I thought were my grandmother's attempts to evade my earnest questions. "She doesn't tell the other girls that she hates them—just me and Mariah. Why would she do that, even if Mariah has problems?"

"Well, when she was little—about six, I think—she still wasn't speaking much or playing with the other kids at school. The principal had me take her to a psychologist. He ran several tests and told me that she has autism."

Autism?! At last, I had an answer! "She has autism? Why didn't anyone tell me this before?" I asked.

"It just wasn't something I ever thought to talk to you about. You know your mother. She doesn't like to talk about stuff like that."

I finished cleaning Grammy's kitchen in near silence, preoccupied with turning over this new revelation in my mind. This was the first time I'd ever heard something about my mother's behavior that made sense.

I didn't know much about autism at the time, but I did know

that it explained her inappropriate outbursts, like when she attacked Grammy for rebuking Lillian; her difficult personality traits, like going out in the yard to howl; and her lack of empathy. It explained why she had never once held an actual conversation with me, why she never asked how I felt or how any of my sisters were doing, why she was always so devoid of expression, why she never drove the car, and even why she couldn't spell even the simplest of words.

It was all because of her autism, I said to myself.

While I was relieved to finally have an explanation for my mother's bizarre behavior, I was very disturbed that so many years had passed without anyone seeking help for her. We might have learned how to deal with her or at least gained an understanding of why she was so disconnected from us and from life in general.

That day in the kitchen, and in the days that followed, I often wondered why something like this had been kept secret. Why had Grammy not told us this before? Couldn't she see what was happening? Couldn't she see how damaging my mother's behavior was to us kids? After all, Grammy herself had been the object of a few of Mom's vicious assaults. Keeping this information a secret had contributed to the damaging effects of Mom's autism on the family. Silence had given her impunity to be destructive.

As I pondered this, it dawned on me that Aunt Clara had told me that Grammy struggled with bipolar disorder. That might explain her lack of involvement in our lives. In fact, that day in the kitchen when she revealed my mother's autism marked our very first deep conversation.

I wondered if even my mother knew she was autistic. Had she ever been told? And if so, did she remember being told? Since she was so adamant that everyone else was "crazy," it was possible she either didn't know or didn't remember.

The revelation suddenly turned my mother, who had been my nemesis for so long, into a fragile human, someone to feel sympathy for. After two decades of resentment, I felt somewhat guilty for being so angry with her. There was now a plausible explanation for all of her terrible behavior.

However, I also knew there was no excuse for hurting a child. I was still mad about being forced to take on a parental role for my sisters at such an early age, and I was angry at my grandmother for not seeing how desperately my mother needed assistance, especially once we kids came along. We'd been left alone to fend for ourselves, even when someone else knew of my mother's limitations. Had Grammy believed my father would compensate for all of my mother's shortcomings and raise us in a healthy way?

Was I supposed to grant my mother a pardon and forgive her for all the damage she'd done to my mind and spirit? Was it okay for me to be so mad at someone who was emotionally, psychologically, and mentally disabled? I had always assumed that finding out what my mother suffered from would bring me peace, but instead, I was even more conflicted than ever. I prayed for answers and for resolution but could not find relief.

I told Jason and Amy what I had learned. Jason, who didn't know anything about autism, took the news as if it made sense but didn't affect our present lives. Amy, on the other hand, spent more time dissecting my family's dynamics.

"I knew there had to be something," she said thoughtfully. "Autism explains everything: why she hit you, why she never told you that she loves you, why she treated you like a slave. Honestly, I can't believe that you and your sisters turned out so normal."

Amy was always there with an understanding ear when I needed it most. She let me vent my anger and, together, we came to understand that all of the bad experiences in our pasts make us who we are today—for better or worse. Our conversations gave me time to process the revelation about my mother.

The following weekend, I stopped by my parents' house to visit my sisters. It was time to tell them what I'd learned. When I arrived, they were all upstairs together in Helen's room, watching television and working on their homework. It was like they were roommates hanging out together in the living room of their apartment.

When I told them about our mother's autism, they were glad to finally have a name for Mom's issues, but knowing what affected her didn't really change their situation—they were still subject to her outbursts, and knowing didn't give them tools to help them deal with her. It did, however, change our perspective on her behavior. We didn't excuse it, but we at least understood it. We finally accepted that *we* weren't the cause of her behavior.

As I was processing my mother's mental disability, I was excelling in all of my classes, mostly due to my knack for studying anywhere and anytime I had a spare moment. I studied with my index cards during my long daily drives to work and school, in waiting rooms, at the grocery store, and during lunch.

In the months prior to graduating with my associate's degree, I met with a guidance counselor at UCONN Extension and started the enrollment process for the four-year university. By this time, I was starting to think that perhaps becoming an MD wasn't as far out of reach as I had thought.

The sciences intrigued me. I was interested in how the patterns of nature repeated themselves over and over again. An atom was like the universe; the veins of a leaf were like the veins of our hands. An amorphous mixture of carbon, hydrogen, and oxygen connecting, twisting, folding, and unfolding into amino acids, proteins, and DNA was just as miraculous to me as the idea of God creating us out of dust. I couldn't get enough. The more I understood the basic makeup of the world and of ourselves, the more I felt I understood God and even my own soul.

I graduated from the community college summa cum laude with an associate's degree in general studies in the spring of 1996. Everyone in the family—except for Mariah, whose exact whereabouts were currently unknown—attended the graduation ceremony. It was a hard-won victory in my life, and I felt wonderful having my friends and family there to celebrate with me.

By obtaining my degree, I had taken a giant leap forward in life. I was proud of myself and determined to continue my education at the satellite campuses of UCONN. Of course, to afford that, I continued my life with Jason, whom I still loved.

My classes at UCONN were an even mix of biology and writing. Because of this incongruity, and in order to complete my degree in two years, I decided to pursue a general studies major under the direction of one of my English professors. My graduating thesis was a creative writing project: the book God had compelled me to write. My professor never questioned the content or veracity of my story; instead, she bought me books—lots of brand-new books—to help me write and develop my story. She used her own income to help me, a random student with whom she had no particular connection, develop into something greater than I could on my own. She gave me the confidence that perhaps someday I'd be able to bring my story to the world. She was an unexpected mentor when I needed one to help me develop as a writer.

My two years at UCONN leading to my bachelor's in general studies were two of the most fulfilling of my life. Ironically, there is little to say for the first of them. Sometimes, what makes life enjoyable is the predictability of stability, the ebb and flow of a comfortable existence, where nothing remarkable happens at all. I worked hard that year and was challenged just enough to realize I was developing into someone new, though not so new as to feel threatened. I was becoming more confident, wiser, and more responsible. The pain and depression of my teen years was now just a memory of a life I was leaving behind. I was becoming an adult, possibly a successful one.

My education continued to remain my top priority. I had A's in all of my classes and began seriously considering a career in medicine again. I spoke with the director of the UCONN general studies program, who also served as the Torrington campus career counselor, about my aspirations.

One day, during the spring semester of my second year in 1997, he asked me to come by his office so he could share some great news. He had met with a local doctor who was teaching an MCAT test-prep course. Typically, he charged around two thousand dollars per person to take his course, but after speaking with our program director, the doctor had decided to donate two spots in his upcoming class to the school. The director had chosen me to fill one of those spots. I was ecstatic.

It was an eight-week course in Waterbury, which was over an hour away, and ran from six to nine p.m., three days a week. While I attended this course, I stayed with Amy, the friend whom I cleaned houses with, since she lived considerably closer to Waterbury than I did. This cut several hours of commuting time out of my schedule each week, which I desperately needed.

This course changed my life, though in an unexpected way. As much as it was a blessing, it was also fraught with drama. One of my classmates, whom I sometimes carpooled with to the course, was a beautiful, funny, and charming young woman with striking red hair. However, she insisted that I photocopy my notes for her after each session, while she sat back and passively enjoyed the lectures.

After two weeks, I complained to her about it, which she did not receive well. When I refused to copy my notes for her any longer, it incited all sorts of chaos. She approached the doctor running the course—who was brilliant, but had a difficult, impatient personality—and complained to him about my not sharing my notes. He took her side and turned me into the class pariah, often making it a point to single me out for not knowing some obscure fact about biochemistry or organic chemistry, while my classmate sat beside me, smiling and still refusing to take notes. Despite this, his lessons were valuable. I learned what areas I excelled in and where I was weak and needed to study more.

And then came the moment that changed the course of my life. A few days before the class ended, our instructor stopped directly in front of me during a lecture. Pointing his finger directly at my face, he said, "You will never get into medical school." He said it dismissively, as if he were talking to himself.

I sat there, speechless and wide-eyed.

Then he moved on down the aisle and continued his regular lecture. The room was awkwardly silent. I could feel my classmates' eyes staring at me in pity and surprise.

My first thought was, *You know what? You're right. I wouldn't want to be in a field where I would have to interact with a jerk like you on a daily basis.* In that one moment, my life was forever changed. I immediately lost all interest in going to medical school; it was as if a switch had been flipped in my mind.

Afterward, I thought that perhaps I should have questioned my knee-jerk decision, as everything else in my life was calculated and planned meticulously, but my intuition applauded my brashness. Instead of, *Wait, what are you thinking? You can't let him win,* my next thought was, *What about dentistry? Maybe I should look into that instead. Isn't that what the personality test I took two years ago actually said I would excel at?*

When the test-prep course finished, I returned to living with Jason and Susan, but I was itching to have my own apartment. I was twenty-two years old now, and I asked Jason if he would be willing to move out with me. I loved Susan, but I was ready to take the next step of going out on my own. My Aunt Clara, who had married late in life just a few months earlier, had given me her furniture when she moved into her new home with her husband, and it was now stashed throughout Susan's house, reminding me daily that I wasn't independent yet. I felt like a reborn phoenix. Now that my feathers had grown to maturity, I felt ready to fly.

Jason was reluctant to make a move. To me, it seemed logical: he now had a job as a mechanic at a dealership forty-five minutes away, and getting our own place closer to where he worked would save time and money. Yet whenever I brought it up, he countered that his mom's house was free, and since she was almost never home, and Matthew and Jennifer had moved out a year earlier, we had the house to ourselves anyway. He didn't understand why I wanted a place of my own. Knowing that I still had a couple of months left before finishing my bachelor's degree, I dropped the subject. With my limited income, I didn't feel I could make the change without Jason's full support. I was still scared of making the leap into the unforeseen.

Chapter 25

We're All Right

Winter 1998–Winter 1999

On a crisp, clear January day in 1998, after cleaning houses with Amy all morning, I dropped her off at her home. I had been ruminating over getting an apartment, but outside of that there had been nothing unusual about the day until I came over the crest of a steep hill. The sunlight shone brightly, washing out the traffic light. I could have sworn it was green, but there was a black SUV directly in my path, crossing the intersection. My foot hit the brake, but it was too late, and my truck crashed into the SUV's rear passenger-side door. I shot forward into my steering wheel, and for a second everything went black.

When I regained consciousness, I remembered the SUV and the panic of hitting my brakes. I looked around. About fifty feet away on my right, the SUV lay on its side. The rear window was smashed out and its glass was scattered across the road. I heard a woman screaming, "My baby, my baby!"

I froze in horror imagining a mangled baby in my head—a baby I had killed—and even when I saw a small girl toddle from the back of the vehicle around to the front toward her mother's cries, the terror continued its hold.

The next thing I remember is standing on the side of the road. Cars and trucks were stopping, and a crowd of people had gathered around me as I stood there stiff, frozen, and staring blankly at my truck. Someone must have called the police because police cars and fire trucks were there. I only snapped back into myself when a police officer shouted into the crowd of people around me, "Whose truck is this?"

I stepped forward.

The officer asked for my license and registration, and it took me several minutes of fumbling around in the glove compartment to find them. I was still shaking off the feeling of having been asleep for the last few minutes. I handed them to the officer, and he started writing down the details.

Another officer approached me and asked, "Do you need an ambulance?"

"I-I don't know."

The people from the other vehicle were standing together on the sidewalk. I was relieved to see they were fine.

The officer walked me over to the ambulance, where the EMTs stabilized my neck with a brace. After I was wheeled into the ER, I gave the nurses Amy's phone number and asked them to call her. Jason was working, but I knew that Amy was home.

Amy arrived within a few minutes of being called. "I heard about the accident," she said as she walked into my room. "One of my friends works near where you crashed, and I somehow just knew it was you. Are you okay? Oh, and by the way, happy birthday."

I had completely forgotten that it was my birthday. "I told you that my birthday's cursed."

"You're not cursed," she stated flatly.

I raised my eyebrow and scowled in her direction.

"Okay, maybe just a little," she acquiesced, and we both laughed.

The doctors informed me that I had whiplash and would be sore for a few days. My truck had held up better than expected. Jason had it towed back to the house, and he replaced my radiator, bumper, and grill later that weekend. Three of his friends came over to help him winch the frame back into alignment. Living with a mechanic certainly had its advantages. On Sunday, once the repairs were finished, he proudly announced that I was ready to hit the road again. But I wasn't. I was sore and stiff and terrified to drive.

Amy called later that night to ask if I wanted her to pick me up in the morning. That would have meant an additional three hours of driving for her. "I'm okay. I can do it," I told her.

And I did.

However, I had to push through an intense fear of driving for months. I kept expecting something to appear in front of me again—a deer, another vehicle, or even a person. I stopped studying while driving and didn't even listen to the radio, but I did keep praying: "Dear God, please don't let anything bad happen to me today. Please keep me safe. Please help me get through this rain without crashing..."

Amy and I continued cleaning houses together and having a blast all the way through to my graduation from UCONN that spring. I told her about my new ambition to go to dental school, and while she was always supportive, I sensed she didn't want me to go. We worked so well together, and she was understandably worried about being left alone to run the business.

I graduated from UCONN in June 1998 with a 3.9 average and a Bachelor of General Studies degree. An A- in one class ruined my otherwise perfect score. I started studying for the dental school entrance exam, knowing that I would need a very high score if I wanted any program to take my application seriously. Applications and interviews for the fall class at most dental schools were already complete, so I had an extra year to study and prepare for the exam.

Of course, enrolling in a professional graduate program is a big investment of time, energy, and money, and I wanted to make sure that dentistry really would be a good fit. I looked for a full-time dental assisting position and couldn't believe my luck when I found one a few towns away that didn't require any experience. I was delighted: I would earn four times what I was currently making, since it was a full-time position, I would gain a lot of valuable experience, and I would find out if dentistry was the right path for me.

Amy, of course, was profoundly disappointed in losing me as her partner, but she was such a great cheerleader. Our parting was exceptionally bittersweet.

I started working for Dr. Melver full time that summer and put some money from every paycheck aside for a deposit on an apartment of my own. I knew it was time I broke up with Jason. He continued trying to convince me to stay with him and his mother. I got the feeling he assumed I would eventually give in and agree with him, as I always had. However, this time, I trusted my intuition, which was telling me to take the leap away from this relationship.

Later that summer, I moved into my own small, one-bedroom apartment in the attic of a three-story foursquare house with large dormer windows. The house itself was much nicer than my parents' foursquare of my childhood. I loved that apartment: the walls were finished and the kitchen cabinets all had doors. It was sunny and warm in the way that makes one want to linger with something warm to drink and a good book to read. I set up my bed directly under the dormer window in the bedroom and cracked it open at night to let in the breeze. It was calm and free from the dark entities that had haunted my childhood.

Despite my newfound comfort and freedom, I experienced an awful period of wavering between painful longing for the security of a stable but dry relationship and the exhilarating promise of complete freedom. For several months, Jason and I continued an on-again, off-again relationship. My heart knew I had to move on emotionally, but my mind was too terrified to fully make the leap. I was letting go of my one consistent source of emotional security and didn't want to hurt the one man who had stuck by me throughout my education. His stable emotional support had helped heal a damaged part of my psyche. My leaving had been a surprise to him. I felt terrible about hurting him and wasn't entirely sure I had made the right decision. I often reasoned that perhaps he was the right man for me, but when we spent time together, I knew this was no longer true.

Throughout the rest of 1998, I continued studying for my dental school entrance exams and working as a dental assistant. I enjoyed working for Dr. Melver, who had grown up in a rough section of Philly. His mother had given birth to him as a young teenager, and in a way, they had grown up together. In many ways, Dr. Melver and I were kindred spirits: tenacious achievers and survivors. His life was subtly heroic, and it reminded me of Oprah's journey.

Dr. Melver took me under his wing and often gave me random bits of advice on how to survive dental school. He was warm and genuine and laughed often. He confirmed for me that I was on the right path.

* * *

Early on Veteran's Day in 1998, my father woke me with a phone call. He was out of breath: "Someone tried to burn down the house. The kids are upset. Can you come get them?"

"I'll be right there!" I didn't bother to ask what had happened or how bad it was. I lived only three minutes away by car and knew there would be time to ask questions later.

As I drove up to the house, I immediately spotted my sisters standing on the sidewalk. Fire trucks lined the road in front of the house, and I could see the lights from a couple of police cruisers glowing in the driveway. I parked at the Elks Lodge across the street from my sisters and ran up to them.

"Someone tried to burn down the house," Helen sobbed when she saw me open the car door. At sixteen, she had just started her junior year of high school. "The neighbor down the road saw flames when he got up to get ready for work. Someone lit the bag of leaves on the porch on fire and it burned down the front door. The fireman said that if they'd arrived ten minutes later, the whole house would've burned down and we'd be dead."

I hugged her, and she held her face in both hands, sucking down her tears in small convulsions.

"Dad said we're all going to live on the street now," Amanda cried.

"Can we stay with you?" Helen implored.

"Of course you can. For as long as you need to. Where's Mom and Dad?"

Gabby stood beside us silently, perhaps in shock at the situation.

Lillian explained that Mom had freaked out, started shouting something incoherent, and then stormed off down Fairview Avenue. Lillian, twenty-two years old and having long since taken over my role of family guardian, was holding it together well. I was proud of her for toughing it out with my parents, even as she worked nearly full time and attended classes at Central Connecticut State University to earn a master's degree in education after transferring from the community college. She navigated life at home much better than I had.

"It was horrible," Helen continued. "A fireman came into the house and woke us all up. We didn't know what was going on. We had slept through it. If the firemen hadn't gotten there in time, we'd..." She burst into tears again, recalling her near brush with death.

"They said they might have to condemn the house," Amanda said softly, trembling. She was a senior in high school, a year ahead of Helen.

"Why would they condemn the house?" I asked, already knowing the answer.

"They said all the stuff in the house is what made it catch fire so quickly, and now it's not safe," Helen answered for Amanda.

My heart nearly broke for them.

The fire chief soon came over to us. I had helped him in the past as a Red Cross volunteer, and I recognized him instantly. He seemed surprised to see me or perhaps surprised that I had lived in those conditions. "Is this your parents' house?"

"Yes, but I don't live here now. My sisters do."

He looked at Helen. "You live here?" he sighed, the surprise gone.

"Yes," Helen said. She had regained her composure. She knew

the chief even better than I did, having been involved in even more volunteer work than I was. She was well known and respected in Winsted.

Helen spoke up for all of us, "What about the house? Are you going to condemn it?"

"I'll see what I can do." He looked at us forlornly. We must have been quite a sight: five disheveled girls shivering in their nightgowns, some without shoes on, and all with red faces. "Can you tell me where your father is?"

"He's talking to the officers in the back," Lillian replied.

"Okay. It's going to be a little while before we can let anyone back in the house. Is there somewhere you can go?"

"Yeah, they can all stay at my apartment," I said, referring to my sisters. I didn't even think to offer shelter to my parents.

At my apartment, we sat around the living room, talking through the emotional shock of the fire. A couple of hours later, our father came over to retrieve my sisters. "The fire department said if we clean the house up, they won't condemn it, and we'll be able to stay," he said. "They only gave us four weeks, though. I don't think that's enough time."

In fact, not only did the fire department give my parents a month to clean out the house, they also directed my father to a federal agency that gives grants to repair historic homes. Without having to come up with the cash himself, my father was able to replace the burned front door and porch floor and the roof, and to repair the side porches, which were literally falling off of the house. Our father agreed that having to repay the grant money if he ever sold the house was better than living on the streets.

I immediately offered to help. I would do anything to make sure my sisters had a roof over their heads, even if it was a less-than-ideal one. The house had fallen further into disorder since I'd left, not because my sisters were messier than I was, but because my parents continued to pile things up. The cats had long since abandoned their litter boxes in favor of the piles of clothes and random garbage strewn everywhere. The smell of ammonia was overwhelming and delivered a pungent punch every time we walked through the door.

A few days after the fire, a twenty-foot dumpster was dropped off in the driveway, and we spent nearly every spare moment of the next two weeks cleaning out piles of junk caked with dried cat feces. Jason, who had grown close to my sisters over the years, came to help, and I was grateful for his assistance.

A week into the job, Lillian and I both came down with a severe respiratory illness and were bedridden for days. Looking back, we probably had pneumonia and needed to go to the doctor, but since neither of us had health insurance at the time, we suffered through it.

During this time, our parents flitted about, blathering on about being careful not to throw out anything valuable or useful. At times, our mother would quietly snatch a few items from the discard pile and vanish with them; at other times, she charged at us, red-faced and with clenched fists, screaming at us to stop throwing out her things. We stopped her in her tracks by reminding her that if we didn't clean up the mess, everyone would get kicked out. For his part, our father picked through the bags of garbage, repeating over and over, "Make sure you don't throw out anything we might use." It became his mantra, so we were careful to inspect every item before throwing it into the dumpster.

I was proud of my sisters. All of them, with the exception of Mariah, rallied to restore their home to a passable level of cleanliness. I knew they were going to be okay. They had successfully navigated the craziness of growing up with our parents and had emerged as competent, empathetic, intelligent young women. Their actions during this family crisis demonstrated their grit and determination. I could see them all developing into wonderful, successful adults, in spite of the many hurdles they had to overcome.

Despite all this chaos, I took the dental school entrance exam in late November. It was held on the UCONN main campus and started at 8 a.m. Since it was a two-hour drive from Winsted, one of my friends, who was attending classes there and living in the dorms, let me stay with him the night before. Since he was the dorm's Resident Monitor, he had his own room with an extra bed. Unfortunately, it was a Friday night, and the campus was raucous far past midnight with the sounds of college students screaming obscenities in a drunken stupor. I worried about how I would perform on the exam with virtually no sleep.

The next morning, I woke at 6 a.m., which gave me plenty of time to get to the exam facility and mentally prepare myself with some last-minute studying.

An unusual cold front had moved in overnight, making the morning bitterly cold. My nose hairs froze in the short time it took me to walk from the building to the parking lot.

Jason had suggested I take the T-bird, since my truck was acting up at the time, and I'd acquiesced. He had bought a brand-new pickup truck and wasn't driving the T-bird anyway. I gave the door to the T-bird a hard yank; just enough moisture had accumulated on it during the night to make it stick. I jumped in, relieved to be out of the cold blustery wind, and turned the key.

Nothing happened.

The battery was dead. I panicked for a moment, then pulled myself together and went back inside to awaken my friend, who was gracious enough to venture out into the cold to jump-start my car. I made it to the exam site with five minutes to spare—just enough time to collect my thoughts and get my ID ready.

I was afraid that my difficulty making it to the exam was a harbinger of how I would perform on the test, but I couldn't have been more wrong. My perseverance and preparation had paid off, and when my results arrived a couple of weeks later, I was thrilled to see that I had scored in the top 99.7 percent of all students who had taken the exam nationally. In fact, of all the students who had taken the exam at that time, I ranked third overall in the nation.

I was going to dental school!

A few weeks later, I gave Paul, my friend from high school who had recently graduated with a degree in English and was working as an editor for a local newspaper, a copy of my two-hundred-page manuscript, which I had completed as part of my bachelor's degree. I gave another copy to Amy, who had asked to be the first to read it, and then I sent copies to several publishers. I was excited and terrified. What if they hated it? What if they loved it?

Two months passed, and I didn't hear anything from anyone. Finally, I asked both Paul and Amy point-blank what they thought. They both skirted around the subject, as if I had asked them whether I looked fat in my pants. From their reactions, I concluded that the book needed a lot of work, and with all I still had to do to make a future for myself, I knew it just wasn't the right time to tell my story. I sensed it was still lacking something, but I didn't realize that my story hadn't yet found its resolution.

I took the one hard copy I had and the floppy disk it was saved on, put them alongside my high school track trophies in the suitcase my grandfather had owned, and placed it under the eaves of my apartment. I decided not to work on it again until I felt compelled to.

"Dear God," I prayed, "I know You asked me to write my story, but it's obvious to me that it's not ready. I don't know how to make it better, and with dental school coming up, I'll be too busy to continue it. When the time is right to start working on it again, let me know, and I'll start revising it, but You have to tell me when that is. Amen."

It would be many years before God and I picked up that conversation again, and I would resist His promptings to begin again for a few more years after that. Meanwhile, I turned my attention to my education and my future.

Chapter 26
Now I Am Found
1999

B y the time I left for my first round of dental school interviews in February 1999, nearly a year had passed since my accident. My truck had survived, but it wasn't the same, even with all the repairs Jason had done. Susan, who still cared for me like a good mom would, worried it might break down on such a long trip, and she graciously offered to let me use her car. Since I couldn't take the T-bird due to a transmission problem, I gratefully accepted. I was relieved not to have to drive the truck in which I had nearly killed another family and myself.

In mid-February, I had three interviews in a row, on a Tuesday, Wednesday, and Thursday. Since they were scheduled when anyone who might normally have come with me was working, I went alone, terrified of the long drive. The first school I visited was the State University of New York at Stony Brook on Long Island. I left early that morning, just as the snow from a major front was starting to fall. It started out wispy but picked up as I headed south.

I made it to the Long Island ferry in Bridgeport just before the Connecticut highways closed behind me. Even with this closure, I was hopeful that I would beat the storm. I crossed the sound as the snow pelted the ferry and drove on to the SUNY campus. Incredibly, by the time I walked in the front door, the dental school had shut down due to the weather. One other forlorn candidate was there with me, along with a secretary and a single administrator. I was told that they'd tried contacting me several times, but because I'd been driving since dawn and cell phones were still a luxury for the wealthy, they hadn't been able to reach me.

Unfortunately, I had another interview in Philadelphia the next morning, so I couldn't return to Stony Brook the following day. The administrator who was still there agreed to interview me without the rest of the committee. In retrospect, I should have rescheduled it entirely, since the administrator couldn't come to a decision without the input of the other committee members, but sometimes God has a way of redirecting us.

In spite of the unusual interview process, I was relieved to leave earlier than anticipated to continue my trip to Philadelphia. The highways had reopened by this point, and although the storm stretched down the entire Eastern Seaboard, I was hopeful that the weather would improve as I headed further south.

I was so afraid to drive through New York City that I traveled a considerable distance west on Route 80 rather than continue on Route 95. I navigated using a map that lay crumpled on the passenger seat, and the route looked fine on paper. Although it was getting dark by the time I reached the Pennsylvania border, I was making good time. I decided to get as close to Philadelphia as possible and then stop at a motel for the night. That way, I would only have to travel a short distance in the morning before entering the city itself and making my way to my next interview.

Once I got on Interstate 476, I began my ascent into the Pocono Mountains. Suddenly, the snow picked up again, and within minutes, a squall blew around me in violent gusts. The snowflakes popped brilliantly in the glare of my headlights like a million blinding reflectors. The snow coated the highway in a white mat, making the lanes impossible to distinguish. I slowed down to better see the road, but my wipers were smearing partially frozen blue-brown muck back and forth. I opened the window, leaned forward, grabbed the wiper blade, and snapped it against the glass to shake off the ice. A pile of slush landed on my lap as I pulled my freezing hand back inside the car. This was dangerous weather.

Scenes from my accident months earlier flitted through my mind—a black SUV flipped on its side, a mother screaming for her baby, glass strewn out of the rear window. Soon, the night and the thickness of the snow made it pitch dark out, and my headlights were of little help, as I was blinded by the snow reflecting in their light. By then, I could no longer tell where the highway ended and the shoulder began. I was starting to panic.

I couldn't make out anything around me, and my mind raced. Would I hit a tree? It seemed prudent to stop, but what if I stopped in the middle of a major highway? What if someone couldn't see that I was stopped and slammed into me? I pictured myself careening off a cliff. I was terrified to continue, yet just as terrified to stop. I began crying—not a little sniffle, but an all-out, hysterical, convulsing, tears-streaming-down-my-cheeks, blinding cry. I was absolutely positive I was going to die out there in that lonely, cruel storm. It would be hours before anyone found my body.

"Please, God!" I begged. "I don't want to die out here. Please save me! It's not my time. I know it's not my time. Please, lead me out of these mountains. I can't do this. I'll never make it. I'll never make it out on my own. Please, God! Please, please, please help me!"

Meanwhile, I continued to trek onward with my face nearly pressed into the windshield, fogging it up with my hot breath as I prayed. I wasn't even sitting anymore; I was using the steering wheel as a support to get closer to the glass so I could spot landmarks, something, anything. I was so nervous, I thought I had wet myself at one point, but then remembered how I had knocked snow into the car when I popped the wiper blades against the windshield.

An eternity passed as I crept forward. I continued along several more miles of highway completely absent of any other vehicles, when suddenly, a large box truck passed me. Waves of relief swept over me. I sniffled down a few final tears, licked the salt from my running nose off of my upper lip, and prayed, "Thank you, God. Thank You so much for sending me this truck to follow."

I could see its taillights, and like a pair of red lighthouses, they guided me through the mountains. Although we were moving slowly, we were nonetheless moving, and we were alive. After an hour, the truck and I made it to the Lehigh Tunnel. That four-thousand-foot stretch was a delightful respite, and I was able to sit back in my seat and relax my aching hands for a moment.

Suddenly, a chunk of snow blew off the roof and back of the truck, and for the first time, I noticed that something was written in red on the roll-up tailgate: large, bright-crimson letters spelled out "J-E-S-U-S." There was nothing else written on the truck.

My moment of reverie ended as we exited the tunnel and returned to the howl and blowing snow of the storm in the Poconos, but I was no longer afraid. I knew I was going to be fine.

I continued following the truck down the mountain. I lost track of time completely. I could have been driving for twenty minutes or three hours, but it felt like a year. Eventually, the snow turned to flurries that lingered in the air and slowly danced to the earth. Once I could make out the lane markings on the highway again, I slid back from the edge of my seat. Moments later, the box truck turned off the highway. I realized then that we had been the only two vehicles on the interstate this whole way. No one else had been out in the storm. I took the next exit off the highway and found a motel to spend the night in.

The next morning, without any further incidents, I made it to Philly. After my interview, I got back on the road for my third interview in Pittsburgh.

Those three days were a whirlwind of activity: traveling, navigating my way to the schools, interviewing, and then finding a place to spend the night. It was exhausting. I was grateful that the remainder of the trip ran smoothly. Except for the unexpected blizzard, I had planned well.

On Friday, when I drove back home after my interview in Pittsburgh, the interstate through the Poconos was now clear, and I had hours of free time to listen to music and reflect on my interviews. As dusk darkened the landscape around me, niggling questions ran through my mind: What mistakes had I made during the interviews? What should I have said? Had I been friendly enough, smart enough, genuine enough?

That's when it finally hit me: *Wait a minute, that truck said "JESUS,"* my mind sang out. *The truck I followed through the mountains said "JESUS!" Oh my God! God sent Jesus to save my life. It was Jesus, the ultimate messenger, who led me to safety!* It seemed like a nearly impossible coincidence that the one vehicle on the highway during that terrible storm would have "JESUS" written on the back. In my exhaustion at that time, I hadn't even realized the implications.

Tears streamed down my face. My epiphany triggered something within me: an awakening. For the first time, it dawned on me that Jesus truly was more than just another human. I finally got it. I finally believed, really believed. I understood within the depths of my soul that Jesus was an extension of God, a part of God, the Son of God, not some random Biblical hippy that happened to look like my father. It was as if I had awoken to a truth I had always known yet had somehow forgotten.

Driving back to Connecticut in Susan's car, I was overwhelmed with emotion, comforted by the darkness around me, and relieved that no one could see my tears. I turned my revelation over and over in my mind, tackling it from all angles, attempting to reason myself out of it, but I had no convincing arguments anymore. The truth flooded through me: God had sent Jesus to save my life, not once, but twice—once for humanity, and once again for one lone human engulfed in a storm. How many others had been touched like this? How many silent believers were out there?

When I got back to Jason's house to exchange vehicles, I was exhausted and kept my revelation to myself. I needed more time to contemplate why God would go to so much trouble to save me and to help me understand Him.

A month later, I finished my rounds of interviews, which included trips to SUNY at Buffalo, UCONN, University of North Carolina, and University of California-San Francisco. UCSF was my favorite school of them all, and I felt drawn to San Francisco, but it was far from my family. I worried about being able to pay for flights back home for the holidays. I was ready to move in a new direction, but not that far in a new direction.

I ultimately decided to go to Buffalo. It was close enough to home that I could drive to see my sisters when I wanted. The school had an excellent reputation, and I would have my own dental operatory, which I wouldn't have to share with another student. That meant more clinical time practicing dentistry. I was ecstatic about starting my new adventure in a new city.

That autumn, after the bustle of starting classes at the University of Buffalo's School of Dentistry, getting to know my professors, meeting interesting new classmates, and becoming accustomed to a new living arrangement, I settled into my life as a dental student. I was finally gaining traction in my life and actually accomplishing dreams I had nearly forgotten.

Buffalo was far enough from the scenes of my past to give me a sense of having left all its crazy, negative energy behind and starting life afresh. I was certain that my future had begun and that it would be good.

Late one evening in November, during my first year of dental school, I was sitting in the university's Health Sciences Library, studying for an anatomy test, when I looked up from the long oak table my notes were spread across. Suddenly, unexpectedly, a feeling of well-being washed over me.

A massive fireplace to my left, although unlit, lent the room the perception of warmth. Books filled the mahogany shelves lining the walls. All around me, students were studying. Like me, they were preparing for a better future. Through the large window in the massive front door, I saw the exterior lights illuminating the dancing snowflakes. I remembered that night in the Poconos and the blinding reflection of the snowflakes in my headlights as I struggled to drive through the blizzard to safety. Jesus had led me out of that difficulty. Now, the snowflakes were beautiful. My struggle seemed over.

As I stared out that window, I realized that I was exactly where I belonged. I was filled with a profound feeling of peace with my life and with my past. A rare sense of belonging and of being rightfully part of some group that was welcoming and nurturing settled in my soul. Somehow, in spite of all the chaos of growing up with mentally and emotionally impaired parents, in spite of all the pain and the pervasive fear that life would never change for me, in spite of my attempts to end my life, I had ended up happy and successful in dental school, exactly where God had been leading me.

I had made it out of my crazy past with a lot of help from God and His messenger angels talking me out of my own demise and leading me to safety. I was becoming my own person, and that person was a happy person, a better person.

God and Jesus had been my knights in shining armor all along. It was God who had been there through my darkest hours, watching over me and my sisters, protecting me from my parents' abuse, saving me from committing suicide, and leading me to safety when I was emotionally "lost and blind." It was Jesus who had never abandoned me. My knights, my princes, were with me always. No matter what terrifying misadventure I found myself in, I now knew for certain that I could call on Them to lead me through. I knew I would be all right and that we will all be all right in our own time.

I had come to Buffalo, as I believed, to learn how to be a good dentist—and I did learn that—but I also learned even more important lessons about living my life. I learned about hope, love, forgiveness, and all the things that make our lives wonderful, mysterious, and worthwhile.

That epiphany in the study hall both reassured me and served as a stimulus to keep going through the many challenging days ahead in dental school. I sensed in my core that I was destined to be successful, destined to be someone special.

I just knew it.

Amen.

Afterword

I put my memoir away for several years. During that time, I graduated from dental school then went through an orthodontic residency in San Francisco, where I met my husband. We married a month after my graduation in 2006, the same month my sister, Mariah, passed away in a freak accident at the age of twenty-nine. She passed out and hit her head in the shower of her ex-husband's house after her blood sugar dropped too low from taking too much insulin.

The following month, I began practicing as an orthodontist. Two years later, my husband and I had a wonderful son who fills our lives with light and love. I had achieved everything I had hoped for, but I had forgotten what God had asked of me several years earlier. I was too busy, too preoccupied, and too ashamed of my past to resurrect my book. I was building my practice up to five locations with two associates and over twenty-five staff. Completing my story wasn't even a passing thought. But God had not forgotten, and He waited patiently until I was ready by placing one coincidence then another and another in my path until I picked up my book and began working on it again.

Although I had left home in a grand effort of self-preservation, seemingly abandoning my sisters, whom I loved deeply, they grew up to become amazing women. The only exception was Mariah, who'd had both of her sons taken from her years before her death in closed adoptions because she was mentally unfit to care for them.

Lillian continued to live at home while she attended college. She earned her master's degree in education and now teaches second grade. She has two wonderful little girls with her funny, engaging husband.

Amanda went off to college using the money she had received from the car accident settlement. She earned a bachelor's degree in physical education and now works as a personal care assistant. She has three beautiful girls.

Helen attended college just outside of Boston and earned a master's degree in education from Harvard. She works as a high school guidance counselor and lives in Boston with her extroverted, exceptionally kind husband and two vivacious young sons.

Gabrielle earned a master's degree in social work. Today she is employed full time as a licensed clinical social worker, helping place mentally challenged children and young adults into care facilities. She is also married and is content being the favorite "auntie" to all the little ones—at least for now.

Our parents still live in the same house in Winsted, and it is in perpetual disrepair. Most of us girls have limited our interactions with them to a few visits and conversations per year. We found it necessary to create and maintain strong boundaries for our own mental health.

Despite the chaos of our youth, I am proud that my four remaining sisters grew up to become amazing, successful, wonderful women. I find it no surprise that we all chose the professions we did: health care, counseling, and teaching. After years of fear, abuse, and neglect, we all chose careers where we could directly help others. Throughout our youth, we learned how important it is to love and support each other, and we carried those lessons forward into adulthood. We learned that after the darkness comes the light.

A Small Favor

Thanks so much for investing your time reading through my memoir. I hope you were able to appreciate it as an interesting story but also take away that no matter how difficult the circumstances of your life, you can get through them and become a better person.

If you have a spare moment, I would appreciate it if you would share your thoughts by leaving a review wherever you purchased this book. Readers rely on honest, thoughtful feedback from the wider community to help them make more informed decisions.

I read each review personally and appreciate your honest feedback.

Thanks again!

Denise

About the Author

Denise Brown has been living happily in South Carolina over the past decade with her husband and son while practicing orthodontics. She graduated summa cum laude from UCONN with a BGS degree in both the sciences and creative writing and then graduated summa cum laude from SUNY Buffalo with her Doctorate of Dental Surgery before completing her orthodontic residency at UCSF. Although she no longer plays football or wrestles, her love for extreme sports lives on through mountain biking, kayaking under the Golden Gate Bridge, and trying to keep up with her son on Boy Scout camping hikes.

Lightning Source UK Ltd.
Milton Keynes UK
UKHW010926011221
394888UK00003B/338